BROKEN LIVES

BROKEN LIVES

A Personal View
of the Bosnian Conflict

Lieutenant-Colonel Bob Stewart

HarperCollins*Publishers*

HarperCollins*Publishers*
77–85 Fulham Palace Road,
Hammersmith, London W6 8JB

Published by HarperCollins*Publishers* 1993
1 3 5 7 9 8 6 4 2

A catalogue record for this book is
available from the British Library

ISBN 0 00 255391 0

Set in Meriden by Rowland Phototypesetting Ltd
Bury St Edmunds, Suffolk

Maps drawn by John Gilkes

Printed in Great Britain by
Hartnolls Ltd., Bodmin, Cornwall

This book is dedicated to all those whose lives have been broken by the recent conflict in the former Republic of Yugoslavia, but in particular to Lance-Corporal Wayne Edwards and Dobrila Kolaba

CONTENTS

LIST OF ILLUSTRATIONS

LIST OF MAPS

LIST OF ABBREVIATIONS

APC — Armoured Personnel Carrier

BiH — Army of Bosnia Herzegovina

COG — Current Operations Group

CGS — Chief of the General Staff

CSM — Company Sergeant Major

ECMM — European Community Monitoring Mission

HV — Croatian Army

HVO — Croatian Defence Council (Bosnian Croat Army)

HQ UKLF — Headquarters United Kingdom Land Forces at Wilton, Wiltshire

HQ BHC — Headquarters United Nations Forces in Bosnia Herzegovina at Kiseljak

HQ BRITFOR — Headquarters British Forces at Split

HRH — His Royal Highness

ICRC — International Committee of the Red Cross

JNCO — Junior Non-Commissioned Officer

Juliet — Nickname for COs Warrior

MOD — Ministry of Defence

NAAFI — Navy, Army and Air Force Institute

NCO — Non-Commissioned Officer

ODA — Overseas Development Administration

Operation Hanwood — British Medical Support Operation for UNPROFOR based in Zagreb

Operation Grapple — British Operation for Bosnia Herzegovina

Operation Cabinet — United Nations Operation bringing aid into Tuzla from Belgrade

RSM — Regimental Sergeant Major

Scimitar — Light Reconnaissance Tank

TQMS — Technical Quartermaster Sergeant

Triangle — Supply route through mountains from Tomaslavgrad to Vitez

UN — United Nations

UNHCR — United Nations High Commission for Refugees

UNMO — United Nations Medical Officer

UNPA — United Nations Protected Area

UNPROFOR — United Nations Protective Force

Warrior — Armoured Infantry Fighting Vehicle

1ST BATTALION
THE CHESHIRE REGIMENT

This book covers the period of my life between 22 August 1992 and 11 May 1993, from the time I was warned that I might be sent to Bosnia to the day I handed over command to my successor.

It is a personal view of my experience of commanding 1st Battalion The Cheshire Regiment Group on a six-month United Nations operational tour. I did not concern myself with political or military activities at a higher level than was strictly necessary for me to exercise my Command. Naturally any comments I may make in this book are my own and they are not official Government or Ministry of Defence view-points. However, just for the record, I would like to say that I never fundamentally disagreed with the instructions I was given by my superior officers who assisted both my Battalion Group and myself superbly.

The support I received from the Officers, Warrant Officers, Sergeants, Junior Non-Commissioned Officers and Private soldiers of 1st Battalion The Cheshire Regiment Battalion Group throughout operations in Bosnia was second to none. I am so proud of what they achieved and in many ways feel a tremendous fraud because so much attention has been focused on me personally.

Finally I would like to thank Barbara Levy, Michael Fish-wick and Richard Wheaton for their help and advice as I have written the book. I am also grateful to Colour Sergeant Brian Blackburn, Sergeant Chris Smith, Hilary Bannister and the Clerks of my Battalion Orderly Room who frequently had to sort out the mess I had made on my word processor.

Robert Stewart
September 1993

The Former Republics
of Yugoslavia

N

0   50   100 miles
0   50   100   150 km

HUNGARY

VOJVODINA

ROMANIA

■ Belgrade

• Tuzla   • Loznica

• Sarajevo

SERBIA

MONTENEGRO

BULGARIA

KOSOVO

MACEDONIA

ALBANIA

GREECE

INTRODUCTION

We left the Croat checkpoint behind us as we drove directly into town. Novi Travnik seemed absolutely still. I'd taken my headphones off so that I could hear as much as possible. But all I heard was the vehicle engine. Nobody was on the streets. I led the reconnaissance party of six Land Rovers. I wasn't even sure where the centre of town was but supposed this route led there. I had no idea where to find the local head-quarters. We were simply hoping for the best.

Suddenly there was a huge deluge of noise – from all sides. A firefight erupted from the modern flats and houses lining the street. The noise was terrifying and bullets seemed to be going everywhere. We were in the middle. I saw a burst hit the concrete on my left. I had led the convoy right into a killing area between the Croats and the Muslims. The shoot-ing seemed to be right at us. My shoulders curled in towards themselves, maybe to make myself less of a target. I was really scared. 'Keep going,' was all I could mumble to Nick beside me. What a fool! What about the others? I couldn't see them through the back of my Land Rover – even the effort seemed dangerous. Automatic fire and perhaps an anti-tank rocket splashed over the buildings to our right and then left too. There was no time for anything but getting through it. 'Drive on, drive on, keep driving.' My Land Rover seemed to be through the worst. What about the others? Leaning forward and looking sideways into the passenger-door mirror I could see the next two vehicles following. Maybe we had all made it.

Screeching around the streets as we attempted to get well clear of the shooting, I suddenly saw a man waving crazily at us.

'Pull up near him,' I said. All the vehicles were with us. Captain Nick Stansfield, the interpreter, was driving.

'Ask him where his headquarters is,' I said.

'Are you crazy?' the man replied.

'No, we're not,' I told Nick to say, but at this moment I had my doubts.

'My headquarters are round that corner,' said the man.

'Good. Let's go.'

We drove on and found another man. I had not noticed whether the first one was a Muslim or a Croat. I suppose I should have thought about that, even though it did not worry me which side I reached first. I did, however, recognize the second soldier's uniform. He was a Muslim.

The Muslim Headquarters was in a modern building that looked like a school. The Commander's office was on the second floor, said the soldier, who was friendly but wanted us out of the way. There was still a great deal of noise from firing. The noise of battle was all around us, but the fire did not seem to be directed at us then. The situation was nonetheless fearsome. I hadn't realized it would be as bad as this, but we were committed. Brigadier Andrew Cumming, Nick Stansfield and I entered the headquarters, leaving the rest of our party to go to ground and seek protection where they could. I hoped they would be all right.

That was on 22 October 1992. Eight weeks before I had been on leave in Berlin with my wife, Lizzie, and two children, Alexander and Caroline. We had been eating lunch in Edinburgh House, an Army-run hotel, when I received a call from Major Tim Park, my Second in Command, to inform me that all leave had been cancelled and that 1st Battalion The Cheshire Regiment was to be prepared to deploy to Bosnia under United Nations (UN) command. I had been half expecting that we might go but this was confirmation. A whole series of emotions ran through me in quick succession.

I was excited, but I felt immediately apprehensive about what it would involve and how I would cope with the strain of being there. I told Tim we would travel back to our base in Fallingbostel as soon as possible. I returned to my family to break this news, which was disappointing for them as they'd been looking forward to being in Berlin for much longer.

My Army career had been a good one so far. Despite an initial lack of confidence at the Royal Military Academy Sandhurst, I had soon found my feet in 1st Battalion The Cheshire Regiment and began to thoroughly enjoy myself. I love the comradeship of regimental soldiering. I was promoted to Lieutenant-Colonel when I was relatively young, at thirty-eight, but had been perfectly happy to wait almost four years for command of the Cheshires rather than get command somewhere else a little earlier. By the time I took over command of the Battalion I was thus slightly older than most. In the Army an older Commanding Officer is normally reckoned to be a little more relaxed in his style. I hope that is the case with me too.

As a boy I had always aspired to follow my father into the RAF. It was a great disappointment when, at Chigwell School in Essex and at the age of thirteen, I discovered I was short-sighted and a little colour blind. This fact immediately put paid to an RAF flying career. Quickly I switched my thoughts to the Army. I tried for an Army Scholarship two years later, getting through to the final interview but not quite making the grade. In the Easter holidays of my final year at Chigwell I tried for the Army again by going to the Regular Commissions Board at Westbury. To my surprise, because of my lack of confidence, I passed and that autumn I was an officer cadet.

I was still surprised when later I became an under officer for my last two terms at Sandhurst. However, overall I was not sure that I was good enough as an officer cadet and always half-expected to be thrown out. I joined 1st Battalion of the Cheshire Regiment as a Second Lieutenant on Bahrain Island in the Middle East during July 1969.

As a platoon commander, I gained experience and

confidence over the next few years, in England, Northern Ireland, Malaya and Germany. In Berlin I met Lizzie, who was working for the Foreign Office there, and we married in January 1973 when I was a recruit training officer at Lichfield in Staffordshire. After an Army-sponsored course at the University of Wales in Aberystwyth where I graduated in 1977 with an International Politics degree, I returned to the Battalion to become, successively, Intelligence Officer in Northern Ireland, Operations Officer in Germany and Canada and then an instructor at Sandhurst from where I went to the Army Staff College at Camberley.

Upon being promoted to Major after a year at Staff College, I rejoined the Battalion as a company commander for a two-year tour based at Ballykelly in Northern Ireland. I gained a great deal from this period, particularly in the way I viewed my relationship with soldiers. On 6 December 1982 the Battalion suffered its worst disaster since the Second World War when eleven soldiers were killed in the Ballykelly Bomb. Six of those killed and over thirty of the wounded were in my Company. The loss of so many soldiers was traumatic and I have never forgotten how utterly desperate I felt when we realized so many had died. It certainly reinforced my feelings of responsibility for the care and safety of everyone under my command.

When the Battalion itself ended its time in Northern Ireland and was posted to Hong Kong, I was sent to a staff appointment in the Ministry of Defence – concerned principally with the operational deployment of the Army worldwide. When I returned to the Battalion two years later as its Second in Command, we were based back in England, at Caterham in Surrey, on Public Duties. This assignment to ceremonial duties in London, which are normally a preserve of the Brigade of Guards, was an unusual tour for an Infantry of the Line Battalion, but I certainly enjoyed that time – especially when the Battalion was sent on a six-month tour to Belize in Central America. After Caterham I attended the Joint Services Defence College at Greenwich before assuming the appointment of Military Assistant to the Chairman of NATO's Military Committee in Brussels as a Lieutenant-Colonel. My main task there was to write speeches and I remained in Brussels until I took over command of the Battalion at Chester in March 1991, which was something I had always longed to do.

In November 1991 the Battalion had moved to Fallingbostel in Germany from Chester. I had been commanding for seventeen months when I heard about our possible tour in Bosnia. In Germany we had known for some time that the Government might be sending British soldiers to Bosnia. There had even been bets amongst the officers that the choice would fall on us, but nobody could be certain. All ranks in any Battalion are always excited by the prospect of doing the job that they are fundamentally trained to do. Therefore, the idea of a tour in Bosnia made us all buzz with anticipation.

On the personal side of life my marriage to Lizzie had grown increasingly unhappy and difficult over the years. I do not wish to say much on this subject because of its very sensitive nature. However, prior to Bosnia, we had almost split up during a previous operational duty and on my departure for another six-month tour I realized this time our marital relationship would not survive. Nonetheless both of us were determined to remain good friends whatever happened.

UN involvement in the Balkans had begun first at a diplomatic level and the organization had tried to broker a peace settlement with the Vance Plan, which sought to establish four Protected Areas, and thereafter with the establishment of a UN presence in Sarajevo. However, upon receiving dire warnings from many experts that starvation and cold would soon kill 'hundreds of thousands' in the remainder of Bosnia unless something was done, the Secretary General requested another six thousand troops and it was at this point that the British Government tentatively offered an infantry battalion group with logistic support for UN operations in Bosnia – provided the conditions were right. As this offer was made by Mr Major, my Battalion was placed on standby and our leave cancelled. I started to read some background information on the Bosnian predicament.

Bosnia-Herzegovina – Bosnia, for short – was one of six

republics that had made up the former Republic of Yugoslavia.
The others were Slovenia, Croatia, Serbia, Montenegro and
Macedonia. Additionally there had been two so-called auton-
omous provinces: Vojvodina and Kosovo. A total of about
twenty-four million people lived in Yugoslavia, of which
about five million inhabited Bosnia. A melting pot of different
cultures, Bosnia was made up of forty-three per cent Muslims,
thirty-three per cent Serbs and twenty-four per cent Croats.
By race, all were South Slavs but each ethnic group has its
own religion: Croats are Roman Catholics, Serbs are Ortho-
dox Christians and the Muslims are self-explanatory. The
Bosnian Croats clearly look to Croatia and the Bosnian Serbs
consider Serbia as their natural supporters. The Bosnian
Muslims have no natural motherland, as such.

For the purposes of the account of my tour of duty, when
I say Croats I mean Bosnian Croats rather than Croatians
from Croatia, when I refer to Serbs I mean Bosnian Serbs
rather than Serbians from Serbia, and the word Muslim refers
only to Bosnian Muslims. Historically, relations between
Serbs, Croats and Muslims had been appalling for centuries.
Rivalries between each group had frequently led to wars
and massacres. The place has always been considered a
powder keg.

During the Second World War the German invasion of
Yugoslavia further complicated traditional rivalries. The Communist Party of Marshal Tito, which included Serbs, Croats
and Muslims within its ranks, seemed to offer some hope
though. Prime Minister Winston Churchill fully supported
Tito and sent a large number of British advisers there, including Fitzroy Maclean. After the war ended, Tito managed to
keep the country united until his death some ten years ago.
Since then the powder keg has been waiting to explode again.

Serbia reckoned itself the lead republic because it considered itself the direct successor of the former Republic of
Yugoslavia and hence desperately wanted to hold the country
together. From 1990 it went to war with first Slovenia and
then Croatia in order to keep Yugoslavia whole, but failed. In
early 1992 Slovenia, Croatia and Bosnia were internationally
recognized as independent states. The subsequent civil dis-

turbances in Slovenia and Croatia were only minor compared
to the explosion of violence that occurred in Bosnia in the
spring of 1992. Serbs fought an alliance of Croats and Muslims
for territorial control. The Serbs rapidly consolidated their
hold on east and west Bosnia and maintained the link
between the two by a narrow strip of land in the north. The
Croat–Muslim 'alliance' had its strength in a central wedge of
territory which stretched north from the Croatian Dalmatian
coast. Sarajevo was almost surrounded by Serbs who, as the
successors to the Yugoslav National Army, had great numbers
of trained personnel, weapons and ammunition. In the spring
of 1992, the Serbs began to shell Sarajevo mercilessly.
Images of death, mutilation, shelling, prison camps and the
utter wretchedness of the people were shown on TV screens
worldwide and finally forced the West to intervene on behalf
of the innocent millions caught in the crossfire of this worsening civil war.

CHAPTER 1

THE RUSH TO WAIT

Her Majesty's Government has offered a contribution to the United Nations of a Battalion Group to support United Nations High Commission for Refugees operations in the former Yugoslavia. Time is now needed to assemble and prepare such a force. There is therefore pressure for those elements of the Army likely to be involved to be at a high state of readiness so that they can react should the Government's offer be accepted by the United Nations.

Official press communiqué from Her Majesty's Government

On 21 August 1992, as the official Government communiqué was released to the press no decision had been taken to deploy British troops. We were 'on offer' to the UN. Yet we had to train for real in order to be ready if the decision was taken, which is a standard procedure for the Army, and this assignment brought with it unique problems. Intensive training should be geared to a target, and preferably a specific time on a prearranged date.

First Battalion The Cheshire Regiment was to form the core of any force sent to Bosnia and to all intents and purposes we now had to act as though we were going and soon. In addition a medium reconnaissance squadron of the 9/12 Royal Lancers, of about ninety all ranks, an engineer squadron of about one hundred and thirty personnel and a considerable logistics element were to be involved. The whole force was to consist of a total of about eighteen hundred all ranks and the name allocated to the deployment was Operation Grapple. Apparently, 'Grapple' was next on the

Ministry of Defence's (MOD) list of nicknames, chosen at random in order that nothing should be given away by an operational name. Thus Operation Desert Storm, the conspicuous American name for the Kuwait War of 1991, had been dubbed more covertly by the MOD, Operation Granby.

I chaired the first Operation Grapple conference in Battalion Headquarters on the evening of Friday 21 August 1992. I told my company commanders as much as I knew about the forthcoming operation and that no final decisions had been made. After listing the units likely to be involved, I stated that the Battalion's immediate mission was to prepare for a possible deployment to the former Yugoslavia under the auspices of the United Nations. All leave was cancelled – which was very unfortunate for many in the Battalion who were never thereafter to make it up. I directed that the preparation of vehicles was to begin immediately – work was to continue through the weekend and until late at night each day. A problem arose over numbers: we were short of about one hundred and fifty soldiers because we had been trying to reduce our manpower to facilitate a planned amalgamation with 1st Battalion The Staffordshire Regiment. However, we were soon informed by the chain of command in Germany that the 2nd Battalion The Royal Irish Regiment was to reinforce us with soldiers as necessary.

At the conference we also discussed training in outline. I insisted that we fire all weapons and conduct a short exercise before we went. We discussed a directive that any soldier under seventeen and a half years of age had to be identified and his attendance on Operation Grapple be personally authorized by myself. There were a few such young soldiers – but in the end they were all to come with us. We warned all ranks that the tour length in Bosnia would be six months from deployment and that from now they were at seven days' notice to move from Fallingbostel. However, a reconnaissance party, which at this stage seemed to consist of only myself and the Quartermaster, Captain Mike Winstanley, had already been instructed to be prepared to leave immediately.

The next day I issued a formal written Warning Order to the

Battalion. It contained the first draft Order of Battle detailing names for appointments down to Platoon Sergeant level. The need to match names to appointments and keep within a manpower ceiling was to occupy the Adjutant, Captain Richard Waltier, for many an hour over the next few weeks. The London Conference on Thursday 27 August, to be chaired by the Prime Minister, was the focus for our attention at this time: we assumed that a decision about deployment would be made there. We continued to act as though we were on our way – there was no other option if we wanted to be really serious about training. But I hoped for a final decision as quickly as possible.

Whilst we were working flat out in the Battalion, others in Germany were working equally hard to support us. Tim Park, my Second in Command, attended a training conference at Verden on the Saturday, 23 August, under the chairmanship of Colonel Keith Skempton, my predecessor in command of the Cheshires and now Deputy Chief of Staff Headquarters 1st Armoured Division. A couple of days later Brigadier Colin Groves and Keith Skempton jointly set up a training package for us. The whole world seemed to be at this second conference, which I attended, but the most abiding impression I took away was how incredibly helpful people wanted to be. The training package was to start in less than forty-eight hours: it was to consist of two days firing small arms, followed by two days firing the 30mm Rarden cannon and the Hughes chain-gun on Warrior which was the armoured infantry fighting vehicle with which my Battalion was equipped. We were to end the package with a field-training exercise.

During our training packages all tedious administration was to be done for us. All we had to do was arrive on a range – even the Warriors we were to fire were provided by other battalions in Germany. Our Warriors were being intensively prepared and had to be kept in tip-top working condition both mechanically and in weapon terms. We were also considering at this stage whether to fit them with additional protective armoured plates. Finally they had to be painted white – the UN colour.

The media interest in us, which had flared up with the

news of our possible deployment, had rapidly cooled once the press discovered that no decisions had been taken – despite our own high excitement about a possible deployment. I was interviewed by a reporter from the *Sunday Times* and an article about us appeared in the newspaper on the next day. The report seemed a favourable one, reflecting the press's wish for greater British involvement in Bosnia. However, there was one aspect of it I did not like. A 'soldier who asked not to be named' was reportedly quoted as saying, 'I think we could be sucked into something that's not really a good thing. The point is, where would it stop? It's got all the makings of another Vietnam.' Whether a soldier really did say that or whether it was a little piece of journalistic licence I really cannot say. Nobody in the Army complained about the comment but it worried me. Commanding in Bosnia could be a potential nightmare when it came to handling the press if such things could be printed even before a decision had been taken to deploy. In the apparent maelstrom of Bosnia, it seemed we would be bound to make lots of mistakes and the press could have a field day. I was not sure how we should deal with it all but I was determined not to be overwhelmed by the press. The best thing seemed to be that I should try to bring the media 'on side' as soon as possible – that was, of course, if we deployed.

Using the experience of Operation Granby (the Kuwait War), the Training Organization in Germany rapidly tailored us a package based on the essentials we felt we might need. At the time nobody in the Battalion – apart from people like myself who had been on a Gunnery Course – had live-fired from a Warrior. We also needed to revise our skills with regard to booby traps, mines and field defences. Additionally we felt we needed lots more medical training, not just First Aid but a complete understanding of how to keep healthy in a hostile environment. All ranks needed to be given lectures about the political situation in the Balkans, that was if anyone could understand it. And we had to revise the Laws of Armed Conflict and how to recognize vehicles used by all sides there. Fortunately, in Germany there was considerable expertise on the former Yugoslav National Army from which almost all vehicles used in the Balkans had come. Fitness was also a high priority. Although we considered ourselves quite a fit Battalion there is always room for improvement and all training programmes included physical exercise, normally to start the day's activities.

I felt it essential that we have several snipers in each company, although we hoped, because of our humanitarian mission, we would never have to use them. The sniper's primary skill is to be a highly accurate shot using a rifle with a telescopic sight, but he must also be capable of operating on his own for long periods. In order to be effective he must be able to stalk any potential foe and be a master of camouflage. Snipers are highly professional soldiers in the British Army. To have passed the Snipers' Course is a considerable achievement. It is a qualification in its own right and very difficult to obtain. In media reports from Bosnia, the term sniper was normally applied to anyone who shot his weapon independently, but that is vastly different to how we would define the extraordinary range of talents this specialist needs. My Battalion was lucky here as only nine months before we had run a full Snipers' Course back in the United Kingdom and each of the companies had at least one sniper in its ranks. Nonetheless we also laid considerable emphasis on 'sharpshooting' for as many people as possible. Training a new generation of snipers would have taken too long and so we concentrated on giving good shots some increased training in accurate shooting. We called the soldiers thus trained 'sharpshooters'.

On our tactical training exercises I decided that we should concentrate on convoy drills, anti-ambush drills, route clearance, route picketing (protecting a path through hostile territory), helping refugees, dealing with snipers and how to handle the media. This was organized so that the vast bulk of our training was to be completed at the Sennelager Training Centre, near Paderborn, and it included firing our small arms. Live-firing of vehicle-mounted weapons was to be done much closer to home, on Hohne Ranges, which was practically on our own doorstep as we were right on Luneburg Heath at Fallingbostel.

I went down to Sennelager myself. Not only did I want to see exactly how training was being conducted but I too had a need to fire my Warrior's weapons using my own crew. I was doing just this when Lieutenant-General Sir Jeremy Mackenzie, Commander Allied Rapid Reaction Corps, arrived to visit us. Previously I had worked for him in 1984 when he was a Colonel in the MOD. A tall, thin and good-looking man with a soft voice, he always made me feel very comfortable in his presence. Without my knowing, he had been watching my Warrior firing – and afterwards he jokingly remarked that I was still a poor shot.

During our chat at the back of the ranges, General Mackenzie suggested that I must not expect any sort of direction if I went to Bosnia. There would be no rigid control from above and I must realize this from the outset. I would have to make up my own mind and then get on with it. This was going to be quite an unusual operation – if it came off – and UN command and control expertise was likely to be rudimentary at best. General Mackenzie was suggesting that in Bosnia, contrary to our usual British practice, there might not necessarily be any of the chain of command that normally gives an officer strict, clear guidelines.

The British chain of command might not be in an effective position to direct operations, due to the Battalion Group being placed under direct UN command and control – at least for day-to-day operations. At the time General Mackenzie believed I would probably also report to the British chain through Colonel Mark Cook who was currently running Operation Hanwood based in Zagreb. Operation Hanwood was giving medical support to the United Nations Protection Force (UNPROFOR) and consisted of a field ambulance, which was essentially medical support for other national contingents. Mark Cook was a Gurkha officer whom I had never met before.

General Mackenzie confirmed my thoughts about the importance of snipers if things really went badly. He told me that the Canadian Battalion in Sarajevo had recently been most successful in dealing with about twelve local-force snipers by employing their own snipers. I replied that I had given much consideration to this particular point and told him about our plans for a sharpshooters' course. A good Rear Party, the administrative support left back in Germany, was also required, he said. It was particularly needed to cover welfare matters, as nobody could guess what our casualties might be in Bosnia. He didn't know where we might end up in Bosnia but told me that wherever it turned out to be my command would represent the Main Effort – certainly for the British and possibly the United Nations as well. Finally he told me to be as tactful but as strong as possible and to keep my nerve. I promised to do my best on this. He ended with an afterthought, saying that he felt a time might come when his new Rapid Reaction Corps would be deployed. He hoped so.

Later, on my return from the ranges into the Sennelager Training Centre, I met Major-General Peter Shepherd who was in conversation with Brigadier Colin Groves. General Shepherd was the Chief of Staff of Headquarters British Army of the Rhine and Brigadier Groves was Brigadier Infantry in Germany. General Shepherd suggested that I would have to accompany any MOD reconnaissance sent into the Balkans and that I would therefore be much involved in deciding the appropriate force to send there. He told me that I must be totally honest about that. I must say if I felt something was right or wrong but the absolute ceiling on our total personnel was to be 1822. In terms of our schedule, we all agreed that a 'No Move Before' date was crucial. This phrase is standard Army jargon for the earliest date at which a unit plans to be fully prepared to move. We should have this as soon as possible as all plans could then be adjusted to suit it. I mentioned that I was concerned that a lot of people in my Battalion had had no leave whatsoever for over six months. General Shepherd left having told me to contact him at any time I felt it necessary.

Later that day I discussed the operation at the back of a range with a third visiting general, Major-General Iain MacKay-Dick, who had simply come to see how things were going. It was the first time I had met the new General Officer Commanding 1st Armoured Division and I talked to him about my two immediate aims. Firstly, I wanted to ensure all my weapons systems could shoot accurately – especially those mounted on vehicles, which in their turn must be automotively as perfect as possible. Any shooting we might have to do would have to be exact. Inaccurate shooting might injure innocent parties – and that would be terribly counter-productive in Bosnia. Our mistakes would make very good propaganda to any side that might wish to capitalize on them. The answer was to try to avoid mistakes. Thus we needed to employ weapons which were pin-point in their effects. Using mortars or artillery in the first instance would not be wise as their results are far from precise. Naturally too our vehicles must be as reliable as possible. Secondly, I wanted the Battalion to take some leave – especially those who had served a long spell without any time off. Soldiers are wonderful people but they expect and have a right to leave – particularly if they are going away for six months where they will have very little chance to have a break. Everyone in the Army understands that. 'Have you had enough leave?' is almost the first thing senior officers ask when visiting British units about to go on operations.

But the major worry I had at this stage was the state of our vehicles. We did not have enough spares available and it would take the system some time to procure them. We had also estimated that it would take us about seven days' work to get all our vehicles operational – that is with spares available – another week to fit additional armour and a third week to paint them all white. All this had a knock-on effect for our earliest possible deployment date. At the time we were working on a three-week sea move of vehicles too – although none of us could understand why it would take so long. All of this gave us a minimum of forty-two days in which we could be in Bosnia.

But all my fears about how long it would take us to become fully operational were in many ways academic. The key planning tool was an official deadline for when we were required to be in theatre, and that would only come from the decision to deploy us. Frustratingly, we were once again left on tenter-hooks when, on 28 August 1992, the London Conference ended without a deployment decision having been taken.

The lack of a deployment decision meant that there could be no possible 'No Move Before' order. Without it I couldn't train properly or make decisions on when people might be granted leave prior to their deployment. So I felt I had to commit some thoughts to paper. For eight hours on 31 August, I wrote a formal appreciation for myself in which I made an assessment of when I could get the entire Battalion to Bosnia, when I should ideally go and from that what remaining time I had available for detailed training. Given that no decisions had been taken on the additional armour or the white paint and the vehicle spares had still not arrived, my forty-two-day minimum deployment time still held. But I had also been informed that I must be in Bosnia within thirty-one days of a decision and so this timing had to be cut. I felt we could do it, particularly if the sea move was shortened. I worked out two options: option one enabled us to be fully operational from 5 October, the shortest possible deadline, were we told to deploy within the next few days; option two assumed the decision would be further delayed until mid-September and would require us to be in Bosnia from 17 October. Under either option, my time for detailed training was less than five days but I also wanted at least one week's leave taken into account.

In the event the decision never came in the cut-and-dried way I'd expected. The final decision was only made after a full reconnaissance of Bosnia had been carried out. In the Army reconnaissances are normally carried out before the decision to deploy troops is taken: in this exceptional circumstance we had to make up new rules. When we were first warned about a possible United Nations tour I had felt that events would get us there quite quickly. In this I was naive. It was rapidly becoming apparent to me, because of the lack of information that I was receiving, that the decision to commit British troops to operations in the Balkans had still not been taken. Whilst we were preparing as hard as possible for deployment, and acting as though our move to Bosnia was imminent, the MOD and the Government had still to be convinced by a full reconnaissance on the ground that British soldiers should be committed into the Balkans. Of course I understood the reason for this. There was still much that needed to be cleared – not just within our own Government but also with the UN as well as on the ground itself. After all, no British officers had yet been to assess the situation on the ground. It would have been totally irresponsible therefore to commit British troops to an operation without understanding as much as possible of what was happening in Bosnia. Nonetheless, indecision made little difference to the way we had to behave. My Battalion had to believe it was going in order to get as much as possible from what little training time we had available.

Rumours were rife. Some suggested that the murder of two French soldiers at Sarajevo Airport when their convoy was machine-gunned and mortared would cause the Government to rethink. Major James Myles, who ran Public Information in 1st Armoured Division, implied that an announcement was imminent, but his deadline came and passed. Even so, the Battalion was working flat out.

In the midst of our preparations, the Chief of the General Staff, General Sir Peter Inge, visited Fallingbostel accompanied by Lieutenant-General Sir Jeremy MacKenzie. I briefed both senior officers in my office on how we were preparing ourselves and when we might be ready to go. We discussed how best to keep our armoured vehicles working in severe winter and the Chief of the General Staff stressed how important he felt it was for the Rules of Engagement to be right. He had recently visited Bosnia and felt that the Canadians had the right approach there. He told me that a UN Bosnia Command Headquarters was now most likely and it would probably be commanded by a French general. We would come under his operational control once we were fully deployed.

Together with my senior visitors we toured the tank park so that they could talk to the soldiers, who seemed in very good heart. Thereafter General Inge talked to the officers over tea. He came across very well in a matter-of-fact way that instilled a lot of confidence. Obviously he understood our problems. General Inge said he had been shocked by the devastation in the Balkans when he had visited. He could not believe just how much hatred there was between opposing factions. We had to prepare ourselves for this. On the subject of where we might go within our future theatre of operations, he was not yet clear. But he hoped we would be based in Banja Luka in the Serb-controlled area. This seemed to be a good operational role and one that might be logistically more straightforward than other options. He told us to learn from how the Canadians had carried out their task and I made a mental note to see if I could get to the Canadian Commanding Officer on my reconnaissance. The Chief of the General Staff stated that a decision was imminent and there was now no doubt in his mind that we would be going – which caused quite a buzz around the room as we were beginning to have our doubts once again. Finally General Inge told us all that the prestige of United Nations Forces was not too high at the moment. We were to go there and try to restore this somewhat tarnished image.

This visit by General Inge was a big success. I liked the man and had considerable confidence in him. His visit to Fallingbostel had most certainly lifted morale and when, just before leaving, he privately assured me that the Prime Minister was determined on the operation it gave a further boost to my determination to have everything perfect as soon as possible. I was now much happier because it seemed our period of uncertainty was about to end.

Once the Chief of the General Staff had gone I kept all the officers together and spoke to them. I said that I was sure a decision was almost upon us but that we should not yet get too excited, as the final orders might still be delayed. However, I was sufficiently convinced for us to plan a leave period which would start after I had inspected the Battalion on Friday 18 September.

The decision to commit us to Bosnia finally came on the night of Monday 14 September. During the evening Brigadier Tim Glass, the Director of Public Relations for the Army, had telephoned me at home and told me that an announcement would be made later in the evening. I stayed up until 11 p.m. waiting for some form of newsflash, I presume. It had not happened before I went to bed, but in the morning the decision was all over the BBC Ceefax, which we get as part of the Service Television Service in Germany. For me it was a great relief to see confirmation that all our efforts had not been in vain. This news would put added impetus into our training which was on-going at Sennelager.

On Friday 18 September I inspected every man in the Battalion beside his vehicle. Amazingly all our Warriors had eventually been up-armoured within four days of orders being given for us to do so. Lieutenant-Colonel Paul Cort, Commanding Officer 7th Armoured Workshop and my neighbour in Fallingbostel, gave us incredible assistance. He was in constant touch with me and devoted as much of his resources as possible to help us get our vehicles fully operational, up-armoured and painted. Our vehicles were now painted white and stunning they looked. In fact some of the soldiers started to complain of dizziness: after many hours of working on a brilliant white background they seemed to suffer from snow blindness. We thought this might be a problem in the Balkans, but in fact all vehicles rapidly became greyish-white and soon lost their glare. Whilst I was walking around the vehicles, Brigadier Tim Sulivan, our Brigade Commander, arrived to say goodbye to the Battalion and rather sportingly helped me inspect Headquarters Company as he did so.

Having dismissed the Battalion on leave, I myself received rather different orders. The Director of Military Operations, Brigadier David Jenkins, was already in the Balkans assessing the situation and was returning to London over the weekend. Both Lieutenant-Colonel Malcolm Wood, appointed Commanding Officer of the Logistic Element of Operation Grapple, and I were to present ourselves for a Ministry of Defence briefing on Sunday morning. We were warned that we should not necessarily expect to return to Germany before being sent to the Balkans. I went to my house and started to pack what I felt I would need.

CHAPTER 2

SERBIAN ODYSSEY

At 9.30 a.m. on Sunday 20 September I reported to Historic Room 27 in the Main Building of the Ministry of Defence for briefing as instructed. Within this post-war MOD building, it is by far the nicest room, with its strong sense of grandeur and history, furnished as it is with decent pictures and a large old-fashioned conference table taken from the previous war-time offices. Someone had organized coffee just inside the entrance and so I helped myself. I felt a little bit apprehensive as by now I knew that a great deal might depend on me. As I considered this rather daunting meeting and sipped my coffee, the pleasant surroundings of Historic Room 27, with all the trappings of Empire and military success, only brought this home to me more vividly.

Although I was in good time, the senior officers were attending an on-going meeting of the Current Operations Group, the MOD's main committee for directing operations. It seemed that Brigadier David Jenkins, the Director of Military Operations, was still briefing the Current Operations Group on his assessment of the situation he had found in the Balkans. An hour later than scheduled, the senior officers arrived. Major-General Roger Wheeler, Assistant Chief of the General Staff, was to chair the meeting with Major-General Field and Major-General Rupert Smith, who until recently had been Commander of 1st Armoured Division in Germany, attended along with Brigadier David Jenkins and a host of other people, most of whom I had never seen before. Malcolm Wood, who had come on a different flight to me, sat opposite me at the large conference-room table and seemed to share some of my feelings of apprehension.

There was a buzz of excitement in the room. In many ways it had the appearance of a meeting of a board of directors of any commercial company. Everyone wore suits, which is standard practice in London for Army officers. There was quite a hubbub as people introduced themselves to one another and old acquaintances chatted amongst themselves.

After a short while General Wheeler opened the meeting by stating that the aim was to set up Operation Grapple. He started by announcing that a major-general's command, called in the Army a 'Two Star' Headquarters, had now been authorized and appointed. The Two Star Commander, Major-General Philippe Morillon, was already in Sarajevo. All I knew about General Morillon at this stage was that he had recently taken over the command of Sector Sarajevo from General Lewis MacKenzie. The British contingent was to come under day-to-day command of General Morillon but within his Headquarters Brigadier Roddy Cordy-Simpson was to be his Chief of Staff. Brigadier Cordy-Simpson, whom I had not seen for fourteen years, was present and introduced himself. Once he had been one of my instructors at a junior staff course in Warminster and he had an excellent reputation for being bright, energetic and a good person to work for. Clearly he was keeping fairly quiet at this stage – apart from anything else he had only just been told that he was to be General Morillon's Chief of Staff. There was also to be a separate Commander for the British Forces in the Balkans. At the time Colonel Mark Cook, Commander British Contingent on Operation Hanwood, was felt to be an obvious contender. The British command chain was to stretch back from the Balkans to Headquarters United Kingdom Land Forces (HQ UKLF) at Wilton, near Salisbury, and from there to the MOD.

All United Nations Forces were to operate in support of the United Nations High Commission for Refugees (UNHCR). It had been decided that the British area of operations was to be based around Tuzla in northern Bosnia. The French were to take the Bihac Pocket and the Canadians were to have Banja Luka, which the Chief of the General Staff had originally said was his preference. During our training we had identified a very strong need to have a Field Surgical Team attached to any force that went to the Balkans and so I was delighted when General Wheeler announced that one had been authorized.

After this the Director of Military Operations took over and briefed us all on the impressions he had gained during his visit to the area. He outlined UNHCR operations and how he saw our force structure linking to this. Obviously things were fairly hazy from what he said – particularly when it came to what we might do on any reconnaissance. Such pre-planning was key to how we would eventually operate. We discussed how we might take a few Land Rovers and try to negotiate our way from Zagreb, through the Serb and Muslim lines, to Tuzla and Doboj. These two towns were considered to be the most in need of humanitarian aid in Central and Northern Bosnia. The reconnaissance was to start from London on the following Tuesday. A senior officer passed me a note during all this. It read: 'It looks like a bag of nails. Best of luck.' He was right too. The whole business was still a long way from being put together properly. Not only was it unclear where we could operate but command and control arrangements as well as Rules of Engagement were still in nascent form. It seemed on the reconnaissance we would be breaking new ground in all senses and that knowledge hardly assuaged my apprehension. Naturally I tried not to show it.

Together with about ten other officers, who were also to go on the reconnaissance, I spent most of the afternoon reading through documents in the Military Operations offices on the fifth floor of the Ministry of Defence. Whilst doing so I met Brigadier Myles Frisby, who was Deputy Chief of Staff G3 Operations in Headquarters United Kingdom Land Forces at Wilton and who had commanded a Battalion of the Coldstream Guards when I had been Second in Command at Caterham a few years before. Brigadier Myles was going to lead the reconnaissance on behalf of HQ UKLF. He struck me as extremely nice, mild-mannered and nobody's fool. Together with the Chief of Military Operations 3, Colonel Austin Thorp, we looked at how best to approach the problem of getting to Tuzla. Our other key objective, to which we were now directed, was Doboj. On both counts this meant we had to cross current lines of conflict, which was a fairly daunting prospect as nobody in the MOD had been near either place. Neither did we have much information on what the situation was like there. In the end we decided that an approach to Tuzla from the north-east via Serbia was as good a choice as any other in the absence of more concrete information. We felt that we couldn't write an operational plan until we had been on the ground. All of us fully realized that this reconnaissance was likely to be very testing.

I returned to Putney where, very kindly, Brigadier James Percival was putting me up. He had recently left the Army almost as he assumed the appointment of Colonel of the Regiment. Considerably pre-occupied, I was probably very bad company for Brigadier James and Ann Percival that evening. The Colonel of the Regiment asked me about the briefing and was very concerned that so little was known about the area into which we were about to be launched. I must say I felt much the same myself but didn't want to admit it. That night I sat down in the Percivals' drawing room and examined the maps of Bosnia in as great detail as possible. The biggest problem we had was to determine where exactly the front lines between the Serbs and Muslim-Croat forces ran. On the maps we had only a very rough indication of their positions. However, it looked like we might have to cross the lines of conflict at least once to get to Tuzla and twice more to get to Doboj. Nobody seemed to have penetrated to Tuzla since the war started. Both Tuzla and Doboj appeared to be under constant attack. Nobody knew if we would be allowed anywhere near the front lines anyway.

However, I had to formulate an outline plan – if only as a starting point. I felt that we should aim for both Tuzla and Doboj and set up operational bases, to be manned by the Battalion Group. The logistic support would stretch back from there through somewhere like Loznica to Belgrade, and would have to cross lines of conflict – which was a worry, even if local authorities agreed to us basing ourselves in their area. The dependence of this plan upon the consent from the

Serbian Government for our lines of supply was far from ideal, but it was the best I could think of based on what I knew.

The District Line took me directly into Westminster station early the next day and I was in the Director of Military Operations' office quite early. After a little while Brigadier David Jenkins asked us all to sit down around his small conference table so that he could again go over what he had learnt whilst in the country. Just as we were about to start Colonel Mark Cook telephoned from Zagreb. The Director of Military Operations handed the phone to me and suggested I discuss what we needed on the reconnaissance. I felt this was a little bit of a 'fast ball' but did my best. Mark Cook said he would meet the Reconnaissance Party when we arrived at Zagreb Airport. We would start by basing ourselves with the British Medical Battalion where briefings were to be given. After that we would drive out from Zagreb. Mark agreed absolutely with the direction from which we proposed to approach Tuzla, since going in directly from Zagreb, through Banja Luka, to Doboj and thence to Tuzla would require us continually to cross and then re-cross lines of conflict. Going in from the north-east, possibly from the direction of Sabac, might minimize the number of times we had to cross front lines. It was encouraging that Mark Cook seemed to be in agreement with the conclusions we had reached so far – especially as he was the nearest thing we had to an expert on the area.

Once Mark Cook had rung off Brigadier David recommenced his own personal debriefing. Apparently General Morillon had told him that we must not think in terms of controlling ground – that was not the way to tackle the problem. He wanted the British Forces to have a firm base inside Bosnia itself, rather than setting up outside its borders and sending patrols into the country. It was also very heartening to hear that the United States had offered a strategic airlift to get us positioned in the Balkans. Medical support was also being made available aboard USS *Iwo Jima* in the Adriatic and its Sikorsky helicopters might be used to pick up casualties directly from the area of operations. The President of the town of Tuzla had stated that the airport there was still open and capable of being used by the biggest sorts of aircraft – that was, of course, if they managed to fly there over Serbian anti-aircraft fire. The Two Star Headquarters (later Bosnia-Herzegovina Command) was to be established by 14 October. However, nobody had any idea where such a headquarters might be best located: on the previous Saturday the shelling of Sarajevo had stopped for only ten minutes out of twenty-four hours, which made this key city an unlikely choice. To date, Brigadier David said, eight soldiers from United Nations forces had been killed in Bosnia: seven of them had died on operational service. So-called 'ethnic cleansing', by which ethnic minorities were driven out of their homes, was occurring throughout the length and breadth of Bosnia, and being carried out by all sides involved.

The Director of Military Operations suggested that Scimitars should carry out route reconnaissances whilst Warriors could provide intimate protection for convoys travelling down the routes checked by Scimitars. I said nothing, not because I didn't respect what he suggested, but simply because I wanted to assess the situation for myself before I made up my mind. After a few questions the briefing ended in the late morning. Those of us going on the reconnaissance were to meet early the next day at Heathrow.

That evening I again spent some time trying to put my thoughts into proper order. All officers in the Army are taught that a mission is the vital first step in deciding a plan. Indeed the current thinking is to examine such a mission in the greatest possible detail so that nothing is omitted from any plan. Such a process is called Mission Analysis. Brigadier David and I had discussed what we thought to be the aim of the reconnaissance. In short, it was to find a suitable base (or bases) close to Tuzla/Doboj from which to carry out escort operations in support of the UNHCR. I decided that this was probably as good a mission as I was likely to get and started my analysis based on it. On the reconnaissance I decided that we had to try to find secure bases and lines of communication down which our own supplies must flow. Additionally we should be located as close to UNHCR offices as possible – ideally we should be co-located with them. Naturally any bases we chose should be as far away as possible from the threat posed by indirect fire (artillery and mortars). We must also protect UNHCR in their relief efforts. I felt that a strong liaison officer system was essential. In my opinion this conclusion was to be another crucial decision for our later tour in Bosnia. Last but not least, we also had to be in a position to operate throughout the winter. We had to master working in really adverse weather conditions. Simply surviving would not be enough; we had to be effective at our jobs whatever the conditions were like.

There now seemed to me to be three operational plan options which we had to examine during the reconnaissance. First, we might be based in the Tuzla and Doboj areas with our logistic support trailing back through Serbia, possibly to Belgrade. But that would mean our logistic lines of communication would have to cross lines of conflict every time we needed to be resupplied. Second, we could be based in Serbia proper but operate from those bases into Bosnia. Again, we would have had to cross lines to operate and General Morillon had already made it plain that he wanted at least our operational bases to be inside the borders of Bosnia. Third, I felt we could adopt some kind of compromise plan between the first and second options. None of these proposals seemed ideal and I was still more than a little unhappy with things when I went to bed that night – especially as I had to get up so early the next morning.

I was very surprised that both Brigadier James and his son, Justin, were awake enough to make me a cup of tea before I left their house at 4.50 the next morning. I drove my hire car to Heathrow where I met up with the Reconnaissance Party in Terminal 2. We were all wearing civilian clothes, which was normal procedure since nobody wishes to draw attention to themselves more than necessary on a reconnaissance mission. Via Frankfurt, we flew direct to Zagreb on Air Croatia, an airline none of us had ever heard of. I noticed that there were Canadian troops on the aircraft and that they were wearing uniforms to travel – something we in the British Army never do, even when not on a reconnaissance. It was the first time I saw the UN blue beret being worn by soldiers and I thought it looked far too bright. But later I got used to the colour and by the end of my time in Bosnia I was rather sad to take it off.

In all eleven officers were to take part in the reconnaissance. Colonel Mark Cook was already in Zagreb waiting for us. Brigadier Myles Frisby was to lead the team. Colonel David Glyn-Owen, Deputy Assistant Chief of Staff Logistic Operations from Headquarters United Kingdom Land Forces, was coming to advise us on what logistic support might be required. Both Malcolm Wood and I were to be part of the reconnaissance as prospective commanders on Operation Grapple. John Field, the Commanding Officer of 35 Engineer Regiment, was to advise on engineer matters and possibly deploy himself on Operation Grapple if that proved to be necessary. Lieutenant-Colonel Neil Munro, of the Military Works Force Chilwell, was also to attend and suggest what building might be required. Again, already in Croatia was the Officer Commanding the Signals Squadron in Zagreb, Major Peter Telford, whose task was the efficient running of the operation's communications. Coming with us, although not expected to travel along the same route as ourselves, were Brigadier David Jenkins, Brigadier Roddy Cordy-Simpson and Colonel Roy Lennox. This latter group was to prepare the military-political ground for us at a higher level and they were expected to split off from the main reconnaissance party once we were briefed in Zagreb.

The airport at Zagreb had one runway and as we landed we could see beside it a large UN camp. Regretting that I had chosen to wear so much clothing in the Balkan heat, I sweated out our immigration clearance to be met by Colonel Mark Cook. A fit, wiry and energetic-looking individual, Mark welcomed us and had us bused to Pleso Camp – the UN base – within minutes. The base was an old Yugoslav National Army camp which had obviously seen much better days. It was terribly run-down, except where the United Nations troops had made an effort. Although we could not see them, we were told by Mark that numerous minefields were scattered in the scrublands. He advised everyone to stay on paths as nobody had had a chance to tackle clearing the minefields. I noticed the Swedish UN contingent had built themselves a sauna, which rather amused me.

In a minibus we took a brief tour around Pleso Camp which was the major UN logistics base for Operation Hanwood. Inside the place, all national contingents had detachments of soldiers whose job was to support those people in the field. The camp had an air of having been established in a hurry, with many tents and equipment lying around, and it was still not properly organized as a military camp should be. Mark Cook then escorted us all to the Headquarters of the British Medical Battalion. There, in a makeshift conference room, barely before we could down a quite appalling cup of coffee, Mark asked us to sit down in front of a large map of the Balkans and began his briefing.

Major Jonathon Riley, a British officer on loan to the European Community Monitoring Mission (ECMM) as Operations Officer, spoke first. He reminded us of the three main belligerent parties currently operating in Bosnia-Herzegovina. Firstly, the Serb Army has a strength of about seventy thousand troops operating throughout the area. The land-link corridor between Serbia itself and the Serb Army in the west of Bosnia was of crucial strategic importance to them. Second, the Croat Army, or the Croatian Defence Council (often referred to as HVO), was numerically weaker than the Serb Army at about forty-five thousand in strength. Again, the main strategic link for the Croats was to Croatia, which surrounded Bosnia to its north, west and south. The Croats were trying to close the land-link corridor between Serbia and the Serbs in Krajina in west Bosnia. Finally, the third element was the Muslims with an army of about fifty thousand. There was also word that the Muslims were now being reinforced with so-called Mujahaddin from Islamic countries.

Lieutenant-Colonel Colm Doyle, a regular officer of the Irish Army, spoke next. He had just finished being Lord Carrington's Special Envoy and was shortly to return home having spent the best part of a year in the region. He said that most people in Bosnia were very good at twisting the truth to suit their purposes. 'I never knew how much they can lie,' he declared. In his experience all parties to the conflict were sometimes prepared to attack their own people with the intention of placing the blame on others. He declared that it was 'high time' the United Nations took a more positive stance over the problems in the area. 'Enough is enough,' he said. He seemed very much in favour of enforcement-type action over Bosnia. Colm was aghast at the killings that were taking place throughout the country: 'People are not killed here, they are slaughtered.' Finally he stated that he was convinced the Serbs would not allow themselves to be in the minority anywhere. 'They want the lot!' he announced.

The Honourable Gilbert Greenall was also a briefer, as a representative of the Overseas Development Administration (ODA). Clearly he knew the whole region exceptionally well and his description of the situation was frequently amusing. His job was to assess how much aid was required and report back to the ODA. Later he was also responsible for following up to see how such aid was being used. He recounted the frightful shock the UN Kenyan Battalion had received after placing £120,000 in a local bank upon their arrival in theatre. Unfortunately, when pay day came and they went to make a withdrawal, the same local bank had, unaccountably, no record of such a sum being deposited in the first place. This story simply indicated how close the country was to total anarchy.

At the briefing I met Lieutenant-Colonel Neil Wright, a Royal Corps of Transport officer on loan to the UNHCR with the job of ensuring UNHCR input was included in our planning, since, after all, it was this UN organization that we were coming here to support. Neil was decent, straightforward and honest and I was to spend almost all the reconnaissance in his company.

The series of briefings we received that afternoon was invaluable and stood us in good stead later. I for one knew very little about the detailed situation and it was clear to me that there was a great deal for us to learn from these people, the first we had met with experience of what it was really like on the ground. As we sat listening to them in Pleso Camp, Zagreb seemed very peaceful. There were few signs of war. By contrast the messages we were getting about Bosnia were that it was absolutely lawless. Medieval antagonisms and fears were being fought out in a modern setting with twentieth-century weapons. Nobody and nothing was safe in the place – and we were going to go into it unarmed and in soft-skinned vehicles. That was worrying, to say the least. Nobody at the briefing could assess properly our chances of getting through to Tuzla and Doboj. I suppose that was impossible to judge anyway, since even those briefing us had not actually been there. With no international agencies having offices in Tuzla, nobody was certain how far we would get. But we had to try.

In fact I was very badly organized for the morning's reconnaissance and it was all my fault. I had not packed properly the night before and we were taking very little equipment with us for the operational part of our reconnaissance. And so in a great hurry I stuffed what little kit I could lay my hand on into a Grouse whisky box and pushed it into the back of a vehicle.

Alongside Mark Cook we were also to have Neil Wright and two United Nations Military Observers (UNMOs) to accompany us into Serbia. Our interpreter was to be Captain Nick Stansfield, Royal Army Education Corps, who spoke Serbo-Croat well having studied the subject at university. He had already been in Zagreb for some time as the military interpreter on Operation Hanwood.

Guided by Mark Cook, we left Pleso Camp very early with four vehicles and a party of about twelve personnel and started driving east down the motorway to Belgrade. From Zagreb, the capital of Croatia, we passed through several of the UN Protected Areas – set up under plans made by Cyrus Vance a few months before – en route to the Serbian territory. As we drove east, we quite rapidly lost all other traffic. Approaching the Protected Areas, the road was deserted, with debris lying about and occasional signs of fighting – destroyed houses, demolition holes in the road and signboards shot up. It was a strange sight. We went through a series of checkpoints manned by UN soldiers – Russian, Nepalese and Jordanian. This was strange too. I had just left Germany where for years we had considered the Russians our potential enemies, yet here we were all smiles and friendship working alongside one another under UN auspices. Unfamiliar it might be but there was something good about it too. The motorway took us almost all the way into Serbia and the only vehicles we saw were either UN or UNHCR ones. Obstacles, either natural like trees or man-made like anti-tank defences, suddenly appeared out of nowhere, which, considering the reasonable speed we were travelling at, was fairly hair-raising. For the first time we heard sounds of gunfire as we made our way to the north of the Serb land corridor. It sounded like artillery being fired, although we had no idea by whom. It was a little unclear to me at exactly which point we entered Serbia proper but about seven hours after we left Zagreb we had reached a town called Sabac having turned south off the motorway. An hour later we were in Loznica.

On arrival we heard the news that Yugoslavia, in other words Serbia, had just been expelled from the UN. Our timing was superb. Here we were trying to negotiate our way to Tuzla through Serbia and then Bosnia, at the same time trying to make provisional arrangements to position British UN forces there, while at the highest level what chances we had were rapidly being scuppered – albeit unintentionally. At best this development might have put us into a very awkward, if not dangerous, position with the Serbians and Serbs. It was all a little worrying, though in the event there was a little bad feeling towards us, which was evident when they spoke to us, but nothing too serious.

I am amazed we continued driving south to Zvornik that afternoon, but, not wishing to waste time, Brigadier Myles was determined to get to Tuzla as soon as possible. At Zvornik we approached the long (and highly strategic) bridge over the River Drina, which forms the boundary between Serbia and Bosnia. At the bridge there were checkpoints at either end that appeared to be manned by a mixture of Serbian and Bosnian Serb soldiers, although it was difficult to differentiate them as they were inclined to wear no badges of rank or insignia. The checkpoints consisted of tank obstacles pulled across the road, a barricade and a cabin from which the guards patrolled. There were a lot of soldiers guarding each checkpoint too. Obviously nobody knew we were coming but

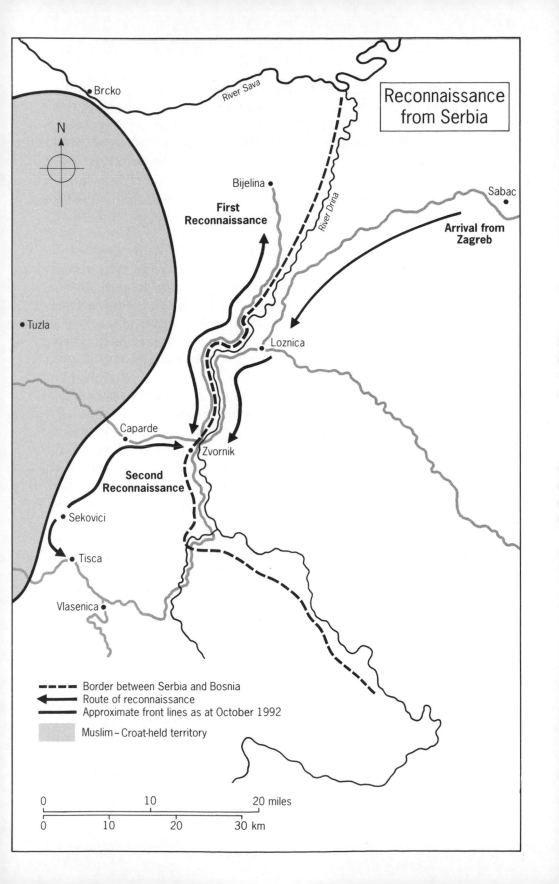

Reconnaissance from Serbia

N

Brcko

River Sava

Bijelina

First Reconnaissance

Sabac

Arrival from Zagreb

River Drina

Tuzla

Loznica

Caparde

Zvornik

Second Reconnaissance

Sekovici

Tisca

Vlasenica

- - - - - Border between Serbia and Bosnia
←───── Route of reconnaissance
───── Approximate front lines as at October 1992

Muslim – Croat-held territory

0   10   20 miles
0   10   20   30 km

Brigadier Myles decided that should not put us off. We drove straight up to the first checkpoint on the eastern side of the bridge. After a short discussion using Nick Stansfield we were allowed across to the western checkpoint. Again we needed to convince the soldiers there that we should be allowed to proceed. Despite our lack of papers – they seemed to have an almost insatiable appetite for 'papers' – we were allowed to go on and we turned right at the junction at the end of the bridge.

But our success was short-lived. About four kilometres further into Bosnia, our travels to the west were stopped by another Serb checkpoint. All our vehicles were searched. We were fairly indignant about this, but our accompanying UNMOs explained this was quite normal – especially as none of us was armed. I made a mental note to myself that we had to address this problem frontally. When we came to the area I did not want any of our vehicles searched at check-points. It was another fundamental conclusion. From the start I decided we must insist absolutely that nobody should stop our vehicles from going where they wanted in accordance with our UN mandate. The experience of being delayed at these Serb checkpoints was a valuable lesson. After a while, though, the Serb commander agreed to let us continue, but north to Bijelina rather than west to Tuzla. Additionally we had to be escorted as we went. Despite this escort, another checkpoint just to the south of Bijelina stopped us again and held us there. Frustrating as it was, we were learning just how difficult things could be. Philosophically we decided to use the time to cook our supper from rations, but after two hours or so Brigadier Myles decided enough was enough. We turned around and headed back over the bridge at Zvornik to spend the night in Serbia at a seedy hotel.

The next day we started by driving to the Zvornik bridge again. This time we were able to get into conversation with a Serb Military Policeman called Splico. Accompanied by the obligatory Kalashnikov with three magazines taped together on the weapon as well as a pistol and knife strapped to his belt, Splico seemed more than willing to talk to us. We explained that we wanted to get to Tuzla, which he found quite amusing. Splico explained, as gently as possible, that we would have to cross the lines to do so and the overflowing graveyard on the hill in front of us was testament to how difficult such a plan was. However, Splico did get us back across the bridge into Bosnia and came with us for a little way. Several checkpoints stopped us. Each demanded to know what we were doing, where we were going and what authorization we had to travel. As we had none whatsoever, things were not easy.

As we travelled on a different route from the day before, first west then south-west, we saw considerable evidence of severe fighting. For the first time we saw houses destroyed by fire. Most of them looked like they had been of very good quality once. Occasionally we could hear sounds of firing, although we never came face to face with any action – indeed we were working our way around it, as we were simply trying to get to Tuzla. Progress through the area was painstakingly slow. At one point, in order to proceed further, we had to wait to join a convoy of vehicles which was then 'escorted' past a place called the 'Black Mountain', although we never saw a black mountain. Our escort was a civilian lorry on to the top of which an anti-aircraft gun had been fitted. The whole contraption looked very strange. We tried to take some photographs of it but had been warned by our accompanying UNMOs that if we were caught doing so our chances of getting any further would be terminated immediately.

As we reached a three-way junction at Tisca we encountered yet another roadblock. This was key to our progress. From here we had to turn east towards Tuzla or we would be wasting our time. I noticed on the wall of the guardhouse about a dozen A5-size notices beneath a cross, each with a person's photograph and some script. I hadn't seen Serb obituaries before. This was the way local people learnt who had been killed and later I was to discover that the system was common to all three sides in the conflict. The commander of the roadblock here was adamant: he would let us turn south-east towards Sarajevo – the same route as the French had come – but there was no way he was prepared to let us go along the Tuzla road. He maintained that there was severe fighting along that way, we didn't have authorization to go and, in any case, he was not prepared to let us proceed. We really could go no further and Brigadier Myles had no alternative but to turn us around.

The next morning we had decided to split up in an attempt to get more done. Whilst Brigadier Myles and the bulk of the Reconnaissance Party stayed on in the Zvornik area investigating possibilities there, Neil Wright had made an appointment for me to meet Lieutenant-Colonel Michel Jones, Commanding Officer of the Canadian Battalion (the so-called Vingt-Deux). After that we hoped to try to get to Banja Luka to talk to the Serb Commander about positioning British soldiers in his area of operations. Early in the morning Neil Wright, Peter Telford, Nick Stansfield, a doctor called Saun and I left our hotel in a UNHCR vehicle in company with a British Land Rover. Very decently, Michel Jones had volunteered to travel from his base at Darovar to the Headquarters of the Nepalese Battalion in one of the United Nations Protected Areas.

It took us about four hours to get there and Michel Jones arrived shortly after us. Peter Telford and Saun continued directly back to Zagreb leaving only Neil Wright, Nick Stansfield and myself in the UNHCR vehicle. Michel was a typical Canadian officer with a straightforward and helpful attitude. It was his Battalion that had so impressed the Chief of the General Staff by its work in Sarajevo a couple of months before and I had always planned to meet him if at all possible. The Canadians had dealt with a series of snipers very successfully having been called into the Bosnian capital by General Lewis MacKenzie and then later they had been returned to their more normal deployment position in Darovar.

Michel briefed me that in dealing with the Serbs it was best to start at the highest levels and then work downwards. I told him that Neil Wright and I wanted to get to Banja Luka so that we could make contact with a senior Serb officer, if that were possible. Michel thought it was a good idea and worth trying although he was not to sure we would be able to get all the way to Banja Luka without authorization. I suggested that we might try to put a Battalion Group base at Bijelina and the main point of our going to Banja Luka was to discuss this – maybe even getting Serb backing.

'In this place,' Michel advised, 'move slowly and consolidate before continuing.' He felt that any Battalion needed about fifteen interpreters and these were a very high priority. I made a note of this again as I had already thought it would be very important to get MOD backing to take on a considerable number of native-speaking interpreters, probably with a mix of Serb, Croat and Muslim backgrounds. He told me that he had had to bribe Muslims in order to get approval for aid to be delivered to their own people. What information he had been given by the UN was worse than useless and he felt that national intelligence sources were essential. Also we would need a highly developed system of liaison officers. 'Nobody in the Balkans is trustworthy,' he suggested, 'maybe that also includes the United Nations.'

We talked about how to get the right mix of armoured vehicles. Here Michel was adamant. He advised, 'Noise impresses, size impresses, and numbers impress. I want more of everything. The French armoured personnel carriers are better than mine but they are not as noisy or impressive.' On the subject of crossing obstacles like barricades or minefields, Michel suggested that if we went through them, then we should put them back together again after we had passed. Everything Michel said made great sense to me – especially about the use of armoured vehicles. I thought his briefing was particularly important as there was still some debate, even amongst the reconnaissance team, about whether Warrior was the right vehicle to bring to the Balkans. Personally I was always convinced it was but there were some who suggested Saxon (a wheeled armoured personnel carrier based on a three-tonne vehicle) was more appropriate for humanitarian aid operations.

Having thanked Michel for coming so far to brief me, Neil Wright, Nick Stansfield and I left the Nepalese Battalion Headquarters and drove south out of the United Nations Protected Area and across the River Sava to Prijedor. Thereafter we turned east and headed for Banja Luka. All along the route we were continually stopped at checkpoints. Again, we had

no authorization but we maintained we were going to see
the Banja Luka Corps Commander and were in a hurry. This
seemed to work better at some checkpoints than others but
in the end we managed to approach the outskirts of Banja
Luka. A modern town, it was nonetheless dilapidated with
few of the traffic lights working, though there was no evidence of fighting having taken place here. Once in the centre
of town, we asked for the Corps Headquarters building and
we were directed to a concrete hall. We requested of the
officer of the guard an interview with the Banja Luka Corps
Commander and were told to go upstairs to a bar and wait
there. On our way we noticed a large meeting was taking
place across the courtyard. There, through a large plate-glass
window, we could see Cyrus Vance and Lord Owen holding
a meeting with the Serb leaders. This came as quite a surprise
to us and both Neil Wright and I immediately agreed that we
must not get involved. But we realized that such a high-level
meeting might destroy any hopes we had of meeting the
Banja Luka Corps Commander.

In the bar we met a Serb major called Jordan Pavlovic.
Apparently he was a logistics staff officer in the Banja Luka
Corps Headquarters. Over a drink we explained to him what
we were trying to do. We told him that we had really come
in the hope that we could talk to the Corps Commander about
basing British UN troops within the area controlled by the
Serb Army, particularly somewhere close to Bijelina. Pavlovic
was most courteous and helpful.

After a while the Vance–Owen meeting started to break
up for what was likely to be a very late lunch. Pavlovic slipped
away and came back with Colonel Mulutin Vukelic, who
introduced himself as the Deputy Commandant (of 1st
Corps). He took us to a small conference room and listened
very carefully to what both I and Neil Wright had to say.
From my point of view, I was trying to get bases and Neil
was talking about UNHCR operations. We seemed to get on
well together. Vukelic stated that he had great respect for the
British Army and would help if he could. Apparently a man
called Colonel Novica Simic was Commandant of the Bijelina
Serb Command and we would need to speak to him before

proceeding further. Vukelic felt that it might be possible, which was heartening news, but at this stage in my tour I was still naive enough to take things at face value. Later I was to learn that such a statement was a very long way from anything happening in Bosnia. At the end of the meeting with Vukelic, during which he had missed his lunch with Cyrus Vance and Lord Owen, we seemed to part on the best of terms. Neil Wright and I felt we had achieved something, if nothing else by getting there and talking to a high-level commander.

Apart from a delay at a checkpoint at the bridge over the River Drina, we had a relatively trouble-free return passage to Zagreb and we were back in the early evening, in time for me to go directly to the conference room. Air Marshal Sir Kenneth Hayr, Deputy Chief of the Defence Staff (Commitments) was in deep conversation with the senior officers including Brigadier David Jenkins and Brigadier Myles. I explained briefly what I had been doing and that I felt we might be able to get aid in from Belgrade. However, it was clear to me that something was wrong. Things had changed. At a higher level it had been decided that such an approach was not going to work – maybe because of Serbia being expelled from the UN or perhaps for some other reason, I don't know. Clearly, our work over the last few days had been largely a waste of time. I was disappointed. Brigadier Myles was furious about it. I do not blame him: it had been a thoroughly unpleasant task that had been well executed, and now we were learning that we need not have bothered.

I now understand that Brigadier David Jenkins had been to see General Morillon. The nightly situation reports we had been sending during our reconnaissance had hardly been encouraging. Having been briefed on our lack of progress, General Morillon had decided we should try a different tack. It had been agreed by General Morillon and the senior British officers that we should now reconnoitre a route to Vitez in Central Bosnia. Our direction of approach was to be from the south, from Split in Croatia. There was already a UNHCR office established in Vitez and our job would be to design a plan to support its operations there. Although an approach from Belgrade was still considered possible, it was unlikely to be adopted.

All of us were very tired and so it was with relief that we heard we had been booked into the International Hotel for the night. It was great to have a proper bath and sleep in a decent bed.

CHAPTER 3

THE PLAN SET

Getting the operational plan properly worked out by reconnaissance in advance is crucial to the subsequent success of
any operation, which was why we were spending so much
time looking at the options before final decisions were made.
For us on the ground it may have been frustrating to have
apparently wasted our time approaching from Serbia, but one
good thing had come out of it: the reports we had sent back
about our lack of progress in Serbia had quickly convinced
those in authority above us that there may be a better option.
We had to find another way.

The next morning we were revising our reconnaissance
plans anew in the conference room at Pleso Camp when Mark
Cook brought Sir Fitzroy and Lady Maclean into the room.
We had all heard about Sir Fitzroy, the most famous of the
British liaison officers attached to Marshal Tito's forces during
the Second World War. Mark Cook explained that Sir Fitzroy
was shortly to present UN medals to the Royal Engineers
under his command. Apparently Tito had given Sir Fitzroy
Maclean a fantastic house on an Adriatic island as a present
in recognition of his wartime services to Yugoslavia and he
was staying there at the moment. It was a real privilege for
us all to meet such a distinguished old British soldier.
Although he now seemed very frail of body, he was very
quick-witted and a fascinating man. Lady Maclean herself
was full of energy. In conversation with Sir Fitzroy he
recounted how during the war he had asked Winston
Churchill which side he should support when he landed in

Yugoslavia. Churchill retorted, 'Support the side that kills the most Germans.' Presumably Sir Fitzroy felt Tito had the best chance of doing that and so joined his cause.

By midday we were airborne bound for Split. In a C–130 Hercules loaded with three of our land cruisers, we were on a route that took us directly out over the Adriatic – to avoid the war zones – and then south-east parallel to the coast. I sat beside Colonel Roy Lennox on the flight and we chatted about how things were going. I was a bit depressed by our apparent lack of progress. We seemed to have been wasting our time a little when we had made our reconnaissance via Serbia. Roy disagreed, saying that it had been worth a try and we agreed that perhaps we would have more luck approaching from the south. At least our port of entry was on the Adriatic.

We had arranged to be met by another UNMO, Major Kent Carswell, a Royal Canadian Dragoons officer, at Split Airport but nobody was there when we arrived. We could do nothing but wait for someone to turn up. On this very hot day, the desolate airport was not the place to be, and we had to wait there for about ninety minutes. We fussed around our vehicles trying to keep cool whilst we waited. A typical Mediterranean airport, Split, like Zagreb, had a single runway and looked as though it had been unattended for some time. There were signs of considerable fighting, with bullet holes evident on some of the buildings' walls, and later we were to hear that there had been quite a battle here when the war had first started.

When Kent Carswell arrived he apologized profusely but it was hardly his fault. He had had very little warning of our impending arrival and had been trying desperately to get us accommodation. Arranging board and lodging for over ten people in Split, which was bulging at the seams with refugees, must have been nearly impossible. But in fact he had done so in a hotel called Medena Apartments.

Led by Kent in his vehicle, we drove out of the airport and turned west on the main road. After ten minutes or so we passed through a place called Trogir and turned uphill along a short drive to the hotel. It was clearly designed for holidaymakers and for happier times. With a superb view of the sea, and tennis courts and a swimming pool, it must have made it a great place for relaxing in the past. Sadly now most of the hotel was full of refugees, as were all the surrounding apartment blocks. In nearby flats every balcony was crowded with washing lines sagging with drying clothes. There were children everywhere. Once again, as in the hotel near Zvornik, it made us feel very uncomfortable to be taking accommodation at all. However, we had been allocated small apartments and I was to share with Malcolm Wood again.

As soon as we had dropped off our bags at the hotel, Brigadier Myles, David Glyn-Owen, Nick Stansfield and I drove the thirty-minute journey to Zagreb with Kent Carswell to visit the ECMM offices at Hotel Split. In a hotel room which doubled as part of the ECMM offices we met an ex-British Army officer called Geoff Beaumont who was on contract to the ECMM and who immediately agreed to give us all the help he could. After a brief discussion about the worsening situation in Central and Southern Bosnia, Geoff took us down one floor to the ECMM's Croatian liaison office where we were introduced to two men, Tomislav Vidosevic, who was in charge, and his assistant Zdeslaw Perkovic (known as 'Elvis' due to an uncanny resemblance to a rather young Elvis Presley). They were charming and very anxious to help. Despite the fact that we had arrived relatively late on a Saturday evening, both men spent two hours doing all they could to make arrangements to get us from Croatia into Bosnia. The telephone lines within Croatia, but especially into Bosnia itself, were appalling, but they seemed to have made progress and in the end we agreed to be back at Hotel Split by 10.30 next morning in order to be guided on our way.

We now had a plan of sorts: Vitez, where there was a UNHCR local office, was our aim. Once there we could assess our chances of setting up an operation to provide aid to Central and Northern Bosnia. Neil Wright, through his contacts in the UNHCR, had booked rooms for us in a Vitez hotel for that night.

All of us were very grateful that the clocks went back overnight as it gave us an extra hour in bed, but in the morning

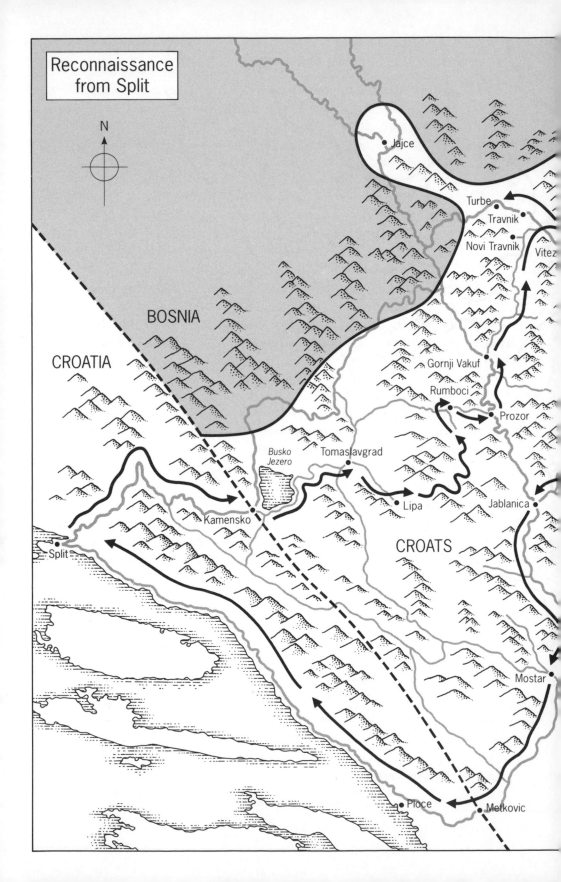

Reconnaissance
from Split

N

Jajce

Turbe
Travnik
Novi Travnik
Vitez

BOSNIA

CROATIA

Gornji Vakuf
Rumboci
Prozor

Busko
Jezero
Tomaslavgrad

Kamensko
Lipa
Jablanica

CROATS

Split

Mostar

Ploce
Metkovic

Maglaj

Novi Seher

Zepce

Zelece

Ribnica

Banovici

Tuzla

MUSLIMS

Kakanj

Vares

Milankovici

Kladanj

Olovo

Breza

Kiseljak

Sarajevo

Tarcin

Routes taken on Reconnaissance

Approximate front lines at October 1992

Serb-held territory

0		10		20		30 miles
0	10	20	30	40		50 km

we were in good time to meet Tomislav at Hotel Split. Overnight he had been as good as his word and a police car was
stood by to escort us to the Bosnian border. In a convoy of
four vehicles, we followed this police car out of Split. We
wound our way slowly up an increasingly steep hill over a
pass and, as I looked back on the relative peace of Split, which
looked exquisite and timeless poised on the craggy coastline,
I wondered exactly what we were letting ourselves in for
this time. As we climbed higher and higher up the pass the
temperature dropped considerably. After ninety minutes we
reached the Croatian–Bosnian border near a place called
Kamensko.

Kamensko did not amount to much, just a couple of Portakabins, a few men in blue uniforms and a building with the
word 'Bank' on it, which was closed. The men in uniform
were Croatians and, though they stopped every car, they
seemed rather indifferent as to whether we went through or
not. We were told to wait at this border crossing point for
our next escort that was apparently due to arrive and take
us on into Bosnia.

After a short while a Croat military police car arrived. Nick
Stansfield spoke to the policemen and then told Brigadier
Myles that we were to follow on behind the car. Crossing the
border we went along quite a good road past a huge, practically dry lake which we identified on our maps as Busko
Jezero. Skirting south and then north around it, we climbed
into the mountains again to the top of a pass. We passed a
river that came straight out of the mountains from an under-
ground source and which seemed to feed the lake. Descending
from a mountain pass we came to a large plain and could see
a town in the distance. On our maps it was called Duvno but,
as the locals all called it Tomaslavgrad, that is what it was to
be for us from then on. Looking at the buildings as we drove
into the town, I noticed that the majority of them had long
wooden planks leaning against the walls in front of the
windows and doors presumably to protect them from shelling
and so we assumed that Tomaslavgrad must be under some
sort of threat. We were taken directly to the Croat Headquarters, which had been set up in an old police station that

had been much fortified. Not only did sandbags protect some of the cellar windows – suggesting that the cellar was a bomb shelter – but most of the external windows up to the first floor were also protected by the same long planks of wood as elsewhere in town. As we arrived a siren was sounding. But nobody seemed to take much notice of it. We parked our vehicles in the Headquarters car park and were guided into the building itself. The guide told us that the siren was a warning of a possible artillery or air attack, but we heard nothing during our visit. Much later, when Tomaslavgrad was the main base for our logistic troops, Serb artillery gave the town a severe pounding – putting over one hundred and forty shells into it from the hills, some of which landed in the British UN base.

Within the Croat Headquarters we asked to speak to the Commander, but were told he was not there. However, we were a little surprised to be greeted in English by his deputy when we were taken upstairs to an office. A man of medium height, relatively slight build and sporting a small moustache, he introduced himself, with a Canadian accent, as Nicholas Glasnovic. He sat us down behind a small conference table in the office and explained that he had emigrated to Canada as a boy. His military experience outside Bosnia had been gained as a soldier serving with Princess Patricia's Canadian Light Infantry. He told us he was not alone in coming from outside to 'help'. There was quite a number of mercenaries fighting alongside Croat forces based in Tomaslavgrad. Whilst we were inside talking to Glasnovic, those left outside the Headquarters met a Glaswegian who had recently arrived in the town. The Glaswegian also confirmed that there were other 'Brits' there too. From him we learnt that the front lines were only about fifteen kilometres away and well within artillery range – thus the protective wood on the openings of buildings.

Glasnovic was a little wary of us but positive. He promised to help if he could. Brigadier Myles asked him for an escort over the mountains to Vitez and he said it could be arranged, but that it would take a while to organize.

Whilst we were waiting Glasnovic explained that he had

returned voluntarily to Bosnia in order to join his people in their fight. He emphasized that the Croats were strongly linked to their land but that they were a very simple people. He suggested that we were in such a 'barren' part of Bosnia that we would be able to find some people who didn't even know that Tito was dead. Clearly he was in some discomfort and, when I enquired about this, he told us he had been wounded earlier in the summer. Two shots had apparently struck him, one through the leg and the other in through the back and out through the chest. From the pain evident as he talked we did not disbelieve him. Obviously he loathed the Serbs whom he called 'Chetniks'. They were beyond contempt and were the kind of people who would 'cut off the leg of a pig whilst keeping it alive so that its screams upset people across the front line'.

Despite being well received by Glasnovic we were anxious to get on our way and so it was a relief when the escort was ready. We were led out of Tomaslavgrad again by a Croat military police car. Initially it took us east from the town until the metalled road ran out at Lipa, then we started to climb up through the mountains on a rough track. We couldn't believe how rough it was but John Field was adamant that, with a lot of engineer effort, the track would be usable for convoys of UNHCR trucks to get aid into the centre of the country. I was not so sure but bowed to John's judgement, which later proved correct – right through the winter. It took us over five hours to pass through the mountains, descend to the town of Prozor, travel over a pass to Gornji Vakuf and then finally journey along a ravine to Vitez. At all the roadblocks our escorts had a brief word and then we passed through. One heartstopping moment occurred as we were entering the outskirts of Vitez. It was well after dark. Suddenly through the darkness we saw a manned checkpoint. We were waved through and, not wishing to lose the initiative, drove on sharply. But, as we did so, my vehicle very nearly ran over some anti-tank mines on the far side of the road block. We missed driving over them by inches. Such mines are commonly used in Bosnia to channel traffic through a chokepoint and were normally left inert, but you can never count on that and later I often saw live mines at such places.

Our destination was Hotel Vitez where Neil Wright, through the auspices of the local UNHCR office, had arranged our accommodation. The hotel, a modern, concrete building, was the Croat Headquarters and did not look too bad from the outside, but it was neglected, dirty and smashed-up inside. Again, I shared a room with my increasingly good friend Malcolm Wood. We were provided with a rather basic supper but I think we were surprised to get anything at all and so were very grateful. This was the first time I saw Vitez. At night it seemed a depressing place, without many lights, people moving about the streets or much traffic.

After supper Neil Wright introduced us to Anders Levinson, who ran the UNHCR office based in Vitez. Anders was a Dane who had been in Vitez for about six weeks at this time and he briefed us thoroughly on the situation as he saw it. He was young and clearly idealistic, energetic and someone who wanted to do his very best. I took to him immediately, but, unsurprisingly, he had very little experience of dealing with military officers. His knowledge of the front lines was impressive and he certainly had a clear vision of how we could help him, but a lot was unrealistic from our point of view. Anders went on to suggest that we should be building refugee camps as well as providing electricity, water and sewers. At this point Brigadier Myles Frisby could hold himself back no longer and said bluntly this was well outside our brief. It was almost midnight, all of us were very tired, and so it was inevitable that tempers were fairly short all round.

During the night we heard many explosions and much firing. A lot of it seemed quite close and so we presumed it was ill-disciplined 'cowboys' simply shooting off a magazine of ammunition. The explosions were more of a puzzle though.

By now our plan was starting to firm up. We were beginning to think that it might be possible to locate three companies in the Vitez area and have the fourth in the vicinity of Prozor/Gornji Vakuf to provide us with security at the 'back door'. We did not envisage Warriors being used over the mountains, since their job would be escorting forward delivery in the most dangerous places. Clearly the route we had crossed would become a major logistics headache if no other one could be found. There was the possibility of using the main road past Mostar but we understood this was often interdicted by Serb artillery attacks. In the winter the mountain route would require immense sapper efforts and would probably need Royal Engineers to be permanently positioned on it in order to facilitate snow clearing, vehicle recovery and maintenance.

Next morning Anders Levinson took us to Travnik, a town about ten kilometres west of Vitez. He wanted to illustrate his problems 'in the raw' and so first stop was the Travnik Refugee Centre. There, in an old high school, about two to three thousand refugees were living in class rooms. They were mainly Muslims who had been 'ethnically cleansed' out of areas controlled by the Serbs to the north and west. What we found most upsetting about their accommodation was the state of the lavatories. Three Asian-type toilets, which were overflowing with sewage at the time, were all that was available for the refugees. Afterwards, with Anders, we went to meet the local Refugee Reception Committee in some nearby offices where they had organized themselves well. They looked to be efficient and businesslike in the way they ran their affairs.

Whilst waiting in Travnik we met two more mercenaries. Both were Danish but they worked for very little if any money. They called themselves 'Stanley' and 'Johnnie', though I suspect these were not their real names. Like most of the mercenaries we met in Bosnia, they were in their mid to late twenties and they claimed to have served in a regular army, although several mercenaries I later met said they had had no military experience whatsoever before they arrived in Bosnia. With their military fatigues, very short hair and rugged fitness, they seemed like archetypal mercenaries to me. Johnnie and Stanley were in the business for 'kicks', or so they said. Like us they were currently living in Hotel Vitez from where they were given missions. Johnnie explained that recently he had 'slotted' a Serb as he was sunbathing on a balcony. Both of them had high-powered sniper rifles equipped with telescopes and they maintained that they were able to kill at fifteen hundred metres – again something I was a little dubious about – and they had their own Japanese jeep. At this stage I really wanted very little to do with such people and, although I listened, I hardly talked to them at all. However, as our time in Bosnia went on, I became less moralistic and found such people an invaluable source of information. When one of these men disappeared a few months later, his disconsolate friend maintained that he had simply failed to return from a mission. But I could see the deep sorrow in the survivor's face and it showed me the intense loneliness of these men with nothing but their instincts on which to survive. This is in marked contrast to Regular Army soldiers who never have to face such isolation. A battalion is a family and that family provides great support in times of trouble.

Poor fools who think that life as a mercenary might be fun in Bosnia are most certainly mistaken in this war. Within Bosnia they are not considered heroes or anything like it. A substantial number have died here and no side will give much quarter to a mercenary working for the opposition once caught. Although there do seem to be recruiting agencies, most mercenaries arrive in the country and simply walk into an army base. I gather this happened a lot in Split, though how they are employed thereafter depends on their level of expertise. Whilst I saw some (actually very few) mercenaries employed in special-forces-type units which operated behind enemy lines, I also saw some who were more of a liability – being kept in a barracks somewhere out of harm's way. The local-force commanders were not impressed by the majority of so-called mercenaries and they had very little time for most of them.

It was important that we saw as much of the area of operations we had been allocated as possible. Therefore we had to try to get to Doboj and Tuzla. We decided to start with Doboj which was not far away and which Brigadier Myles was keen to see that afternoon, although the main town had fallen to the Serb Army in the last few weeks. We were not exactly sure where the front lines towards Doboj were, and the Croats warned us that even getting as far as the small town of Maglaj may be a problem, but we had to try.

Setting out from Vitez, we travelled forty-five minutes along the main road to Zenica, beside the spectacularly beautiful rivers Lasva and Bosna that ran through deep gorges with many sets of dramatic rapids. Just after the town of Kaonik we had to pass through a narrow passage caused by a major rock-slide from the cliff above. It looked like an explosive demolition charge had collapsed the rock.

Zenica itself was a large industrial city, typically communist in style, where urban planning took second place to the overwhelming desire to create one of the largest steelworks in Europe. The steelworks itself stretched for four kilometres to the north of the city along the west bank of the River Bosna. But no steel was being made now: the works were dormant and had been since the start of the war. The town is a mass of concrete, and badly made at that. Not one of the roads has decent tarmac and the town authorities would certainly not have survived in the UK. We found the Croat Headquarters in the northern outskirts of the city. There we had a brief meeting with the Brigade Commander who readily agreed to help us go north towards Doboj. But he said there was no way we would be able to get to Doboj as it had fallen to the 'Chetniks' and he was not sure we would be able to get into Maglaj, which was under severe attack at the moment. Again, the Croats provided us with a police escort.

North of Zenica, with the River Bosna running parallel to the road, the countryside was even more beautiful. The mountains were wilder and there was less evidence of human habitation. Even the rivers seemed less tamed. A few miles short of Zepce we were diverted off the main road because a bridge had been blown down and we took a rough track for about a mile looking for the next bridge. On this detour we saw a whole village burning. Every house was on fire and there were groups of soldiers standing around. We presumed we had just seen 'ethnic cleansing' in the raw but were not sure who was being 'cleansed'. When we tried to stop to take photographs our escorts quickly grew angry and insisted that we travel on immediately. Here was the first time we had seen evidence that people were being forcibly expelled from their houses. We all wanted to do something about it but realized we were in no position to take effective action. I never wanted that to happen again.

In Zepce, a small ugly town without a single handsome building to its name, we went directly to the Croat Headquarters. Once again, air raid-type warning sirens were sounding in the town as we arrived but there was no sign of any shelling. The Commander was not there so we spoke to his deputy, Bozimar Tomic, a thin man in his mid-twenties who seemed very hesitant to me. After the introductions, we asked what was happening in Zelece, the burning village we had just witnessed. He replied that it had been set on fire by 'Chetniks' using artillery from the surrounding hills. We certainly did not believe this as every single individual house seemed to be on fire. There was no way that artillery fire could have done that. Later, when we returned for the tour proper, I was to discover that Zelece was mainly a Serb village.

Tomic was most unenthusiastic about us going further north. He stated that Doboj had been lost and he felt that Maglaj would fall soon. This was depressing for us as Doboj was one of the towns to which we were supposed to deliver humanitarian aid. Brigadier Myles decided that we had exploited as far as we could directly north from Zenica and so we returned to Vitez.

Whilst we had been away John Field and Malcolm Wood had remained behind looking for suitable places to accommodate our troops. Together with the President of Vitez, a man called Santic, they had identified a secondary school about three kilometres from the centre of town on the road to Travnik in the village of Bila. It seemed a possible site for the main Battalion base. John and Malcolm also said that they had heard there was a garage available – a heavy-goods vehicle test station – that might make a good base for our Echelon, my Battalion Group's essential administrative support.

Over supper in Hotel Vitez we revised our plans. It seemed that we might be able to operate in the area, although not being able to get to Doboj was a bit of a blow. With the lines of conflict towards Doboj seemingly impassable, the next objective was Tuzla, which we decided to try for in the morning. If we could get to Tuzla, Maglaj, Zenica and Travnik, with a base at Vitez and a main supply route that ran back from there to Split, we might have a workable zone. Getting to Tuzla would be a major advance, especially as we had been thwarted in this during our reconnaissance from Serbia.

Two very young Croat soldiers arrived next morning to guide us to Tuzla. We left early and made our way south of Zenica, through a village called Kekanj, and into the mountains where we passed by a Franciscan monastery at Kraljevac Suseska. This is a magnificent structure made of grey stone and seemed at least five centuries old.

The mountain road was tortuous and very demanding, with its rough, narrow surface and steep inclines. This time John Field was very much less optimistic about getting through the route in the winter. At one stage we put our flak jackets and helmets on after being warned at a local checkpoint that we might come under sniper fire further down the track. Certainly we heard firing as we proceeded but it was not directed at us. After a seemingly unending journey we reached the outskirts of Tuzla at 2 p.m.

Like Zenica, Tuzla is a large city with a predominantly Muslim population. It has all the hallmarks of a 'master' communist design. As we approached it, we passed a huge chlorine works, which seemed to be functioning but was very ugly. In Tuzla, there were some very wide avenues, which suggested that city planning had been evident once, but as in Zenica, the dilapidated concrete apartment blocks that sat on either side of these thoroughfares looked like they were on the point of collapse. It was not a pretty place. In the City Hall we met the President for Refugees, a man called Lukic St Jepo, who was in his early thirties and wore a beard. He seemed to be very competent and highly intelligent. St Jepo was accompanied by a trainee doctor, a woman called Nikita Tulic, who interpreted for him. After Brigadier Myles had met the Mayor we split up. John Field and I travelled for about twenty-five minutes to the outskirts of the city where we had a look at the airfield. Nikita Tulic accompanied us together with the Deputy Commander of Tuzla Garrison who was a

Muslim officer. I remembered that the Director of Military Operations had briefed us in London that the inhabitants of Tuzla wanted the airfield to be opened and certainly the Muslim Air Force Commander there, as well as the Deputy Commander of Tuzla, were desperate to demonstrate its viability to us. John Field, as an engineer, grew very excited when he saw the runway. It was clearly to international specifications but we did not see one aircraft there, unless of course you included those that had been destroyed where they had stood. We were told they had been deliberately disabled by the old Yugoslav National Army as it had withdrawn from the base. Our guides suggested that the airfield could accommodate up to three thousand troops and we saw enough prospective accommodation to back this claim up. I envisaged Tuzla airfield as a possible company base of the future. Neither John Field nor I had any authority to suggest that we might be able to open up the place to air traffic, but we promised to pass on our report to the UN.

Our journey back to Vitez seemed even longer and more tedious than our outward trip. We tried another route back in the (mistaken) belief that we must have gone wrong to have taken so long getting there. Thus we drove due south from Tuzla on the main Sarajevo road. We reached as far as Kladanj before we were forced to go into the mountains to avoid the front lines. Again the track was treacherous, dusty and difficult. It took us a great deal of time just to reach Vares. From there we took a metalled road south to Breza, by which time it was well after dark. A Croat checkpoint controlled a dirt track that ran over an exposed piece of countryside for about four miles. We were told that the track was in full view of Serb artillery on the hills around Sarajevo and that it was dangerous to proceed as we might come under fire. Therefore we decided to use only convoy lights. Luckily we still had our Croat guides with us but even they became uncertain where we were on this track. Halfway, when our guides were unable to advise which route we should take at a fork in the road, we doubled back to the checkpoint to ask which way we should take. During the ensuing discussions, the rest of us stretched our legs and leant against our vehicles, and some people smoked, while we were able to watch and hear with eerie detachment the battle raging in Sarajevo, some fifteen kilometres away. The flashes and bangs made it look like a fireworks display.

When we eventually arrived back at Hotel Vitez, Malcolm Wood, who had stayed behind to have a look at possible accommodation in Zenica, had had a couple of dramas of his own. Twice during the day he had come under air attack from MIG fighters whilst he was in Zenica. Serb aircraft had attacked first when Malcolm was with the city's Director in his office – being forced to take his obligatory slivovitz under the Director's desk as he took cover. On the second occasion Malcolm was looking around the steelworks when that came under attack. Corporal Burns, a medic travelling with Malcolm, did great work in saving an old man's life after his heart had stopped in shock.

That night a severe burst of firing suddenly started outside our room window. Malcolm had had enough. In mock hysteria he declaimed, 'I can't believe this is happening to me. I'm a "Loggie". Leave me in peace.' 'Loggies', logistics officers, were supposed to have a quieter life than the rest of us but poor old Malcolm seemed to be in the thick of all the action at the moment. Next morning we discovered that the burst of firing was from Croat soldiers firing over the heads of looters who were apparently trying to take humanitarian aid from a UNHCR convoy parked overnight outside the hotel.

No water in the morning was all we needed. Malcolm borrowed 'our' electric razor from me with the promise that he would 'see me right' when he was controlling logistic support for my Battalion. I can stand most things but loathe not having any water in which to wash in the morning and I thereby re-learnt another old lesson: carry a jerrycan of water wherever you go.

We had enough facts and information now to make a sensible plan and so Brigadier Myles decided it was time to return to Split. We took the route via Mostar out of Central Bosnia, which involved a metalled road to Kiseljak, a mountain route to Tarcin and then a good route all the way past Mostar to the Adriatic coast. The Mostar road was exceedingly danger-

ous, with six drivers reportedly having been killed by Serb
gunfire on it the week before, and so obviously we were
very wary. There was evidence of severe fighting as we looked
at the devastated houses en route. Several bridges had been
totally destroyed and makeshift constructions – looking
highly dangerous – spanned the gaps created. We had to go
around a tunnel because a demolition charge had collapsed
the roof. It was a hair-raising journey and we did not feel
safe until we entered Croatia at Metkovic. When we reached
the coast we turned right and travelled towards Split, breaking
our journey for a late lunch at the top of a cliff. Whilst the
others ate I went for a wonderful swim in the Adriatic.

That afternoon we loaded our vehicles into a C–130 and
flew back to Zagreb, where we were treated again to the
relative luxury of the International Hotel, with its hot running
water. But I awoke the next morning with a filthy cold, as
did Peter Telford. That did not help me much as we spent the
whole morning reviewing our recommendations and writing
them up. Brigadier Myles had to present our findings in
London to the Current Operations Group, aided by Colonels
David Glyn-Owen and Roy Lennox as well as John Field.
Malcolm Wood and I were to fly directly back to Germany.

The proposed plan was quite simple. The Battalion Group
Headquarters was to be positioned at the school in Vitez,
accompanied by three squadron/company groups. A company group was to be deployed in a factory complex in Gornji
Vakuf. We decided to get established properly before thinking
about deploying to Tuzla which was another one hundred
and eighty kilometres into Bosnia. The logistic support we
would require was to be located at various stages along what
we considered to be a very long main supply route from
Split. The Headquarters National Support Element (Malcolm
Wood's Command) was to be based at Tomaslavgrad with its
detachments stretching from Vitez and Gornji Vakuf through
to Split. The Headquarters of Commander British Forces
(COMBRITFOR) was to be based in Dijoule Barracks close to
Split Airport. In Split most logistic resupply would come in
via the port.

Malcolm Wood and I travelled with the others as far as

Frankfurt courtesy of Air Croatia. There we left them and took a flight to Hanover. I had written my debrief report as we had travelled as I wanted to issue it the next morning when I briefed all officers and warrant officers on the results of the reconnaissance. Much would still depend on what the Current Operations Group in London thought of the plan.

CHAPTER 4

LAST CHECKS AND BALANCING

The atmosphere when I returned to Fallingbostel on Thursday 1 October was very charged. We now felt that our deployment was inevitable and officers and men were both excited and apprehensive about the possibility. The reconnaissance I had just completed was crucial to what we were about to do. Now we had a workable plan and it was my job to put it into effect. I started passing on what I had learnt early on the morning after I had returned at a conference in Battalion Headquarters.

It took me two and a half hours to brief all officers and warrant officers on the results of the reconnaissance, including a description of the main events and some of the conclusions we had reached. Finally I outlined the plan we were recommending to the Current Operations Group in London. Everyone seemed to pay great attention and there were lots of questions. What seemed to surprise people most was the amount of fighting that was taking place. I stressed to everyone that it was quite unlike anything we had seen before – but it was most certainly not outside our competence. When we deployed to Bosnia we would do a great job.

That day I noticed in the newspapers the growing press scepticism about the rationale behind a possible deployment. It was rather amusing, considering the press had demanded British involvement there in the first place. Surely these journalists need only read their own columns to discover why we were going.

Shortly after I returned I heard that Brigadier Andrew

Cumming had been appointed to command all British forces in Bosnia and Croatia. I had known Brigadier Andrew since Staff College and his appointment was very good news. He had commanded the 17/21 Lancers and had been rapidly promoted thereafter to his present rank. He was really good fun at Staff College and had been something of an amateur jockey. I also learnt that Brigadier Andrew's Headquarters would be established on the ground first, before my Battalion Group deployed. This made sense as it would allow him to make the proper command and control arrangements.

Within days I heard that the Current Operations Group had approved our suggested plan for the operation and soon after that the Chiefs of Staff Committee and Secretary of State for Defence had also agreed it. However, the plan needed the final sanction from the Prime Minister, much of whose attention was taken up by a sterling crisis as the pound was being forced out of the ERM. Many thought that no final decision would be forthcoming anyway until after the Conservative Party Conference, which was to begin soon. This lack of final sanction was very unsettling for us.

Much of my time was now spent considering how best to set up the Battalion finally for Bosnia. Assuming that the mission was to remain giving assistance to the UNHCR in the delivery of humanitarian aid throughout Central Bosnia, I felt we had to link closely with the UNHCR at all levels. From Split, all the way up to Vitez and then beyond to the points of delivery we would support their operation, though this may not necessarily involve close escort at all times. The principal reason we had gone to Vitez in the first place was that the main UNHCR office had already been established there. Added to this, our main supply route from Split to Tomaslav-grad and thence to Prozor, Gornji Vakuf and Vitez was the only route upon which interdiction by Serb artillery action was unlikely, even though travelling was still very difficult. The UNHCR delivered its aid by use of heavy trucks, often articulated ones, and such vehicles needed to travel up decent routes. The quality of the road would have to be improved not just for ourselves but also for the UNHCR convoys, but if we could keep the route open through the winter then the convoys could probably travel most of the way to Vitez without the need for escorts. The much quicker roads which would have offered us more direct access, particularly the Mostar route, were still far too dangerous, although I had just learnt that the Spanish, who had recently announced their intention to send a battalion to Bosnia, would be made responsible for securing the Mostar road.

A fair division of responsibilities would be for the UNHCR to get its convoys to their Vitez warehouse and then for us, using Dutch Transport Battalion vehicles, to escort the aid forward to the places it was needed. The Dutch Transport Battalion was also due to move its Headquarters into the Vitez area and eventually arrived in Central Bosnia a few weeks after we did. Warriors would be used for the highly volatile areas, and indeed I could foresee situations in which we might have to establish all-armoured convoys using some of our vehicles, such as our armoured personnel carriers, as humanitarian aid load-carriers. Thus we would be prepared to take aid anywhere it was needed, almost regardless of the conditions.

But I was also sure that escorting UNHCR convoys meant far more than simply putting armoured vehicles to the front and behind. Without a mandate to force a passage through, we would have to negotiate all the way to our destinations. It would be no good simply launching a convoy and hoping that it would be able to get through the many checkpoints to its destination. We had to create the right conditions in which to operate, which might entail a ceasefire or at least a containment of the fighting between local forces. I saw it as being well within our UN mandate to encourage local forces to cease hostilities and to broker peaceful resolutions to conflicts. After all, if there was no fighting then aid could much more easily be distributed, and it might even reduce the need for it.

The large number of checkpoints throughout our area worried me. I was determined that we should never be stopped from doing what we wanted. Faced with a choice between either forcing our way through using military power or negotiating, I would obviously use the latter option unless there was no other way. Therefore I needed to have excellent contacts on the ground. We would need an extensive system of liaison officers – a decision I had already made. In Germany we did not routinely have liaison officers within our ranks but in Bosnia I felt they were essential. I intended to set up five liaison officer teams that would be self-contained insofar as they would be commanded by a captain, have two vehicles, their own communications and be prepared to operate independently away from the main base, if necessary. They would help create favourable conditions in which the escorts were to operate and they would be our everyday means of talking to local commanders. They would ascertain problem areas in advance of our operations and explain what we were trying to do. In addition I proposed to have an armoured infantry platoon in Warriors and a close reconnaissance troop in Scimitars directly under command of Battalion Headquarters as emergency standby troops. Both the liaison officer teams and the standby troops were to be closely controlled by the Operations Room. I decided that we would need to have two operations officers, which was not the normal requirement but I felt in Bosnia we would need as much help in the Operations Room as possible.

We seemed to have time for a little more training and so the officers of the Operation Grapple force went back to Sennelager. For the first time Brigadier Andrew Cumming was able to assemble the members of his staff, almost all of whom were taken from Headquarters 11 Armoured Brigade. We ourselves had met a few days earlier when we had both flown back to the UK together for meetings at HQ UKLF and it was good to meet up with him again. Sennelager gave everyone an additional chance to get to know one another and, of course, it gave Brigadier Andrew and his team the opportunity to tell the rest of us how they wanted things to work.

Brigadier Andrew opened up our study session by introducing himself before giving his first thoughts on a possible policy directive. After this I gave a talk on the way I saw the Battalion Group operating before both John Field gave the engineer plan and Malcolm Wood his logistic concept.

Over the lunch hour I heard that the Prime Minister had finally endorsed the plan. The Chief of the General Staff was about to sign a signal confirming it and the so-called 'Ship Committee' was in urgent session working out how to move us to Bosnia by sea.

During the afternoon each company was put through a small command-post exercise which served to remind us to get our Casualty Evacuation and Notification of Casualty Procedures better. It also highlighted our need to get in order what the Army call 'Zap' numbers, a code which can be used on the radio or the telephone to identify an individual without using his name. Obviously such devices are necessary in order that the names of casualties are not made public knowledge before relatives have been properly informed. The Army lays great stress on getting such matters right after many years of experience in Northern Ireland. Major-General MacKay-Dick, General Officer Commanding 1st Armoured Division, visited us during the exercise. He told me that everyone in the Army envied us for the opportunity we had been given and he was sure we would do our very best in what looked to be an impossible situation. Personally I wondered if the Army might be quite so envious of us in a few months' time.

Whilst we continued our preparations an Activation Party, whose job was to make reception arrangements and initial plans for the force coming into Croatia and going up-country into Bosnia, was deployed from Headquarters United Kingdom Land Forces and Headquarters 11 Armoured Brigade to Split. They occupied the Medena Apartments and started working to prepare the way for the rest of us. For my part I received word that I should try to get to Split in advance of my Battalion Reconnaissance Party so that I could be updated before the remainder of my officers arrived.

On 16 October the Secretary of State for Defence, Malcolm Rifkind, formally announced our deployment at a press conference in London. At the same time Brigadier Andrew Cumming was confirmed as Commander British Forces (COMBRITFOR). As things stood, though, there was still some confusion over how the chain of command would work, particularly because it had not been established whether Headquarters British Forces (HQ BRITFOR) was within the

United Nations chain of command. General Morillon felt that battalions like my own should be commanded directly by his Headquarters, in which case exactly where HQ BRITFOR was to fit into the command and control mechanism had yet to be decided. This ongoing problem – not for us in the Battalion Group so much – was unresolved for some time, with HQ BRITFOR and Headquarters Bosnia-Herzegovina Command (HQ BHC) continually unsure of the other's degree of control. Amongst other matters, being outside the UN chain of command would mean that those serving in HQ BRITFOR would not qualify for a UN medal. It was of course later resolved that all British military personnel with UNPROFOR who served ninety days in theatre became eligible for such a medal. At the time these matters seemed daft and during the ensuing discussions life could not have been easy for Brigadier Andrew Cumming.

Martin Bell of BBC TV came out to Fallingbostel. It was the first time I had met this extraordinarily decent man and we tried to look after him as much as possible. Having completed a piece about our preparations for deployment, Martin volunteered to give the officers and their wives a talk about Bosnia. He had recently been quite badly wounded in Sarajevo and was still not fully recovered but his knowledge of what was going on in Bosnia seemed profound. Martin emphasized that to regard those fighting in Bosnia as three broad camps – Serb, Croat and Muslim – was far too simple a classification. The place had seen in-fighting throughout history and this was only the latest phase of that larger conflict. He felt that the West in general had to do something much more positive to help the situation, even if such action did present severe dangers. We could not just sit and watch – or, at least, it would be at our peril if we did. But Martin explained there were residual good feelings for the British throughout the area because of our support for Tito during the last war. He had been repeatedly asked when the British Army would be coming to Bosnia. On the subject of UN missions Martin stated quite strongly that he felt such tasks were the future for the British Army in the new world order. More and more such opportunities were going to present themselves.

Martin Bell's talk to us was an ideal way to end our preparations and gave all of us, including our wives, an intuitive insight into what was going on from someone who was highly respected and talked great sense. After dinner in the Officers' Mess, Martin departed for his hotel with the promise that he would, 'See us all in Bosnia very soon.' For those of us in the Battalion Reconnaissance Party our journey to Bosnia started early the next day.

CHAPTER 5

CARDS RESHUFFLED

I was the only person in 1 Cheshire Battalion Group that had actually been to Bosnia, so we needed our own reconnaissance. We had to make a comprehensive plan of how we were going to arrive, deploy and operate, and of course my subordinate commanders needed to have as good an idea as possible about the problems they would face. I also planned to leave a few people behind when the majority of us returned to Germany to ensure continuity and to tie up final details for our arrival in Bosnia.

A total of sixteen officers from the Battalion Group formed the Reconnaissance Party, including the Company Commanders, an Operations Officer, the Quartermaster, the Paymaster, the Electrical Mechanical Engineer Officer and five Liaison Officers. However, our ranks were swollen to twenty-five in total as we needed some soldiers and non-commissioned officers (NCOs) to help us as drivers, mechanics, cooks and the like.

In order to be fully briefed on the latest situation before my reconnaissance party arrived, I travelled to Bosnia with Captain Simon Ellis, my first Operations Officer, on 16 October, a day early. Flying in a United States Air Force C–130 aircraft with us human beings squashed on either side of the vehicles we were taking with us, I must say I did not travel well. On the long, bumpy trip, I was very hot and felt sick for a lot of the way, as did several members of the British reconnaissance teams from other units on the flight.

On arrival at Split a movements NCO arranged transport

for Simon and me to the Medena Apartments, where there were even more refugees than last time, if that were possible, crammed into every available spare room. Dogs appeared to have taken refuge here too, with great numbers of them playing around the children in the street. I was never to get used to seeing people who had all the looks of British citizens living in such awful conditions. It always gave me a very uncomfortable feeling and I was embarrassed to witness such scenes. Colonel David Glyn-Owen gave us a comprehensive briefing on the latest situation and suggested the refugee situation was getting worse, which was evident all around us. Apparently now the Croats in Tomaslavgrad and the Serbs across the battle lines to their north-west had a 'hotline' which would allow commanders on both sides to talk to one another in course of a battle. Potentially this was useful to us too as we might be able to employ it to talk to the Serbian commanders as we had no direct means of communication with them at the moment. David also told us that the deployment of Sea King helicopters on Operation Grapple was being considered, although we both had severe doubts about their usefulness as it would be very dangerous to fly in Bosnia. Divoulje Barracks, right alongside Split Airport, had been rented for HQ BRITFOR, although no one was living there yet.

Later in the evening Brigadier Andrew Cumming called a short meeting with John Field, Malcolm Wood and myself at which we discussed how everyone was going to 'play' the reconnaissance; not just the Battalion Group but all other elements of BRITFOR were completing their own reconnaissances at the same time. For my part I briefed Brigadier Andrew on my ideas for Liaison Officer Teams and suggested that they remain under his operational control after my Battalion Group Reconnaissance (when I would personally go back to Germany) until my return. He agreed to this and to my invitation, since the Brigadier had never been into Bosnia itself, to accompany my Battalion Group Reconnaissance when it went up to Vitez.

Next morning I accompanied Brigadier Andrew to meet with the two officials of the Croatian Liaison Office in Hotel Split. Tomaslav Vidosevic and 'Elvis' seemed pleased to see us again and as anxious as ever to help. This time we did not expect any problems about travelling up-country but we simply wanted to make sure of this by talking it through with Tomaslav. After a press conference at which the Brigadier outlined our plans for the reconnaissance and for when we deployed completely, Brigadier Andrew and I drove to the Split UNHCR office. Having learnt that Anders Levinson was also in Split, staying at the Park Hotel, Simon Ellis and I went on to find him and over a drink Anders reported that our previous reconnaissance had made quite an impact on the locals around Vitez – particularly because Corporal Burns had saved someone's life in Zenica. Anders told me that he was intending to travel up to Vitez using the Mostar road very shortly and hoped to be in Vitez by the time we arrived tomorrow.

The remainder of my Battalion Group Reconnaissance Party arrived on the evening of 17 October. I gave out orders to them later, stressing the worsening situation and instructing how we should move up to Vitez on the next morning.

The next morning the Reconnaissance Party was held up by the inadequate preparation of our vehicles and equipment for the journey into Bosnia, primarily due to the lack of NCOs available to carry out the necessary checks. My Land Rover, which had arrived a day after me, was in a parlous state. The radios did not work properly and there was no spare fuel or water on board. I blamed myself completely for not thinking the matter through enough back in Germany. After a considerable amount of rushing around and the odd bad-tempered exchange, all thirteen Land Rovers, most with trailers, were just ready to go on time. We left the Medena Apartments at 8.15 a.m.

Progress was slow because of the weight each vehicle was carrying. In addition, personnel were crammed into every spare space in them. The journey was hardly pleasant and it was with relief that we stopped at Tomaslavgrad.

Last time I had halted here the Commander had been away but on this occasion Colonel Zelko Siljeg, an ex-Yugoslav National Army officer who now commanded the Croat operational area that stretched from Livno to Gornji Vakuf, was in his office. He was thirty-two years old and had black hair, dark eyes, a strong face and a determined look about him. I thought he looked a hard man. He told us over slivovitz, the national drink of the Balkans and ever-present at all meetings with the local-force commanders, that his opposite number in the Serb Army had been a colonel in the Yugoslav National Army when he had been a captain. He left me with the impression that he felt the lines of conflict around Tomaslav-grad might not change much in future. To end our meeting with Siljeg and as a gesture of goodwill, Brigadier Andrew presented him with a Regimental plaque which he seemed to like.

The mountain road had far more traffic on it than when last we took it and our maximum speed was much reduced by the many trailers we were dragging behind us. En route between Tomaslavgrad and Prozor, which seemed to take an age, we passed an abandoned Croat M−48 tank on a plateau in the mountains. Having dropped off Major Alistair Rule, Officer Commanding B Company, and Captain Mike Hughes, the Liaison Officer I had allocated to Alistair, in Gornji Vakuf, where they were to be based throughout our tour, we pressed on.

Our first hint of problems came on the road some five kilometres south of Novi Travnik. It was well after dark when we ran into a Muslim roadblock. The soldiers at it refused to let us pass because they said there were big problems ahead. I insisted on our right to go through and eventually, after a short delay, the soldiers reluctantly agreed. But a few hundred metres along the road we came across a Croat checkpoint. There was great tension in the air and obviously considerable animosity between the Croats on one side and the Muslims on the other. I thought with dismay, 'Oh no, we haven't even got to Vitez!'

Using Nick Stansfield as interpreter I told the Croats that we were to pass and a heated discussion then took place. The Croat officer stated that we had no special rights to pass through his checkpoint, and I immediately sprang to the attack. As I had already discovered, in these confrontations

you had to take a very firm line and a lot of bombast, noise
and aggression often paid dividends. I always deliberately
gave the impression that I was on the verge of walking back
to my vehicle and driving across regardless of what was said.
I told the Croat Commander he was wrong and that we had
very special rights to pass. We were here on the instructions
of the UN Security Council. Moreover, the Commanders of
the Croat Army would be embarrassed to discover that he
had barred our way. I was not prepared to wait any longer
and stated that I was going to go through his checkpoint
regardless. In the end, he conceded that we could pass. This
was the first time I had put one of the lessons of my reconnaissances into action. I was determined that we should not be
stopped by checkpoints under any circumstances, but at the
same time realized that I did not have the power to force
my way through. Negotiating passage through checkpoints in
Bosnia was always a gamble, which consisted of a combi-
nation of bluff, determination and good luck.

However, we were not the only ones stopped at this checkpoint. A UNHCR convoy travelling in the opposite direction
was also halted there. The leader of the convoy, a Swede,
asked for our assistance to get through. Although we were
about to go, I got out of the Land Rover and, having taken a
deep breath, went back to the Croat Commander. I told him
that the UNHCR convoy must also be allowed to pass too.
Again, after a little while, this was agreed and we stayed to
watch the UNHCR convoy proceeding on its way before we
left in the opposite direction. This was the first time we had
directly assisted the UNHCR and I felt good about it, as we
had done something positive to help.

The rest of our journey to Vitez went without any further
problems. We decided to see if we could stay overnight in the
school as I did not really want to go back to Hotel Vitez. As
we approached the school a man who seemed to be a care-
taker came out. He was perfectly willing to admit us and so
we slept that night on the floor of the gymnasium.

The school's director arrived the next morning and
stated that the school was available to be hired. We were
slightly concerned for the obvious reason that we might be

inconveniencing a lot of children, as we were here to help not complicate a situation, but the Director assured us that the school was to remain closed. I agreed that it would be suitable, provided appropriate contracts could be negotiated.

Thereafter I spent that first day back in Vitez getting the feel of the place. Brigadier Andrew and I went to see the local UNHCR Office. Anders Levinson was there, having returned from Split the day before. He introduced us to all the other members of the UNHCR staff and for my part I introduced Simon Ellis in particular, who was due to remain in Vitez from then onwards and so would be the continuity man. I briefed the UNHCR staff on how I saw our joint operations running with the utmost cooperation between us. We agreed that we must work very closely together. For their part they seemed more than satisfied at the way we intended to do things.

A visit to the Director of Vitez town was next on our agenda. I had met Jean Santic before and he was to be the main point of contact for the contractual arrangements. He always struck me as looking like a gentle businessman, well out of place in Bosnia. Once, later when I knew him well, he told me that he hated both the Croat and Muslim armies. They caused so many problems, he said. We agreed with Santic that the school seemed the most appropriate place to base the Battalion and that proper contracts needed to be agreed.

Our next meeting was ominous. In the Hotel Vitez we saw Mario Cerkoz, Croat Commander in Vitez. He was with Marijan Jukic, Police Commander, and Marko Knezovic, Deputy Defence Minister for the town. Over a cup of coffee Mario Cerkoz stated that we were welcome in the area but that trouble was just about to erupt between the Croats and Muslims. This did not fill us with too much joy – we had already seen evidence of the fact that things were very tense as we travelled into the area.

However, we had no time to waste and that afternoon I held a meeting with the Sapper reconnaissance team to decide how we might improve conditions in the school. At a first glance, using all classrooms, we might get about three hundred soldiers accommodated under hard cover, but we needed to be prepared for up to five hundred more personnel than that. The Sappers started making plans which involved a perimeter track, inside which additional accommodation would be built. We needed to construct considerable lavatory and washing facilities as well as a kitchen/dining complex.

Later in the afternoon Andrew Cumming and I travelled into Travnik to meet the local Commander of the Muslim forces. 'Brigadier' Ribo was a large, avuncular man with a huge moustache. He entertained us to coffee and slivovitz and listened carefully to what plans we had. I made sure that Simon Ellis and the liaison officers met him and we left having been assured that we were welcome in his Headquarters at any time. Both on the way into Travnik and on the way out there was an unusually large number of roadblocks and a great deal of firing throughout the evening.

On our return we decided to eat out at a restaurant in Vitez. We had invited the UNHCR staff to join us too but they sent a message saying that they felt the syreets of Vitez were becoming too dangerous at night and that they preferred to stay in their house that evening. Maybe because we were new to the area we went out anyway. We ate well in a pizzeria in town despite the fact that nobody was on the streets. However, as a precaution, all ranks including Brigadier Andrew took turns at guarding our vehicles outside the restaurant.

That night we had a good sleep, but the next morning we discovered that the situation had developed much for the worse. We returned to Vitez where we were to meet Tihomir Blaskic, the Croat Commander for Central Bosnia, but now things were very different. There was absolutely nobody on the streets. The place looked deserted. But we could feel the tension as we drove through the town. The atmosphere was electric.

Approaching Hotel Vitez, where we were due to meet Blaskic, we noticed armed soldiers in fire positions. Then, as we got out of our vehicles beside the hotel, some shots rang out. We took cover quickly and cocked our weapons. But nobody could see from where the shots had come. After a couple of minutes though things became quiet again. Some

Croat soldiers then told us it was they who had fired – at Muslim snipers, they said.

Inside Hotel Vitez we could not locate Blaskic. Mario Cerkoz was there though and he told us that Blaskic had had to go to Novi Travnik because serious fighting between Croats and Muslims had erupted. We could now hear clear evidence of this in the distance, but there was also a worsening conflict nearby, with not only small arms being fired but also the sounds of mortars and heavier anti-tank fire.

Cerkoz explained that what we were listening to was fighting between the Croats and Muslims in Vitez itself. It seemed to both Brigadier Andrew and myself as though we just ran into one obstacle after another. I asked Mario Cerkoz to try to control his forces as no possible good could come of it. In particular would he open up all roads to us. His reply was that he would do so provided the Muslims did so too. With Brigadier Andrew's agreement, I left to try to see the Muslim Commander with Zelko, Mario Cerkoz's Second in Command, who insisted on coming in our vehicle.

This was not as straightforward as it may seem, as I had heard that United Nations soldiers were not supposed to take local forces – particularly those that are armed – within their vehicles. But, since I had no choice if I wanted to get to see the Muslim Commander, we took Zelko as our guide. After a few minutes' driving through Vitez's deserted streets, we arrived at what looked to be a high-school building where most of the glass in the windows had been blown out. With considerable caution, unsurprisingly, Zelko took us into the entrance where we were stopped by some heavily armed Muslim soldiers. They all seemed to know Zelko, although they exhibited little antagonism towards him, which I found quite strange. For my part, I was driven by the desire to see the Muslim Commander and indeed convince all commanders to stop the fighting immediately. I felt that time was not on our side and everything was going wrong. I had to stop the fighting somehow because it might interfere with our deployment plan that had taken us so long to set up. This may sound silly, but I was desperate to avoid what had happened when we had approached Bosnia from Serbia and the chain of command had had second thoughts after the first reconnaissance.

Upstairs, in an office which looked like it used to belong to the head teacher, we met Dzidic Sefkija. A middle-aged rather stout man with a moustache, he introduced himself as the Commander of the Muslim forces in Vitez. Later I was to learn that he was in fact the Brigade Commander there. Sefkija was sitting at a desk surrounded by the glass remnants of the office window. He told us that during the night he had been working there when a large explosion had blown glass all over him. He was a lucky man. We had already seen from outside where a projectile, possibly a Soviet-designed anti-tank rocket called an RPG–7, had struck – about two inches below the window itself on the wall of the building. A little higher and Sefkija would definitely have died.

Whilst we were talking the fighting outside seemed to be intensifying: the sounds of a considerable battle both in Vitez itself and further away, presumably Novi Travnik, were getting louder. Zelko and Sefkija were old friends, they told us. They had been to school together and were clearly very upset by what seemed to be happening. However, Sefkija told me that he was not prepared to remove any barricades or road-blocks as he believed a force of Croat soldiers would then pass through to Novi Travnik where they would kill Muslims.

Both Cerkoz for the Croats, and now Sefkija for the Muslims, told me that the real problem was what was happening in Novi Travnik. Brigadier Andrew had already suggested that we would have to go there and now it appeared he was right. I asked Sefkija if he would warn Muslim forces in Novi Travnik that the British UN force would be going there and requested him to pass on that we wanted both sides to stop firing at 3 p.m. We would try to go into Novi Travnik at that time. Sefkija said he would do it but to be honest I did not have much faith in his ability to follow it through.

Just as we were about to depart Sefkija received a telephone call that a journalist had been ambushed near to the school and was asking for our help to get out to safety. The receiver was handed to me and, at the other end of the line, Dan Damon of Sky News, one of the first of the many journalists to report on our activities in Bosnia, told me that he had been on his way back to the school and had been stopped at a Muslim checkpoint. As he was talking to the soldiers some shots had been fired at his vehicle. They seemed to come from a hill to the south and the Muslims told him they were from Croat snipers. Rapidly Dan and his wife Sian had evacuated their vehicle and taken shelter in a nearby house. They were still in the house and asked if we could extricate them. I said I would do what I could when I returned to the school having picked up the remainder of the Reconnaissance Party, which was still waiting for me at Hotel Vitez.

Back at Hotel Vitez I passed a message to Mario Cerkoz, through Zelko, asking him to try to get a ceasefire agreed for 3 p.m. in Novi Travnik. I also asked him to warn the Croats in Novi Travnik that we were coming. To the best of my knowledge neither message – via either Sefkija or Cerkoz – was ever passed. But at the time I felt it was worth trying.

On the way back to the school we came across Dan Damon's vehicle that was parked in front of a bus that had been pulled across the road. Mines with anti-tilt switches were also positioned around the bus. Two shots had hit Dan's vehicle and one of them had shattered the glass in one of his rear windows. I asked the Muslim soldiers taking cover around the bus to direct me to Dan Damon's party, but Dan showed himself quite quickly after we arrived. In rather a heated exchange I told what looked to be a Mujahaddin soldier that the bus and mines were to be moved and we were to pass through. Surprisingly he obeyed me and we then drove back to the school taking Dan's vehicle with us. Nobody shot at us as we drove away from the checkpoint. Perhaps they had some respect for the fact that we were driving white United Nations vehicles.

But at the school the situation was very different to that which we had left behind earlier in the day. An anti-aircraft gun was firing from the hill behind at the road we had just come down. RPG–7s and small-arms fire were constant and snipers wearing black uniforms were using the school itself for cover. I went up to two of these and told them to get off the property as it was now occupied by UN troops. I was fairly apprehensive when I did this as I had no idea what their reaction might have been. I was probably the first UN soldier they had seen and it seemed likely they would have scant respect for international authority. When they did what I asked, I was gratifyingly surprised. Maybe these people responded best to orders when they were shouted – whether they understood the words or not.

John Field and his Sapper reconnaissance team were also at the school. They had tried to get down the main road to Kiseljak earlier but had been turned back by fire. Their original intention had been to return to Split via the Mostar road but now John decided that they would have to go back the same way as we had come – provided, of course, he was able to get through and we had no way of knowing that. It made sense for both John Field's party and the Sky News people to accompany us as we travelled to Novi Travnik for 3 p.m.

Thus a small convoy of vehicles left the school shortly after 2.30 p.m. Brigadier Andrew, John Field, my Company Commanders, some soldiers for protection and Dan and Sian travelled together. We encountered no problems whatsoever and just outside Novi Travnik we watched the Sappers and Dan Damon on their way south before we turned into the town itself.

At this point our troubles began in earnest. In the incident I described in some detail in the Introduction to this book the streets of Novi Travnik were instantly transformed from almost total stillness to a pitched battle.

Having careered through an enormous storm of bullets in the streets of Novi Travnik, we found the Muslim Head-quarters. Brigadier Andrew Cumming, Nick Stansfield and I entered that Headquarters as directed by a soldier in the street, finding the Muslim Commander upstairs. His name was Lendo and he was a very calm man in his mid-thirties. Trying to regain our composure, we introduced ourselves and told him that we hoped it might be possible for a ceasefire to be arranged. In conversation I asked him to release seven prisoners he was reputed to hold and, after some minutes of claiming that was impossible, Lendo suddenly made it clear that he would be able to give someone to us. This was great news, as we could take him to the Croats as a sign of good faith. After a few more minutes a man called Illya was produced. He looked thoroughly frightened and I suppose might have thought he was being led out to execution, I do not really know. Brigadier Andrew and I tried to reassure him that all would be well and that he was going to be protected by us, but from his frantic eyes we could see he was in no state to believe anything. Either way he was now in our possession and we took him with us when we left. Outside on the ground there had been a great deal of firing around the officers and soldiers left guarding our vehicles. Luckily nobody was hurt.

Using Illya as a guide, we went back across Novi Travnik. There was still a lot of firing in the streets as Illya directed us to the Croat Headquarters. At the Croat Headquarters in the Novi Travnik Hotel — the Croat Army seemed rather partial to hotels — we asked to see the Commander. We were led to the Café Grand close by and, up some stairs, in a bar we met Dario Kordich, a thin man with a crew-cut and over-large glasses who tended to shout rather than speak. He had been a journalist before the war and was now a Vice President of the HVO — and a military commander too — although I always found the Muslims to be scathing about his military competence.

Dario Kordich was surrounded by other officers who were all nervously excited in this extremely dangerous situation. Whilst the fighting continued outside, we explained that our task was to move into Central Bosnia and assist in the distribution of humanitarian aid, but that our job would be made almost impossible if the current fighting taking place between the Croats and Muslims continued. Therefore we wanted to try to help restore peace so that we could get on with our mission. I indicated Illya and told Kordich that we had just brought him from Lendo's office. Kordich did not seem to be too impressed by this and instead told me that he considered Lendo to be a war criminal. In a lengthy discussion between Kordich, Brigadier Andrew and myself, Kordich claimed that fourteen Croats had already been killed in the fighting and the man responsible was Lendo. Therefore he would not be prepared to talk about ceasefires with him. However, he was prepared to discuss the matter with a man called Merdan who was probably in Zenica.

To my surprise a mobile telephone was produced and in a few moments Kordich had Merdan on the other end of the line. We explained, through Nick Stansfield, what we were trying to do. Merdan was quick to agree that a ceasefire was possible. Kordich asked for a draft document and Merdan said he would fax one through. Again this took me by surprise: mobile telephones and faxed ceasefire documents were not what I had expected to find in Bosnia. Local forces seemed to have more modern amenities than I had ever imagined. However, Kordich insisted that Merdan's draft ceasefire should be authorized by the Bosnian Government in Sarajevo. Merdan stated that this would be impossible as he had no way of making contact with the Government of President Izetbegovic. In addition Kordich said he wanted Lendo surrendered to the Croats for trial as a war criminal. Matters were not going well but as we continued to talk (and drink) with Kordich a ceasefire fax appeared.

Amidst the ensuing discussions I was handed the mobile telephone. Somehow or other Anders Levinson had managed to find out where we were and was on the other end.

'Things are so bad in Vitez now that I may have to withdraw the UNHCR staff,' he said.

I replied that I hoped that did not happen but, of course, accepted his decision.

Kordich was still dissatisfied with the draft document: it had only been authorized by the Bosnian Chief of Staff in Zenica and made no mention of Lendo as a war criminal. But after a little while longer, during which both Andrew Cumming and I pressed him, he agreed that he would agree to ceasefire 'discussions'. I think it was Brigadier Andrew who suggested we hold the talks in our school at Vitez and this was also agreed. The final problem was that Merdan had to be present and he was in Zenica. Once more on the mobile telephone Merdan agreed to be present – provided we, the British, would collect him from and return him to Zenica when it was all over. This we agreed to do.

We had now been inside the Café Grand for several hours

and so it was a relief to get out of the dark and oppressive place. But at least we had been safe there. Those we had left outside, in order to guard the vehicles and signify our UN presence, had again been in considerable danger as the battle raged around them. Thank goodness they had been all right. The Croats guided our small convoy out of Novi Travnik and, in stark contrast to our arrival, nobody fired at us once. We were back at the school within forty-five minutes of leaving but it was now about 9 p.m.

The breakdown of law and order and the consequent ferocity of the fighting had come as a great surprise to me. But even more of a personal challenge was how to deal with the situation. I had no experience of running negotiations or arranging ceasefires, yet it seemed that unless we did so all our efforts would come to nothing.

Brigadier Andrew and I decided that he would remain in the school preparing for a meeting whilst I went to fetch Merdan from Zenica. Taking four Land Rovers with me, I left shortly after our arrival at the school but was stopped within a kilometre by an apparently unmanned road block. To make matters worse it was dark and I could see mines around it – some of them with tilt switches. The choice was either to turn around, and thus fail, or to take a risk by moving the mines. This was one of the most difficult decisions I can remember making in Bosnia. I had attended several lectures on mines and the advice was always clear and unequivocal: do not touch them, leave it for the experts. After a few moments' further thought I decided that I had to risk it otherwise all our efforts would have been for nought.

I knew I was taking a considerable risk, since all these mines had tilt switches (highly sensitive vertical rods with which the bellies of tanks trigger the mines) and they could also have been booby-trapped. As I placed my hands around the first mine I was frightened but strangely remote from what I was doing too. I said a small prayer and lifted the mine. Nothing happened and I moved it aside. Others helped me move several other mines and, growing in confidence all the time, we soon created a gap big enough for our vehicles to pass through. In fact I was never to come across anti-tank mines that had been booby-trapped in Bosnia but at the time none of us was to know that.

We travelled down the Sava–Bosna valley route to Zenica without seeing any other vehicles at all. There was the odd barricade, normally unmanned, but we entered the town about forty-five minutes after we left the school at Bila. We were directed to the Opstina building, the Town Hall, where we met Merdan accompanied by six other men, including a couple of bodyguards.

This was the first of many times I was to meet Djemal Merdan but I liked him from the start. He was my age, forty-three years old, and had been an officer in the Yugoslav National Army before the war. Of average height and build, he was good-looking with a moustache that went well on him. A fanatical footballer – I think he had only recently given up playing seriously – he was also one of the most honest men I encountered in Bosnia. It was unsurprising therefore that the Croats should want to deal with him.

After introducing myself and a brief conversation it emerged that Merdan would prefer to meet at the Hotel Vitez. As the arrangement was that we would pick up the Croat representative from there en route, this did not involve too much of a change of plan, except, of course, that Brigadier Andrew was preparing for the conference at the school. Unfortunately our high-frequency radio could not communicate back to the school. This was the first instance of the problem that high-frequency did not work in Bosnia at night. We ended up using satellite telephones to communicate down to Company locations but we could never absolutely guarantee to be able to talk directly to soldiers in the field and this remained a constant source of worry for me.

At Hotel Vitez I sent someone to tell Brigadier Andrew about the change of plan and we were shown into the office of the Croat Commander. Colonel Timomir Blaskic was again someone I was to come to know very well later and who was a crucial 'player' in Bosnia as he commanded the Central Bosnian Operational Zone for the Croats. Aged thirty-two, with dark hair and fine features, Timomir Blaskic had also been an officer in the Yugoslav National Army before the war. He always struck me as a man under pressure but never so much that he did not receive me well. That evening he was to represent the Croats in our ceasefire talks.

We sat around in easy chairs in Blaskic's office, which was really part of a suite in the hotel, and frankly I did not know quite how I was going to convince both sides that they had to stop fighting. I had never done anything like this before. To start with nobody said anything and so I felt I ought to lead. I made a short statement outlining British plans and the need for peace in order that we could proceed with these. I invited both Merdan and Blaskic to agree to issue orders to stop the fighting immediately as it was counter-productive and pointless. Blaskic stated that the Muslim forces should surrender unconditionally to the Croats and, in particular, Lendo should be considered as a war criminal. Merdan's viewpoint was that fighting should stop regardless of preconditions. After about thirty minutes of discussion, I was delighted when Brigadier Andrew walked into the room, since we had worked together so well in Novi Travnik and I was getting very tired. Brigadier Andrew whispered to me that we might try a harder line and I handed over the chairing of the meeting to him.

The Brigadier suggested that the Muslims should remove Lendo as he was obviously causing so many problems for the Croats. Blaskic fully accepted this and it was, at least, being considered by Merdan. But then Blaskic announced that he had written instructions from a 'higher authority' that no compromise was possible. There seemed little further point in continuing the discussions. Having asked both sides to get higher-level agreement to some form of ceasefire, and an 'absolute' guarantee that instructions would be given out that both UN and UNHCR convoys should pass through the area unimpeded, Brigadier Andrew ended the meeting. He presented plaques to both sides and we all chatted informally over a bottle of whisky produced by us. Everyone seemed much more amenable then but obviously nothing further was to be gained.

I was tired out. Having asked Captain Mark Cooper and his liaison team to escort Merdan and his party back to Zenica,

I returned to the school with Brigadier Andrew. We arrived to be greeted with the news that the BBC World Service had reported the extraction of the UNHCR from Vitez. The report stated that French armoured personnel carriers, sent from Sarajevo, had carried out the mission. I was not surprised as Anders had warned me he might have to withdraw if things got too bad, but now I was not sure how we stood. It seemed that the very reason for our coming to Vitez, the UNHCR office there, had just unilaterally withdrawn itself. At the end of this very long day, during which nothing had gone right, I was too exhausted to worry any more. It was nearly 3 a.m. before Brigadier Andrew and I unrolled our sleeping bags on the floor of the gymnasium.

The next day, Wednesday 21 October, I drove into Vitez to see if the UNHCR really had gone. The town was much quieter but clearly there was still a great deal of tension. I drove to the UNHCR office, which was positioned above a café, to find nobody around except a little boy who told me in gestures (I had no interpreter with me − I had let Nick Stansfield sleep on as he was more tired than anyone) that armoured vehicles had taken people away during the night.

Despite the fighting I was determined that we must continue with our plans and so I went to see Jean Santic, Director of Vitez town. The whole centre of town was in a dreadful mess, with broken glass and signs of serious fighting everywhere. The Town Hall did not have one whole pane of glass in the front of the building and there was a pile of about thirty 120mm shell-cases from a recoilless gun littered about the Town Hall car park. What a change twenty-four hours of fighting had made to the place. I was a little surprised to find Jean Santic in his office at such an early hour but was glad as it enabled me to tell him that I was going to leave nine British Army personnel at the school. I explained that they must be protected by both sides and the school should now be considered UN property. After Santic accepted all of this, I said I would be back in a week or so and wished him luck.

But, with the return of Nick Stansfield to Split, those who were to remain in Vitez badly needed another interpreter in order to assist them as they prepared for our arrival. Captain

Simon Ellis and the liaison officer teams could not operate without one. Luckily Major Alan Abraham, B Squadron Commander, had located a woman who might be able to do the job and so we went around to her flat close to Hotel Vitez. After coffee, she agreed to a salary of 200 Deutschmarks – the best currency to use in Bosnia – and we had our interpreter.

We were all ready to leave the school at 10.30 a.m. for Split, but both Brigadier Andrew and I were worried that our stay-behind party was being left out on a limb with very little support. Simon Ellis was reassuring. 'Don't worry, we'll be all right,' I remember him saying, but nobody could know how the conflict might escalate and we all realized the risks if it did. Neither the Brigadier nor I could have stayed anyway and so that was that. We drove south to Gornji Vakuf where Alistair Rule showed us around the factory selected as his base. The situation seemed very much more calm there (although it was not) and so I had few reservations about him remaining behind.

From Gornji Vakuf we travelled to Split and from there back to Germany by civilian aircraft. I had left a number of people behind in theatre. The senior officer there was Alistair Rule who was charged with setting up his base in Gornji Vakuf. Simon Ellis and two liaison officer teams (Captains Martin Forgrave and Bob Ryan) were to remain in Vitez. Their job was to link to the local UNHCR office and get to know how local politics worked. Three other liaison officer teams (Captains Matthew Dundas-Whatley, Mike Hughes and Mark Cooper) were to work the route between Split and Vitez, getting to know it and being prepared to guide people up and down it. The Technical Quartermaster Sergeant, Mr Salisbury, was to remain in Split and work with the Headquarters of the National Support Element. Everyone I left behind was to be under the operational control of Brigadier Andrew Cumming's Headquarters. But I flew back to Germany more than a little unhappy about the situation facing those left behind.

CHAPTER 6

THE ART OF THE POSSIBLE

On the last of my few days in Germany before I took the Battalion Group to Bosnia, Malcolm Rifkind, Secretary of State for Defence, visited us with Lieutenant-General Sir Jeremy Mackenzie. In my office I gave the Secretary of State a short briefing on how we had prepared ourselves and what we had found during our reconnaissances in Bosnia. He seemed well satisfied and thereafter we toured around the tank park where the soldiers were preparing their vehicles. After a short press conference Malcolm Rifkind had lunch with the officers and their wives before leaving. Personally I already had a high regard for Malcolm Rifkind and this feeling was confirmed by our first meeting in Fallingbostel.

The Operation Grapple Advance Party flew to Split on Thursday 29 October. Again our flight was by means of United States aircraft and we arrived in Croatia soon after 6 p.m. For the third time I went back to the same room at the Medena Apartments, which again I was sharing with Malcolm Wood. He had stayed on after the last reconnaissance and so was getting quite used to the inadequacies of the Croatian water supply.

The Advance Party had the task of preparing the operational area for the Battalion, having remained long enough in Germany to complete their training with their companies. The liaison officers were already in place and they would guide the company commanders completely in the early days after their arrival. However, Alistair Rule (B Company) was already in Gornji Vakuf and I brought Alan Abraham (B

Squadron) with me on the Advance Party because his Squadron's initial task would be to act as the guides, or the Regulating Organization, to get the whole force from Split to Central Bosnia. Thus the majority of the Advance Party consisted of administrative support personnel such as Mike Winstanley, the Quartermaster, and Mark Weir, the Regimental Medical Officer.

My biggest concern at this point was what had been happening in Vitez during our absence. I had kept in touch with Alistair Rule and Simon Ellis only very intermittently because the communications to Gornji Vakuf and Vitez were almost non-existent. Of course I'd known this would be the case when I had departed and had made arrangements for HQ BRITFOR to help. Thus I had received periodic reports on what was going on and learnt that things had not been easy for any of them – particularly Simon in Vitez.

After our departure Simon Ellis, together with Anders Levinson of the UNHCR, who much to my delight had returned with his staff to Vitez, had worked terribly hard to get a ceasefire. Prior to leaving I had told Simon not to take too many risks as he was totally unsupported. Although I still do not know the full story I am sure that he almost totally ignored this instruction in his efforts to get a peaceful resolution in the area. In soft-skinned Land Rovers, Simon and the liaison officer teams travelled extensively in order to bring both the Croats and Muslims to ceasefire meetings. Together with Anders, Simon had jointly chaired ceasefire meetings and over a period of several days their efforts had started to pay off. Eventually Simon and Anders managed to get a 'real' ceasefire signed – and it stuck. To have achieved that in the short period that I had been away was a great coup.

Alistair Rule had been working equally hard in the Prozor area, south of Gornji Vakuf. In Prozor also considerable fighting between the Croats and Muslims had broken out. Most Muslims had been forced to flee the town. In fact the Muslim-owned café where we had had lunch on 21 October, as the Reconnaissance Party returned to Split, was now a burnt-out shell. Again Alistair managed to help resolve the crisis. I was very proud of what those officers left in Bosnia had achieved.

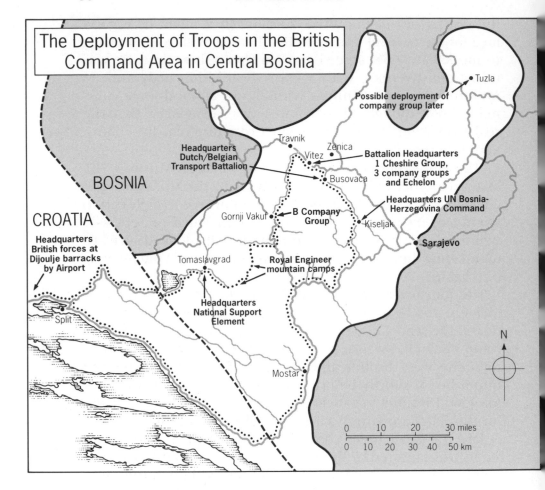

The Deployment of Troops in the British Command Area in Central Bosnia

Tuzla

Possible deployment of company group later

Travnik

Zenica

Headquarters
Dutch/Belgian
Transport Battalion

Vitez

BOSNIA

Busovača

Battalion Headquarters
1 Cheshire Group,
3 company groups
and Echelon

CROATIA

Gornji Vakuf

B Company
Group

Headquarters UN Bosnia-
Herzegovina Command

Kiseljak

Headquarters
British forces at
Dijoulje barracks
by Airport

Tomaslavgrad

Royal Engineer
mountain camps

Sarajevo

Split

Headquarters
National Support
Element

N

Mostar

| 0 | 10 | 20 | 30 miles |
| 0 | 10 | 20 | 30 | 40 | 50 km |

——— Front lines as at October 1992
········ Main Supply Route, codenamed Route Triangle
░░░ Serb-held territory

By their success they made it far easier for us to deploy the remainder of the Battalion Group into the area and equally they were instrumental in showing everyone that our role in the area would not be entirely passive.

Travelling back into Bosnia by the mountain route for the third time, Alistair Rule accompanied us, having come down to Split to meet us. In Prozor he took me to see the local Croat Commander whose Headquarters was in a factory to the north-west of the town. Alistair felt it might be a good idea for me to meet this man, Ilya Franjic, who could not see us immediately but agreed to do so after a short time. He was in his mid-twenties, with a wispy beard, thin body and no rank insignia – in common with almost all local-force commanders. Although Alistair and I were convinced that the real trouble in Prozor had been Croat-inspired, Ilya had a very different view.

'The whole problem was started by fanatical Muslims,' he assured us. 'Because of problems caused by the Muslims at the checkpoint close to the front lines, west of Prozor, eighteen to twenty of my soldiers have either been killed or seriously wounded.' I left Ilya with the remark that I looked forward to meeting him next time, but in the event I never saw him again.

The journey onwards from Prozor to Vitez was without incident and I was pleased to get back. I immediately requisitioned the school director's office and set up my desk and my camp-bed in it. I was to continue to use the place as my office right the way through the tour although I moved my bed into a house shortly before Christmas. Now that I was back for good I wanted to concentrate on getting everything ready for the Battalion Group's arrival. But then Jajce fell.

Jajce, a small town some fifty kilometres north-west of Vitez, was captured by the Serb Army on Saturday 31 October – only two days after I had arrived back. Although the town had been under serious threat for some time before and its 'fall' was fairly predictable, nonetheless it precipitated panic on the ground, as streams of refugees swarmed eastwards, and caused something close to panic up my chain of command to HQ UKLF. What particularly worried the chain of command was the new front line. The Serb Army advanced rapidly to new positions, just to the west of Turbe which was some twenty kilometres from Vitez. Only Travnik now stood between the advancing Serbs and the proposed main British Base in Central Bosnia. Some people maintained that Travnik would also 'fall' rapidly. Personally I was always much more of an optimist than that, but, to be honest, nobody really knew what were the Serb intentions.

The school at Vitez sat exactly on the main route east out
of Travnik. Streams and streams of disconsolate and utterly
wretched people passed by, more often than not crowded on
to over-burdened carts drawn by a single horse. Whole lives
were crammed on to those carts. The scenes were traumatic
and had a tremendous impact on those of us who saw them.
But what was most upsetting of all was the fact that the
people walking or riding on the carts looked so much like
our own families. My soldiers kept making this point and
asking me why it was happening in modern Europe. I couldn't
give even an approach to a decent answer. These people were
not the 'traditional' displaced persons – if there is such a thing
– these were people who never expected to be displaced in
their lives. They were mixtures of all types and classes of
people. Clearly they had had no perception of what they
might need on the road and most were in a total state of
shock. They dragged themselves past our school in a long line
and that line kept going both day and night. I asked the
sentries to try to keep a tally of the numbers going by but
they rapidly lost count as there were so many. We estimated
that as many as twenty thousand people could have passed
by in the aftermath of Jajce's fall. Where they all went to –
presumably Zenica was a favourite target as they were mostly
Muslims – we never really discovered.

The Refugee Centre in Travnik was working at full tilt.
Every corner in all parts of the big building was crowded
with refugees. When I visited it with Captain Mark Weir, the
Regimental Medical Officer, I asked Mark if he would organize a makeshift surgery in one half of the Refugee Office. We
piled up desks and used old blankets as curtains to provide
privacy. As soon as this 'surgery' was ready the first patient
was carried in to see Mark. She was a very old lady whose
breathing was scarcely discernible. Mark's feeling was that
she just did not want to live any more and was willing herself
to die. Having checked that there was little he could do for
the old lady she was taken outside again. I wonder if she is
still alive. This surgery of Mark's stayed in place for over a
week. We managed to get drugs for it, not from UNHCR who
were not equipped with them, but from Patrick Dagassan

who ran the French aid agency, Pharmacies Sans Frontières. Mark Weir's efforts were greatly appreciated by the Refugee Centre in Travnik and again it was proof that we really did mean to help the situation.

From Split Brigadier Andrew organized a convoy to carry UNHCR goods, amongst which were lots of blankets, under the command of Major Mike Healis. Travnik was being shelled on the evening of its arrival but there had been urgent requests for blankets as some refugees had absolutely no cover at all. Together with some volunteers and a UNHCR representative I travelled from place to place around Travnik giving out these blankets. In one field I remember there being about forty carts, I don't know where the horses had been placed, and each cart had its owners huddled underneath or on top of it trying to keep warm in the pouring rain. It was sometimes very difficult to find these owners; they had buried themselves very deeply in their piled possessions. Perhaps they did this for protection from either shelling and cold or perhaps it was their way of trying to get away from the hell they were undergoing. I don't know. However, I do know that those blankets and the plastic sheeting that went with them were vital. For our part, we felt at least we were doing something. It was far better than simply just watching all those swarms of people trudging past our base.

Not that this was our sole occupation at this time. Captains Bob Ryan and Martin Forgrave with their liaison teams came under fire as they were carrying out a reconnaissance west of Turbe, where they had been trying to ascertain exactly what was going on in the area of the Karaula group of villages. They managed to withdraw without too much difficulty. The next day though a BBC cameraman working with a news team, although driving alone in his vehicle, received a direct hit with an armour-piercing round on the side of his armoured Land Rover. The vehicle careered off the road and tumbled down an embankment. The remainder of the journalists in this team, travelling in a second car, managed to escape back to Vitez where they told us what had happened. Although they could not be certain, they felt sure that the cameraman, a Croatian called Timomir Tunokovic, had been killed in the incident. As Martin Forgrave knew the area I tasked him to try to get the body back, but with minimum risk to himself or his team.

Martin went to the Croats who confirmed that Timomir had been killed and, after dark, Timomir's body was recovered by a couple of brave Croat soldiers who had known him. Martin brought his body back and the armoured Land Rover was abandoned – although much later I was to receive word from another journalist, Jim Hooper, that the Serb Army had it and had offered to return it to the BBC if they wanted it. However, since the vehicle had hardly been in any state to move when last seen, we assumed they were only making this offer because it was hopelessly unworkable. Subsequently we helped the BBC take Timomir's body down to Split from where it was flown by RAF aircraft to his home in Zagreb. I had met Timomir a couple of times when he was visiting the school and so wrote to his parents.

The incident in which Bob Ryan and Martin Forgrave had come under fire and the murder of Timomir both served to emphasize just how dangerous travelling close to the front lines was and we re-examined our policy on soft-skinned vehicles in those volatile areas. More than ever I was grateful that we would have Warrior which seemed to me fairly invulnerable to almost all kinds of fire we were likely to encounter. However, at this stage the arrival of any form of armoured vehicle was still over two weeks away. In Vitez we had only Land Rovers and about forty all ranks.

But I was determined that we should act to the maximum extent – even if we were still only small in number and capability. Glynne Evans, Head of UN Department in the Foreign and Commonwealth Office, visited with Lieutenant-Colonel Neil Wright who had accompanied us on the first two reconnaissances. It was great to see Neil again and interesting to meet Glynne Evans who had a reputation for getting things done. I was about to go into Travnik to meet the Deputy President of the HVO and she accepted my offer to come with us. In an upstairs conference room in Travnik, we met Perica Krizanoc and, as I did at every meeting with local leaders when I first met them, I outlined our mission to Krizanoc and informed him how I intended to operate in Central Bosnia. Glynne Evans also asked him about the situation and he told us that he was very worried about Serbian intentions, particularly about a possible attack on Travnik itself. We talked about the fall of Jajce and the possible threat to Travnik. Krizanoc told us that Travnik consisted of forty-three per cent Muslims and thirty-nine per cent Croats. In Bosnia everyone seems to know the ethnic percentages of each town, village or even street – no wonder that large Muslim influxes across the front lines cause so much worry to the Bosnian Croats. Clearly Krizanoc was very concerned about the fall of Jajce; he felt that now Travnik would come under severe pressure.

Leaving Krizanoc, I took Glynne Evans on to the Refugee Centre so that she could see the extent of the problem. After she had left, I went to the Muslim Headquarters and again met Djemal Merdan, who was visiting the Headquarters in Travnik in his capacity as Deputy Commander of 3rd Corps and who greeted me as an old friend and recalled how I had come to fetch him from Zenica in the middle of the night the month before. Having asked him about the current situation with regard to the advancing Serb Army, he took my map and marked on it the front lines in very great detail – using map symbols I recognized as being straight out of Soviet Army textbooks. I noticed that there were still forward detachments of the Muslims positioned on the outskirts of Jajce that were well in front of the main front line and were extremely vulnerable. Merdan explained that the area between the forward detachments and Turbe was not really controlled by anyone at the moment. He felt the forward detachments were safe enough for the time being but accepted that they may have to withdrawn quite soon.

Meanwhile the Croats were to be faced with further tremendous challenges. The threat posed to Jajce before it fell persuaded them to draft in a considerable number of troops from other areas – particularly Tomaslavgrad. Now that Jajce had fallen, those 'external' troops wanted to go home. In Bosnia most forces fighting on all sides are from the local area; it is really a domestic war in many more ways than it at first appears. Suddenly a very large column of dispirited Croat soldiers, mostly in old cars and on tractor-driven trailers, appeared in Vitez. They really did look a miserable sight. They all were perfectly willing to say what was happening, which was a clear indication to us that morale was very low. In fact they just wanted to go home and were going to stay together until they did so. They were not soldiers at all; very few had had any real training. They could handle their weapons all right but were really civilians in uniform. I asked them what they were paid and they laughed. They were paid practically nothing and certainly had had no money at all for several weeks. In a normal army what they were doing would properly be called mutiny but no army in Bosnia was normal. For two days this large column stayed around Hotel Vitez, although once it tried to head west and then south to Gornji Vakuf but was turned back by its own side. It was clearly very embarrassing for Timomir Blaskic, the Croat Commander of Central Bosnia. When I asked him about it he simply shrugged his shoulders in a gesture of resignation. Eventually Blaskic agreed that the soldiers could go home but they had to hand over their weapons in Kiseljak as they did so. The last we saw of the mutinous column was as it headed towards Kiseljak.

Although, in principle, I had previously decided not to have anything to do with mercenaries, as I wanted very much to disassociate our activities from theirs, it was not easy in practice. Actually they could be a considerable source of information and so I began to talk to some of them. In Travnik I saw 'Stanley', the Danish mercenary whom I had first met on my second day in Vitez during the initial reconnaissance. Stanley told me that 'Johnnie' had been missing for some days now and so was their jeep which they had jointly owned. Johnnie may well have been killed or captured, he felt – or simply disappeared, I thought. Either way, Stanley himself seemed very lost and completely uncertain as to what to do. I never saw him again and did not have too much sympathy with his plight as both Danish mercenaries seemed to have derived great pleasure from killing people on behalf of the Croats, at long range with their sniper rifles.

However, I did not feel quite the same about two other mercenaries I met at this time. Kevin 'Ted' Skinner and Derek Arlow McBride worked with the Muslim Army and I first met them outside the hospital in Travnik when I went to see the director there. Ted stood up as I approached, called me 'Sir', and introduced himself. He was middle-aged, slightly under average height, plump and certainly did not look like a standard mercenary. He explained he was a captain in the Muslim Army and that his job was training and medical evacuation. Originally he had come from Blacon, outside Chester, although he had never served in the British Army. I think he said he had emigrated to New Zealand when he was young; he claimed to have been a sergeant in the New Zealand infantry and certainly he wore a New Zealand badge in his beret. But Derek Arlow McBride had been in the British Army, or at least said he had. He seemed far more a soldier; again middle-aged, but large and wearing an Argyll and Sutherland Highlanders cap badge. Both men wore their own uniforms and carried a selection of weapons. They told me they lived in the Muslim barracks at Travnik and received hardly any pay. Calling themselves 'helpers' rather than mercenaries, they claimed that they were in Bosnia because it was such a tragic situation. The Muslims needed all the help they could get, they said.

Ted Skinner was greatly dismayed about the fall of Jajce and particularly the way some of the refugees from there had been treated as they tried to escape in front of the Serb Army. On the day we met they had just attended the funeral of a six-year-old boy. Apparently the boy had been killed by a grenade thrown by a Serb soldier into the back of a truck where he was travelling. As his father rushed around to help the boy, he was shot too. For these two 'mercenaries' I had much more time, even though I still could not understand their motivation, and we received a considerable amount of useful background information from them.

Whilst I was trying to set up the Vitez Base, Brigadier Andrew in Split was keeping in close touch with HQ UKLF and the MOD about the Serb Army advance. The biggest worry of all was that we would be cut off by such an advance,

or even that the Croats might simply abandon the area —
effectively leaving the Muslims to their fate. There was a
growing feeling amongst some that the Croats might be preparing to expand the HVO-controlled area to the east of Mostar, where the more radical Croats wished to establish the
so-called Herze-Bosna state, its capital being Mostar. This
manoeuvre, were it to take place, would place us, the British,
who were trying to establish the biggest operational force on
mainland Europe since the Second World War, in the middle
of what looked to be the most threatened area. It was thus
hardly surprising that the chain of command above me was
so worried. I was tasked by Brigadier Andrew to try to make
my own assessment of the situation so that we could get a
more complete picture.

Until my Battalion Group was fully established in our operational area, I was to remain under direct British command
through Split to HQ UKLF. This made absolute sense as we
needed to build up properly and it was a national responsibility to do so. In any case Brigadier Roddy Cordy-Simpson, as
Chief of Staff at HQ BHC, was not yet in a particularly good
position to take us under his wing. HQ BHC was trying to get
established at an old Olympic skiing hotel in Kiseljak, just
outside Sarajevo, and was faced at this time with enough
problems without us. In the event we were put under day-to-
day control of HQ BHC at midnight on 17 November.

Following Brigadier Andrew's instructions I went to see
local commanders. To start with I visited Mario Cerkoz, Croat
Commander in Vitez. He indicated quite strongly that he had
no intention of abandoning the area, but then he might not
have been aware of higher-level HVO decisions to leave the
local Croats to their fate. In the Muslim headquarters in Vitez,
Sefkija had similar views and gave no indication of any fears
that the Croats might abandon the Muslims in the area. I also
went to see Timomir Blaskic and asked him how he thought
things were going and what his aims were. To be honest, he
didn't seem to have any — unless just maintaining the status
quo was his aim. Certainly I detected little suggestion that
the area was about to be yielded up, but I took careful note
of Brigadier Andrew's worries and wrote an appreciation

about how I might make an emergency withdrawal from the school, in a worst-case scenario. My main conclusions were that it would take us up to five hours to break away from the place, provided of course that we took only vital equipment, that I needed to devise a hasty defence plan for Vitez and that I needed to know what kind of artillery was held by the Bosnian Serb Army on the Vlassic Feature some fourteen thousand metres from the school. The Vlassic Feature was a high mountain which dominated not just Travnik but also, at a greater distance, Vitez and the remainder of the Kiseljak valley. The Serbs had a headquarters on the top of it in the old Olympic skiing village there. At fourteen thousand metres, our base would easily be within range of the Serb artillery. But in my reply to Brigadier Andrew's request I emphasized that, as far as I could ascertain, the Croats had little intention of abandoning Central Bosnia.

In fact Central Bosnia was fast becoming the main effort in all senses for British involvement in the country. In particular the Overseas Development Administration, a branch of the Ministry of Overseas Development, was beginning to send a lot more people into the area. Gilbert Greenall was often around and the First Secretary (Aid) from the British Embassy in Zagreb, Doug Houston, was almost permanently in Zenica. Over the course of my time in Bosnia Doug was to become a good friend who helped and advised me a great deal. Doug's job was mainly to coordinate civilian aid efforts, such as Bovis putting up sheltered accommodation for refugees. I was happily surprised by the enormous amount of British-donated aid that was to flood into the country over the next few months.

I first met General Nambiar, Commander of UN Forces in former Yugoslavia, and Major General Philippe Morillon, UN Commander in Bosnia-Herzegovina, on Tuesday 10 November when they visited the school in Vitez. We briefed them, gave them lunch, showed them around the base and then I had a private talk with them in my office. General Nambiar was charming and quite obviously talking way above my level.

General Morillon struck me as an energetically fit man who

was determined to do well in his new appointment as Commander in Bosnia-Herzegovina. Wiry, good-looking and silver-haired he was a fine figure of a soldier – in contrast to myself. He chain-smoked small cigars throughout his visit and seemed quite unable to sit still. As he talked, in good English, he almost always put his hands inside his belt and leant forward with his shoulders hunched. He talked lovingly of the French Foreign Legion, into which he had been commissioned, and seemed very pleased to have the British Battalion as part of his Command. We laughed about how the press were saying that my Battalion Group were the first British troops to be under a French General since the First World War. I admired his style and we got on well.

The day after Generals Nambiar and Morillon visited I met the local representative of the International Committee of the Red Cross (ICRC) for the first time. Up until then I had almost forgotten the implications of Security Council Resolution 776 to the effect that UN forces in Bosnia were required to assist the ICRC in the escorting of detainees if requested to do so by the ICRC and provided the UN Commander agreed to do it. And so when I received a telephone call from Yves Mauron, Head Delegate of ICRC in Zenica, rather guiltily I invited him to come for tea that afternoon. Yves arrived on time in a Toyota Land Cruiser painted in ICRC insignia. He was a dapper, good-looking man in his early thirties and was accompanied by another delegate, a lady called Claire Podbielski. She was a lovely girl, stylishly dressed in Timberland shoes, jeans and a short jacket. I gave them tea in the room beside my office and then briefed them on the front-line situation. They were particularly interested in the situation around Olovo and Maglaj. I asked how I should deal with the increasing number of atrocity stories we were hearing and Yves suggested that we report them simultaneously to both the UN and ICRC. Although I invited Yves and Claire to remain for dinner they had to get back to Zenica.

The problems to the west of Vitez continued to worry me greatly. We were now getting reports from the Muslim Army that a two-brigade-sized attack was being launched on Turbe by the Serbs: tanks and infantry were being used and two thousand civilians were trapped in the Karaula area. The Muslim Commander in Travnik, Colonel Ribo, asked for our help to organize a ceasefire and evacuate the two thousand or so civilians who were trapped. I passed on this information to both HQ BHC at Kiseljak and HQ BRITFOR in Split, but I was very unhappy. At this stage I still had only one armoured infantry company of Warriors in my area, which was B Company in Gornji Vakuf, and we were right in the middle of getting our Warrior companies up from Split. I warned off Alistair Rule that he may need to go into the Karaula with his Company – but only if a ceasefire could be arranged between the Serbs, Croats and Muslims. HQ BHC was trying to do its best to organize this but I couldn't really see it happening.

Then General Morillon announced to the world's press that he had ordered the British Battalion to go into the Karaula. He did not accompany the announcement with any publicly stated pre-conditions such as the fact that there must be a ceasefire first. In the resultant worried telephone calls between HQ BHC, ourselves and HQ BRITFOR this matter was clarified. It then became clear that no UN troops were to go into the Karaula unless such a pre-condition was met. However, there was something I might try.

The next day I thought I would attempt to talk to the Serb Commander on the radio. Captain Nick Stansfield, our military interpreter, had often told me that all sides often listened to one another's radio nets and would sometimes interrupt them. I drove into Travnik with Nick early in the morning and spoke to Ribo who thought it might be possible to contact the Serbs on the radio, though clearly everyone in his Muslim Headquarters was in a high state of anguish about what was happening to their west. After a while a man called Dalje Sahinovik arrived. I had met him before and he was very much a professional soldier having been a major in the Yugoslav National Army. Tough-looking, clearly a field soldier and a man of about the same age as me, he was treated with tremendous respect by both Croats and Muslims alike. Dalje offered to try to make contact on the radio for me with the

two local Serb Commanders, Brigadier General Galic in the
Komar area and Colonel Trivic around the Vlassic Feature to
the north. However, we had to go into the hills south of Turbe
to do this, although I had never been to the area.

I followed Dalje up the Turbe road to a point just outside
the town, at which we went south and west into the hills.
At various points Dalje stopped and tried to make contact
with the Serbs on the radio in his Range Rover. Eventually
he managed to get through to Brigadier General Galic's Headquarters, but Galic or his officers refused to speak to me.
Apparently they had received instructions from their Headquarters in Banja Luka that they were not to speak to anyone
from UNPROFOR. That was the end of that then, but I did
make as much use of the expedition as possible. From our
positions I could clearly see down into Turbe – and could
watch the battle – but equally I could see further forward
than that. Using my binoculars I scanned the Karaula area on
the forward slopes beyond Turbe and could see no evidence of
anyone being there – let alone two thousand displaced
persons. I decided to stand down Alistair Rule on my return,
much to his extreme disappointment. I did not think the risk
was worth it, especially as nobody had guaranteed a ceasefire
by all sides. Later I was to discover that the reports of so many
refugees had been wildly exaggerated as so many things tend
to be in Bosnia. My decision had been right.

That evening I was working in my office when I was told
that the Mayor of Gorazde wished to see me. He was at the
front gate. Hadzo Efendic, the Mayor, had walked the forty
kilometres from Gorazde in order to plead for international
help. In the room we were using for an officers' mess he told
me that there were still a total of seventy thousand people
living in Gorazde, of which fifteen thousand or so were under
fifteen years of age. He said that his town had been effectively
surrounded for so long now that it was about to run out of
food. My heart went out to him but there seemed very little
I could do because it was well outside my operational area,
but I promised to represent his case to HQ BHC. Nonetheless
I felt ashamed that we seemed so impotent, though later I was
greatly relieved to learn that a UNHCR convoy did manage to

get through to Gorazde. Hadzo Efendic accepted my offer of dinner, which was, I felt, the least we could do.

When the Mayor of Gorazde left I finally had some spare minutes for the first time in days and decided to make use of the newly erected mobile-bath unit. I don't wish to imply that I hadn't had a wash since I arrived because each morning I stood stark naked in a bowl and cleaned myself all over, but I had not had a proper shower. It was fabulous to go into this tent and have high-pressure 'hot' water squirted at me. The soldiers that organized this and the fantastic laundry unit we were allocated for the tour deserved medals.

Whilst trying to establish ourselves with the Advance Party, I felt it particularly important to try to work out how we would travel to Maglaj and to Tuzla. Both towns were key targets for aid delivery. Maglaj was a so-called front-line town and was apparently always under fire. And although we had briefly visited Tuzla on the reconnaissance commanded by Brigadier Myles Frisby we had not been back since.

Maglaj was much the closer of the two towns and I felt we should easily be able to get there and back inside a day. Starting early I took a few vehicles with me to Zepce where, once again, I met Bozimar Tomic, the Deputy Commander. He introduced us to his Commander, a man called Ivo Lozancic. After a brief conversation, during which Lozancic allowed us to mark our maps with the current state of front-line play, he contacted Maglaj by radio and arranged for us to rendez-vous with the Croat Commander of Maglaj at a roadblock just four kilometres south of the town.

We drove to it without incident and there we met Alois Gasparic who led us into Maglaj by a circuitous mountain track, part of which was in full view of the Serb positions. But it was preferable to the main road, which was much more likely to be targeted. The track was rough but not more than three miles long. We approached Maglaj finally through a couple of tunnels which were full of trucks.

Maglaj itself was in ruins. Every house along the route we took had been hit by artillery or mortar fire, most of them with gaping holes in their roofs and relatively few still had windows with glass in them. Most of the power lines and telegraph poles were down. We drove across some railway lines on a rough road and everywhere there was evidence of shelling. Every house had planks positioned over the windows and door entrances. Nobody was in the streets. This was hardly surprising as the place was under shellfire at the time – we heard and saw incoming artillery and even some going out too. We moved swiftly into the centre of town and there in a cellar of a large office building was the Joint Operations Room for both Croat and Muslim Commands in Maglaj. The place was dark – it was inadequately lit by bulbs hanging from the ceiling – and full of cigarette smoke. Every-one seemed to be smoking. A large table, with about twenty chairs around it, dominated the room. Cups, glasses and ash-trays in turn dominated the maps that were spread on that table. Three or four telephones were also positioned on the table, their wires leading up to the ceiling. Alois Gasparic introduced us to Herzog Sulejman who commanded the Muslim forces in the town and was obviously a good friend of his.

After I'd again explained our purpose in Bosnia and how we might help the UNHCR deliver aid to Maglaj – if necessary, under fire using armoured vehicles – we left and Alois Gasparic took me across the bridge over the River Bosna to the old town. In fact we ran across because many people had been shot by snipers as they crossed the hundred-and-fifty-metre-long bridge. The old town was in an appalling con-dition – all buildings were in ruins. Very few doors were left on their hinges, there was no glass in any of the windows, all the roofs were destroyed and the area was almost totally abandoned.

Returning from the old town, we were taken to see some of the inhabitants who lived in the cellars. In one cellar was Radio Maglaj and the radio-station controller wanted me to go 'on the air'. I agreed to make a short statement and started by saying that I had heard about the plight of Maglaj from a radio appeal made a couple of months before. The BBC had re-broadcast the original message sent out of Maglaj, I explained, and thus their plight was known to the outside world. I assured them that we would do all in our power to help by delivering aid. After my broadcast I met a lady called Barbara Baric, a Croat who operated the local Red Cross Office. She pleaded with me to return to Maglaj with some medical supplies as soon as possible, which I agreed to do.

Two days later and in company with an eight-tonne truck loaded with medical and other supplies from Pharmacies Sans Frontières and the UNHCR, I returned to Maglaj. Gilbert Greenall of the ODA, and Doug Houston, First Secretary from the British Embassy Zagreb, accompanied the group. This time, having checked that there had been no shelling on to it for several hours and moving as fast as possible, we ran the risk of entering Maglaj directly down the main road from the south. With Barbara Baric, Alois Gasparic and Herzog Sulejman we gained great credit for returning so quickly. Mark Weir, our doctor, went to the local hospital whilst we unloaded our supplies as quickly as possible at the Red Cross office. We needed to be fast as there was still the odd artillery round incoming and a good deal of sniper fire too – some of which came very close to hitting our escorts while I was in the Operations Room.

As we drove out of town I had to make a choice: either take the mountain track or risk going straight down the main road. I decided to be cautious and opted for the mountain track. In the vehicle immediately behind mine I gather Gilbert Greenall summed up my decision to Doug Houston by the one word: 'Chicken!' However, as I led our small convoy of vehicles up the start of the mountain track, a fast-moving lorry – presumably one that had started in the tunnels – rushed past. We had only gone a further fifty metres or so when we heard the reaction. An enormous barrage of shellfire was directed at the truck on the other side of the hill to us. Doug Houston has since confirmed to me that Gilbert Greenall hastily revised his judgement of my decision with a short expletive – 'S—t!' Later I told Gilbert that he should have more faith in military decision making.

We had proved that delivering aid to Maglaj was possible but now we had to find a workable route towards Tuzla as well. On Saturday 7 November, we went to Maglaj. Captain Bob Ryan led a small packet of vehicles out from the school and set off for Tuzla. He was accompanied by Captains Mark Cooper and Chris Leyshon as well as Major Jamie Sage, who commanded 42 Field Squadron Royal Engineers. Jamie went along to advise on what routes might take heavy traffic. Some press vehicles accompanied them too.

All went well for the first few hours but then suddenly at a place called Ribnica the convoy was ambushed. To start with a few shots were fired over the first vehicle. Bob stopped in dead ground – an Army term meaning a place protected from enemy view and fire – to consider his position. He believed the shots had not been aimed at his patrol and so decided to continue, but down another route. This track passed along the left side of a cliff with the right side exposed to the east. Suddenly a great volume of fire was directed at his vehicles, with 20mm high-explosive shells taking out large chunks of the cliff beside them. One of the Sapper vehicles was hit by small-arms fire. At high speed the convoy turned and raced back out of the danger area. A press vehicle was caught up in the action and raced back neck-and-neck with Bob's Land Rover. Bob Ryan ordered fire to be returned and about thirty shots were fired as the convoy withdrew. Nobody was hurt.

An ITV news crew filmed the incident which was later shown on British television. For my part our communications allowed me to hear a first report of the contact – including, thankfully, the fact that nobody was hurt – before nightfall wiped out any chance of talking to Bob Ryan on the high-frequency radio. Bob Ryan and his party returned to Vitez the next day. Although our first attempt to get to Tuzla was therefore a failure, we knew we would have to try again because it was one of the main aid targets I had been given.

Nine days later, on Monday 16 November, I decided to have a go myself and another small convoy of vehicles left Vitez early in the morning. Bob Ryan, Jamie Sage and Martin Forgrave came with me – as well as nine press vehicles. The media, having had quite a 'scoop' on the last occasion we had tried to get to Tuzla, felt that the chances of us having similar problems this time were quite high. Major Andrew Venus, the Public Information Officer I had inherited on arrival in Bosnia, advised me that it was preferable to take the press with us 'under control', amongst other things for their own safety, rather than have them follow us anyway – doing what they wanted. Thus I briefed them on how I wanted them to join us, how they should act and made certain guarantees so that they could get a good story from the trip. Most important, I settled where the press should travel and we agreed that the press convoy – for it most certainly was that at nine vehicles – needed to be a 'tactical bound' behind us. The definition of a tactical bound being far enough behind me so that they did not get directly involved with any contact situations yet not so far that they could not see what was happening. In the earlier contact situation at Ribnica, press vehicles had very nearly caused casualties by being too involved. Ribnica taught us that we had to take full account – and most certainly a little responsibility – for press vehicles accompanying our patrols.

The route I was to try this time avoided going directly through Ribnica and took us via Milankovici and Kladanj. Bob Ryan, who obviously knew the way as far as Ribnica, led to start with but I took over once we swung away from there. The roads were difficult and seemed potentially impassable for trucks and I dreaded to think what they might be like in the winter. The bridges were also very suspect – Jamie Sage was definite that there was no chance of Warriors going over them – and the passes through the mountains were very high. The views were tremendous though. We could see for many miles down into the wooded valleys and across to the breathtaking ranges in the distance as we climbed up these huge, snow-topped mountains.

In Pogar we met an ICRC convoy, led by Claire Podbielski, on its way to Vares. We talked for a couple of minutes about our respective destinations and then our convoys went their separate ways. For our part we went close to Ribnica where we took cover as some shots were fired – though I wasn't sure if they were at us – but instead of going through the town we turned towards Olovo and then took another pass through Milankovici to Kladanj. There was some snow in the mountains but it was only light. We finally made it to Tuzla by approaching from Kladanj. I took a slight risk travelling north from Kladanj on the main road as I knew that vehicles had often been attacked there from Serb positions about a thousand metres to the east. In the event nothing happened and we were in Tuzla within six hours of leaving Vitez, with which I was very pleased.

Once in the town I went to see Lukic St Jepo, the President for Refugees. A Croat in his early thirties, he was obviously dedicated to trying to sort out the dreadful situation in Tuzla. I told him that I intended to start escorting aid to the town as soon as possible and that that might mean as early as one week's time. I gave Lukic a bottle of whisky and our rations. I wanted to get back to Vitez as soon as possible, so we left soon.

The journey back was fairly uneventful, except that the ITN news team's Granada car broke down. Before we had started I had warned that any media vehicles coming with us should be equipped with four-wheel-drive and an armoured Granada (ex-Northern Ireland Police) was certainly not the sort of vehicle that should travel to Tuzla. Eventually we had to leave the Granada behind, looked after by a family in the area of Milankovici.

Immediately on my return I held a conference that night at 10.15. I told Jamie Sage that he was to make a plan as to how aid should get to Tuzla. We now had a route – albeit a difficult one – and I had decided we needed a Forward Company Base in the area of Kladanj. This Forward Base would act as our springboard to get aid into Tuzla until the weather stopped us. At this stage I thought there was no way we would be able to sustain a Tuzla humanitarian aid operation through the winter on the roads we had found. I was to be proved wrong there – much to my delight – but I was not to know it at the time. Warrior could not be used at least initially but I wanted it to be employed up there eventually because of the protection it offered and the impression it would make on the local forces. In the meantime, Jamie was to have Scimitars at his disposal, particularly to protect convoys on the dangerous stretch for some ten kilometres north of Kladanj. I stressed that I wanted aid to Tuzla to start immediately after the main body of the Battalion Group arrived in Vitez. We set a date of 19 November to start the operation.

The next morning Brigadier Andrew Cumming telephoned on our INMARSAT to express his displeasure. He said I had disobeyed his directive after the Ribnica incident in which he had prohibited any further reconnaissances towards Tuzla until we had armoured vehicles. I felt a little aggrieved at the reprimand, as I had achieved what we wanted, but he was right: in my enthusiasm I had honestly forgotten that conversation. In short I had disobeyed him and I understood why he was a little angry. I apologized absolutely saying that I had entirely forgotten in my enthusiasm and was very sorry. Being a decent sort he accepted my apology immediately and then we discussed how we were to get aid to Tuzla. Brigadier Andrew endorsed the plan I had devised.

But now at last I was beginning to see the arrival of the main body of my Battalion Group. Having taken slightly longer for the sea journey than we had estimated, the armoured vehicles had finally arrived aboard the roll-on/roll-off ferry *Rosa Dan* on 11 November. From the final decision to deploy until the arrival of Warriors in theatre it had taken twenty-seven days, but we had been fully ready to go for some time before that. Once on the quay at Split, the Warriors were taken by low-loader up to Tomaslavgrad and from there they were driven over the mountain road to Gornji Vakuf and Vitez. B Company arrived first in Gornji Vakuf followed by A Company, who had a horrendous journey through the ice and snow which fell shortly after B Company had made it through. C Company came next followed by Support Company. Finally B Squadron 9/12 Lancers arrived in Vitez on 18 November having been released from its duties regulating the move of all British forces into Bosnia. By this stage Brigadier Andrew Cumming had already passed tactical control of all British forces in Bosnia to General Morillon with effect from midnight the night before. Now we were complete in Bosnia and the real work of getting aid through could start.

CHAPTER 7

INTO THE TUZLA FINGER

The Battalion Group was in Vitez but electric power was most certainly not. For the first five days after the main body arrived we had no electricity whatsoever. A fierce storm had struck in the early evening on 11 November. Power lines throughout Vitez had been brought down and live cabling was everywhere. The tented camp we had carefully constructed to shelter over two-thirds of the Battalion Group was devastated. Several tents, with space for twelve men each, were totally destroyed as they were ripped from their stays and carried into the air. Members of the Advance Party, particularly the Sappers and Medics, worked frantically and at some danger to themselves to try to save what they could. When the storm subsided, though, we had lost a great deal of canvas. We had no electricity for seven days after this – just as the Main Body of the Battalion Group arrived. Some emergency lighting was set up and I worked in my office by the light of a Tilley lamp. Life was fairly miserable – especially as the lavatories, of which there were very few, rapidly blocked and were placed out of bounds by Mike Winstanley, the Quartermaster. Everyone had to use buckets in tents outside until the end of January.

However, it was very comforting to have everyone in Vitez, and particularly to see the Warriors and Scimitars. Both kinds of armoured vehicles had taken the journey from Split over the mountains in their stride. Not one Warrior had broken down in any significant way and great credit for that must go to the crews and vehicle mechanics who worked so long and hard to prepare the vehicles.

Now we began to operate with the UNHCR in detail. I started by appointing Captain James Askew to be a liaison officer with the local office in Zenica. His job was to keep us informed of what the UNHCR wanted to do so that we could ensure that our part of the operation was as well planned as possible. Once the UNHCR decided where they wanted particular aid convoys to go to, we would calculate what escorts and other arrangements were necessary in order to get that aid through to its target. José de la Mota, a Spanish UN officer whose father also worked for the UN in Geneva, took over as Head of UNHCR Office from Anders Levinson in the middle of November. It took a little time for José and me to get to know one another well as neither of us understood how the other's organization worked. But I respected José from the start and rapidly we began to trust each other. Escort operations had begun even before the arrival of the main body and so all we did was extend them fully when the armoured vehicles arrived. I explained to José that I did not want only to place armoured vehicles to the front and rear of UNHCR convoys but wanted to think much more broadly than that. In particular we should make every effort to ensure that the areas into which aid was to be delivered were as peaceful as possible. Both José and I were agreed that we wanted to minimize close military protection for UNHCR convoys as much as possible. Confidence patrolling throughout Central Bosnia should create a 'climate' into which aid could be delivered without too much danger. That was the way we started our cooperation with the UNHCR and essentially it did not change throughout the tour.

Although I was happy to have everyone in Vitez and Gornji Vakuf, still I needed to get a base that could effectively support operations towards Tuzla. Apparently the dangers from starvation and cold were greatest there and it had always been our main objective from the start and I did not want to waste what little time we had before winter set in. I couldn't envisage us being able to sustain any operations through the mountains to Tuzla once the severe cold came and wanted to do

all I could before then. Jamie Sage had been given the task
of planning how to get aid to Tuzla initially and he had set
himself up in a small operating base at Kladanj, which was
just on the far side of the mountains. From there it was a
short, although dangerous, run along a main road to Tuzla.
The plan was that we would initially position a company
group in the factory. Convoys from the UNHCR warehouse
in Vitez would travel through the mountains to Kladanj – if
necessary overnight there – and then continue on to Tuzla
with a military escort. We reckoned that there was no need
for an armoured escort until convoys started to go north of
Kladanj. Thus such armoured escorts would rendezvous with
the convoys just before going through the most dangerous
stretch of the route and accompany them through it.

Major Martyn Thomas, Officer Commanding A Company,
was tasked by me to develop the Forward Operating Base at
Kladanj having taken over from Jamie. Martyn would then
stay there whilst we pushed as much aid as we could through
to Tuzla before the winter really struck deep. At the time I
thought it was quite a big gamble. To start with we could not
get Warriors to Kladanj and the escorts had to be done by
the much lighter (less protected) Scimitars. Thereafter I was
worried about how I could possibly get the company group
out again if I continued to push aid up to Tuzla until the
roads became impassable. I might just be left with a Company
Group marooned the other side of the mountains all winter.
How I would resupply them in such circumstances worried
me greatly. I explained the situation to Brigadier Roddy
Cordy-Simpson, General Morillon's Chief of Staff, and he
thought we should do our best to get there. Brigadier Andrew
Cumming was also concerned about how close we might run
to disaster if we pushed our luck. For his part he had to satisfy
HQ UKLF who must have been very concerned too. However,
I decided that we would take the gamble and I was fully
backed by Brigadier Andrew on this.

It was snowing at 4 a.m. on 19 November when Martyn
Thomas left to escort the first convoy all the way to Tuzla. I
am very proud of the fact that we were so quick. The last
armoured vehicles had only arrived in Vitez the day before.

Most certainly nobody could say we had wasted our time. Jamie Sage was waiting for Martyn in Kladanj but Martyn had decided to run all the way through to Tuzla and then try to get back that evening to stay overnight in Kladanj. Everything seemed to go to plan – at least until reaching Tuzla.

On returning from Tuzla, the escort Scimitars were involved in a fairly horrific accident. Apparently just after last light a 'mad' Bosnian had tried to overtake another car just as the light tanks were approaching from the other direction. The overtaking vehicle clipped the side of a Scimitar and several people were badly hurt. Lieutenant Mike Dooley, a platoon commander, did remarkably well in the follow-up. He placed a man's foot back on the stump of his leg, bound the two together and later surgeons in Tuzla Hospital rejoined the two parts successfully. Kate Adie, of BBC News, who was present at the time of the accident, told me later that she had been terrifically impressed by the actions of Mike and the other soldiers present.

At about the same time, the forward detachment ahead of the troops involved in the traffic accident also ran into problems. Suddenly we heard on a very bad radio link that there had been a contact seven kilometres north of Kladanj as the convoy was returning. The contact was incoming small-arms and mortar fire directed at our convoy. In the Operations Room at Vitez we heard a report that nobody had been hurt but nothing more for the rest of the night, which was worrying. A lack of direct and immediate communications between operations rooms and troops on the ground was a matter we always had difficulty rectifying throughout our time in Bosnia, despite repeated visits from high-ranking communications experts who were trying to do something about it. In this instance we reported what had happened up both our chains of command – to HQ BHC and HQ BRITFOR – and I was most grateful to both superior headquarters for not demanding more information. I was sure that Brigadier Andrew Cumming would be under enormous pressure to provide additional information to HQ UKLF and yet he did not hassle us once. Just to reassure the Rear Party in

Fallingbostel we also gave them a report of what had happened using our INMARSAT telephone. In fact this became standard procedure whenever an incident occurred. I had always understood that the section of the route north of Kladanj was probably the most dangerous – after all that was one reason for putting a Forward Operating Base close by – but I did not like the fact that we had a contact on our very first convoy up to Tuzla. That did not bode well at all.

The first official British visitor we received in Vitez was Lieutenant-General Sir Michael Wilkes who was Commander of the United Kingdom's Land Army based in Wilton. As such he was the man to whom Brigadier Andrew Cumming reported from HQ BRITFOR in Split and he had come to see how we had set ourselves up and to get a feel for what the situation was truly like. I met General Wilkes in Gornji Vakuf on 20 November. He was accompanied, as became normal for VIP visitors, by Brigadier Andrew Cumming. In the Base at Gornji Vakuf Simon Ellis (Operations Officer), Chris Leyshon (Intelligence Officer), Alistair Rule (Officer Commanding B Company) and I briefed the General on the situation as we saw it. We all had lunch in Gornji Vakuf Base and then took the General on a quick tour around.

Travelling back to Vitez with the General only took about an hour and so I had time to take him almost directly into Travnik where I had arranged for him to meet Djemal Merdan, Deputy Commander BiH 3rd Corps, and Colonel Timomir Blaskic, HVO Commander of Central Bosnia. Also present was Ahmed Kulenovic who had recently replaced 'Colonel' Ribo as BiH Commander in the town. The word was that Ribo was now on 'leave', whatever that meant. Ribo was a large avuncular man who might not have had the determination or drive for command of a sector so vital to the Muslims. There in the conference room of the Muslim Headquarters we discussed the situation. General Wilkes invited the local-force commanders to make their assessment of what was happening. They replied that there was great pressure on Turbe (and thus Travnik) from Serb forces to the east and neither commander seemed fully confident about holding the line there. They accepted that the Serbs had better heavy weapons than they did. When General Wilkes posited that the Serb Army might be trying to cut Bosnia in half by striking from the west along a line from Prozor to Jablonica, both Merdan and Blaskic agreed it could be a possible Serb intention.

From when we first arrived in Central Bosnia, our lack of intelligence on the situation was a matter of real urgency and we spent a great deal of our time trying to estimate the intentions of the various sides. The Serbs were really the 'action players' in late 1992. They were attacking, they had 'taken' Jajce and caused thousands of displaced persons to flood east and they were now putting pressure on places like Maglaj, Tescanj, Turbe and Bugojno. We received most of our intelligence on Serb intentions from the Croats and Muslims, who were always willing to identify positions and lines for us on maps. But we helped ourselves as well. We talked widely to people who lived in the area and made extensive use of such conversations to build up our knowledge. Our patrols were frequently tasked to observe and report front-line positions, which they did from vehicles in static positions for a long period of time. B Squadron was particularly good at this; it was, after all, a primary role for Scimitar crews in Germany and they were well practised at it. For their part, once we met the Serbs we found them to be by far the most secretive of the local forces in Bosnia. They distrusted us completely and were neurotic about their own security. Although we rapidly built up a large information store in Vitez, never did we pass information on from one side to another – even Croat to Muslim or vice versa when they were allies. To have done so would have been a compromise of our neutrality and would have been a severe mistake. Quite rapidly the Intelligence Cell at Vitez, under Chris Leyshon's control, became an essential source of information for visitors wishing to be briefed on what was going on in Central Bosnia, particularly the briefings by Sergeant Connelly.

General Wilkes seemed to like going to meet Merdan and Blaskic and it occurred to me that taking VIP visitors to meet local commanders was probably a very sensible use of their time. I was to make such meetings almost a standard part of a visit package from then onwards.

That evening, Friday 20 November, we held a dinner night in our large mess tent. It was the first time we had been able to relax since arriving in Bosnia and I thought it highly appropriate to do so when General Wilkes was with us. The night also offered us the opportunity to invite some of the people we would be working with throughout our tour, including a number of multinational officers from HQ BHC at Kiseljak as well as members of UNHCR, ICRC and the press. I also invited both Merdan and Blaskic who seemed to enjoy the evening as much as anyone. The French Battalion in Sarajevo was particularly kind and sent us sixty bottles of Beaujolais Nouveaux 1992 with Sarajevo labels on them. Once empty the bottles were eagerly sought after as souvenirs!

We were also lucky to have the excellent services of a Royal Irish piper in the form of Corporal Keery whose music made the evening for everyone.

I had discussed how I should tackle the worsening situation west of Travnik with General Wilkes. He was very keen that I should actively patrol right up to the front lines at Turbe as a logical extension of confidence-patrolling and that suited me down to the ground. I was very happy about that. Warrior patrols right up to the front line at Turbe were to begin as soon as possible.

The spur to action on my behalf came on Sunday 22 November when I was shaving and listening to a report on the BBC World Service (they were frequent at this time) that Travnik was about to be filled with many more refugees and might fall like Jajce had done. I decided that before any patrols went near Turbe I should go myself and, as I finished shaving, I began to formulate a plan in my mind. Lieutenant Alex Watts and his Standby Platoon of Warriors and two Scimitars were to go with me. I would use Juliet (Callsign Zero Alpha) which was my own Warrior. During breakfast I warned everyone involved and gave formal orders out at 8.30 a.m. Two liaison officers, Captains Martin Forgrave and Matthew Dundas-Whatley, were to inform the local Croat and Muslim headquarters of my intentions at 9.30 and an hour later the reconnaissance party would leave Vitez for Turbe.

I was writing a letter in my office at 9.30 when the door opened and in walked a Canadian Lieutenant-Colonel. He was accompanied by another Canadian officer. Having introduced himself as Tom Gebirt, the Commanding Officer of the Royal Canadian Regiment, and his companion as operations officer, Major Andrew Butters, the colonel told me how, unfortunately, his Battalion had not been able to get into its allocated operational area on the Serb side of the lines. An advance party was stuck in Banja Luka, hemmed in by the Serb Army and the main body of his Battalion was positioned at Darovar with the first Canadian Battalion in UNPROFOR. His situation was intolerable and I couldn't understand why the UN did not do something more about it. Tom told me that he had crossed the front lines in the Bugojno area last night and had spent the night at HQ BHC in Kiseljak. He intended to re-cross the lines again later on his way back to his Advance Party in Banja Luka. I was somewhat surprised that the Serbs would allow Tom to move around like that and yet restrict the rest of his soldiers to a small compound in Banja Luka. But I was also very pleased that crossing the lines could be done – with agreement on all sides – and it encouraged me greatly. Tom and I discussed how we might jointly open up a corridor between Vitez and Banja Luka; that was if he could get the remainder of his Battalion deployed into Banja Luka and able to operate. As Tom was going back across the lines later I quickly wrote out a letter (translated into Serbian) asking Galic, the Serb Commander in Donji Vakuf, to stop firing on the towns of Turbe and Travnik. Tom realized I was in a rush as I had to leave at 10.30 for Turbe but it was very good to meet him at last. I wished him luck and he left.

This was the first time I used Juliet in an operational role. My crew on board the Warrior normally consisted of four people including myself. I had selected them very carefully before coming to Bosnia. Beside me as commander in the turret sat Company Sergeant Major (CSM) Lawson who was a huge man of over six feet four inches in height and enormously powerful physically though with a terribly gentle personality. I had known him for well over ten years: he had been one of my platoon sergeants in A Company on a two-year tour in Northern Ireland from 1982 to 1984. His task was gunner but in reality he was far more than that as he ran Juliet for me. I had absolute trust in him. Later during the tour he was promoted to Warrant Officer 1 and I think everyone in the Battalion was delighted for a man who generated such tremendous respect. In contrast to 'Tiny' Lawson, my driver was small physically. Corporal Gill, who I had also known for over ten years and had served in my Company in Northern Ireland, was a fine soldier and my admiration for him had not changed over the years. He was an accomplished signaller and a driving instructor on Warrior. I knew he was a superb driver and he repeatedly proved it in Bosnia. The rear of Juliet was designed as a command post with radio sets and map boards ready for commanding an armoured battle. In Bosnia the rear compartment was rarely used for that but I always carried a signaller with me. Lance-Corporal Higginson, whom I had left to complete his signals course in UK, joined the Battalion a few weeks after the main body and soon re-established himself in the crew. A bright, fast-thinking and highly popular soldier, he was ideally suited for the job of keeping me in touch with both the Operations Room at Vitez and any troops deployed on the ground. It was sometimes very difficult to obtain and he spent a great deal of his time switching radio nets and repositioning radio aerials to try to improve our communications.

Although not a full member of the crew, the Regimental Sergeant Major (RSM), Warrant Officer 1 Charlie Stevens, was a man I rarely went anywhere without. I never ascertained whether RSM Stevens was taller than 'Tiny' Lawson or not, but both men were huge. RSM Stevens had been appointed Regimental Sergeant Major of the Battalion in March earlier in the year, having been rebadged from the Gloucestershire Regiment to the Cheshire Regiment on appointment. Coming in as RSM of a different battalion is never easy but Charlie Stevens had adapted perfectly. He was more 'Cheshire' than anyone now and I had great respect and liking for him. On this particular trip to Turbe I also had a French officer with me, Major Olivier de Bavinehard, a liaison officer from HQ BHC, who had asked if he could come if we had enough space.

The Warrior itself is a superb piece of military hardware. Relatively new in design it was first introduced to infantry battalions in Germany during the late 1980s and from the start was an instant success. Juliet and all the other Warriors with us had been fitted with additional protective armour as I had so wanted during the planning of the operation and the total weight of the vehicles was now about thirty tonnes. Warrior provided a tremendous feeling of protection and this gave us a great deal of confidence when going about our business in Bosnia. Once in Warrior everyone felt safe. But Warrior could also fight, if necessary. It had a 30mm Rarden cannon which could fire high-explosive and Armour-Piercing Discarding Sabot shells to about two thousand metres. We tended to load with high-explosive shells in Bosnia. Warrior also had the Hughes chain-gun which fired 7·62mm Linked Ball ammunition at a tremendous rate. The sights for both weapons systems were excellent, by day and night.

Everyone travelling in my Warrior was always linked to the intercom so that they heard everything that was happening. Sitting in the turret I could normally listen to two radio nets – one in each ear – and talk on the intercom to everyone else in the vehicle, if necessary. Naturally 'Tiny' Lawson and Lance-Corporal Higginson were also listening in and would pick up on things I missed.

At just after 10.30, as I was completing final checks with the vehicle and gunnery system just before leaving the school, I received a radio message from Matthew Dundas-Whatley, who I had sent on to give the local-force headquarters warning of what I wanted to do.

'Could you meet me outside HVO Headquarters in Travnik as Colonel Blaskic wishes to see you,' Matthew asked on the radio.

Juliet and the other vehicles with us took only fifteen minutes to get into Travnik and I stopped the small convoy

on the road beside Croat Headquarters. Inside I met Timomir
Blaskic again. He looked unusually tired and had not shaved.
Blaskic came straight to the point.

'Could you find and recover two of my dead soldiers from
Turbe when you are there?' he asked.

He insisted that they were both accredited to UNPROFOR
once and so there should be no problem. I did not know what
he meant by that. Picking up dead bodies was not really our
job, yet I felt it should not cause too many problems, if all
sides agreed to it. I replied that I would do my best but could
promise nothing until I had seen the situation. Blaskic
explained where he thought the bodies were and we left to
continue our journey to Turbe.

Going west out of Travnik we could not help noticing the
destruction caused by shelling. The high blocks of flats on the
left have prominent shell marks against their sides and many
of the buildings have no windows. It is also easy to see where
shells and mortars have landed: from the impact position, the
scouring effects of shrapnel are obvious. The whole of Travnik
is overlooked by forward Serb positions on a huge mountain
feature to the north of it. This is the so-called Vlassic Feature
on the top of which there is a television tower and an old
Olympic skiing village. Travnik must look like a shooting gallery from that high vantage point. The top floors of Travnik
Hospital, which we passed on our right, had had to be abandoned because shells were landing directly on top of the building. All operations were now being carried out in the
basement. I was a little apprehensive as we travelled down
the seven kilometres of road that links Travnik to Turbe. I
felt we were being watched all the way on all sides. The Serbs
could see our every move as we drove along. The road itself
was still in good shape but nobody in his right mind would
travel along it without the greatest caution. The Serbs had
perfected their targeting of that stretch of highway: their forward observation posts watched the road, judged the speed
of vehicles, and fired their mortars at a selected point so that
the bombs impacted some twenty-plus seconds later at exactly
the position the target vehicles had reached.

Turbe was a dead town – at least that is the way it looked.

In fact the very word 'Turbe' refers to a Muslim headstone, which, seeing it that day, seemed almost appropriate. Every building had received extensive shell damage and there were signs that ferocious fighting had taken place there. Telephone and electric lines, walls, street lamps and signs were all down. Wrecked vehicles littered the streets, everywhere carried the marks of shelling and the only living things that we saw were dogs and cats. Nobody was on the streets because of the fear of snipers and the constant sounds of battle. The centre of Turbe was two hundred metres from the front line and there in the heart of town was the command post of the Muslim forces defending the place.

It was in a building which had been as protected as possible. Lots of sandbags and wood leaning against the walls were the best that could be done and, from the damage to surrounding buildings, it had obviously been the target of artillery attacks. The Headquarters had a few cars 'hidden' in the protection of surrounding buildings. I positioned Alex Watts and his Warriors all around and then placed Juliet as close to the Headquarters as possible. There was a lot of incoming artillery and small-arms fire as we arrived and it was to continue throughout our visit. However, I noticed that the nearest shells seemed to be landing about two hundred metres away and certainly no small-arms fire seemed to be directed exclusively at us. Therefore I decided the risk of dismounting was worth taking, though I ordered that all Warriors were to remain closed down – that is with all hatches closed and as protected as possible.

As I got out beside a tractor, I noticed a body lying in an attached trailer. At first I thought it might have been one of the Croat bodies that Timomir Blaskic had requested me to recover, but quickly it became obvious that it was a Serb soldier. He was immense in size, a real giant, and he had been shot. He lay on his back with a huge beard and large boots, rather like Goliath. He was exactly like the Serb soldiers we had envisaged in training. The Muslim soldiers around were particularly aggressive to the body, prodding and spitting on it. I did not like that and asked them to leave it alone, but it made little real difference and they continued to abuse it.

I had let only Nick Stansfield, RSM Stevens and Olivier de Bavinehard come with me when we debussed from Juliet. Having walked past the dead Serb we went into a door at the back of the building which led along a short corridor. Inside a smoke-filled room in the Headquarters I met Sulejman Leko, the Bosnian Muslim Commander of Turbe. A gentle-looking man of medium height, Leko had been a lecturer in a local college until a year before. He really did not look much like a soldier. However, he was very hospitable and made the four of us very welcome indeed. He told me that this was the only command post in Turbe and that really Turbe was almost completely defended by Muslim forces. Only a very small percentage of the defenders were Croats.

On asking about the dead soldier outside, Leko confirmed that it was a Serb body. He said he himself had ten dead soldiers at the time. I asked about the two Croat bodies and at this Leko became quite excited, saying that we would not be able to take them – wherever they were – unless we took the other ten bodies he had. I replied that I simply did not have the space and so would take no bodies back with me. This seemed to satisfy Leko but I found this disappointing because, although we only had room for two bodies, I know just how important it is to families to have the remains of their sons back for a proper burial.

In the middle of our meeting into the room strode another big man with a beard. But he was no Serb. He introduced himself as General Ante Prkacin. Apparently he was a Croat on the Joint Croat/Muslim Council for the Prosecution of the War and he acted largely as an intermediary between the Croats and Muslims. From the way he was received by the Muslims in the room, he was very popular.

After about an hour talking about the threat posed to Turbe by the Serbs, I decided it was time to go. Throughout the meeting I had heard Alex Watts and his Warriors 'jockeying' – moving their vehicles in order to provide less chance for any potential enemy to engage with accuracy – as the battle continued and the situation was quite dangerous. The four of us who had been inside walked, rather quickly I admit, to

Juliet, and mounted up. I gave quick orders to withdraw and we all left Turbe.

The journey back was no problem but I stopped briefly in Travnik to brief Timomir Blaskic on my lack of success over recovering the bodies of his dead soldiers. I was glad that Prkacin joined us in Travnik a few minutes after I arrived to confirm my account of what had happened. He endorsed my decision, anxious as he was to avoid bad feeling between the Muslims and Croats. It was interesting to see Dario Kordich with Blaskic and I wondered, not for the first time, who was in charge of whom. I discussed with the three of them the theory, currently growing amongst local forces, that when the British were in Travnik less shells fell. They agreed that there might be a link as the Serbs had a clear view of the town and so, when I left, I instructed Alex Watts to keep his Warriors in Travnik until 7.30 p.m.

By the time I returned to Vitez I had decided that there were no reasons at all why we should not patrol Turbe with immediate effect. Later I telephoned Brigadier Roddy Cordy-Simpson on the INMARSAT telephone to brief him on the outcome of my trip stating that I was not at all convinced that Turbe was about to fall. The defences seemed to be quite well coordinated with about two to four hundred Muslim soldiers and an unknown number of Croats manning the defences. I estimated that the town still had about two hundred civilians living there. The trip had confirmed my feeling that the threat to Travnik was probably not as great as some people suggested. Tom Gebirt, the day before, had told me that he believed the Serbs had no intention of taking Travnik. All this seemed very good news indeed.

That evening I was invited to watch a video film by Major Andrew Venus, the PINFO officer. I walked over to the house that had recently been taken over as the briefing and meeting point for all media representatives. Andrew sat me down, gave me a beer, and switched on the video. But that is all I can remember as I fell asleep immediately. I understand that the PINFO staff were very 'nice' to me – they turned the volume down a bit.

At this point I needed to review the conditions and requirements of what had by now become Camp Vitez, though this waited till the next day, since even 'Nora', our local Croat howitzer, would not have been able to wake me on my return from Turbe. This howitzer, by the way, was a source of some concern in itself, since it was often very active – presumably firing at Serb positions on the Vlassic Feature. The Croats did not have very much artillery and so what they had needed to be well protected and Nora, a 152mm howitzer, was positioned in a large quarry some fifteen hundred metres from the base. It occurred to me in passing that at some point counter-battery fire from the Serbs was possible and that that would leave our base very vulnerable.

We had always planned that Sea King helicopters might be used in an emergency and the Royal Navy had deployed a flight of them to Split. But there were real problems about flying over Bosnian territory. Anything that flew was deemed 'fair game' to the local forces and so it was unsurprising that extreme caution about flying our helicopters had to be exercised. In the event it took a very long time before anyone was satisfied that it was sufficiently safe to fly, though Commander John Bond and his Sea King pilots were terribly keen to help. They frequently visited Vitez and reconnoitred possible landing sites. When eventually John and his pilots were able to fly they were superb, particularly over casualty evacuation and going into the eastern Muslim 'pockets' of Bosnia.

Naturally we were subject to the normal sort of problems any vast organization faces when it tries to get itself set up. For example, great efforts were made by the Army to get each soldier a locker for beside his bed. These lockers had been procured in the UK, sent by ship all the way to Split and then transported two hundred and forty kilometres up a very difficult main supply route to Vitez. My soldiers were pleased at the prospect of these, until they discovered that the 'System' had purchased stationery lockers into which it was almost impossible to get any clothing and equipment. In the end, of course, the soldiers managed to 'adapt' them to their purposes. They always do.

Warrior was sometimes not the easiest of vehicles to use because of its size and weight but I wanted to be able to deploy it as often as possible because its protection was second to none. Having already begun to use the vehicle for patrols into Turbe, I now wanted to extend its use to both Maglaj and Tuzla. I decided we would start by trying to get Warrior to Maglaj as I did not want soft-skinned vehicles regularly patrolling into a town which was constantly under shellfire. We had brought Warrior to Bosnia essentially so that our soldiers should have the best protection possible and it was vital that it be employed in all places where the threat was greatest. Maglaj certainly qualified there. The problem was that to the west of the village of Selece were two bridges which apparently would not be able to take almost thirty tonnes of armoured vehicle. Jamie Sage warned me that it would be a risk to take Warrior over them but I wanted to see for myself at least.

The journey north from Zenica is wonderful. A good modern road runs up the side of the River Bosna which flows through some marvellous mountains. Occasionally the road crosses the river and it was at one of these bridges that we encountered a problem worse than had been anticipated. A main road bridge over the river, which Jamie Sage had doubted would take the weight of Warrior, had been destroyed with a demolition charge. Therefore the locals had improved a track by-passing that point, but this detour crossed two small streams on fairly unreliable wooden bridges. We had tried to work out another way of getting past: one viable suggestion was a railway bridge close by, but we simply could not get Warrior on to the railway tracks.

With me I had Juliet, a Spartan and FV 432 (armoured vehicles), two Scimitars, my Land Rover and a recovery vehicle. When we approached the first bridge I dismounted and we assessed our chances of getting across. The bridges were simple but effective. They consisted of four or five tree trunks laid across the gap with planks on top of them. The trouble was that the main trunks looked fairly rotten. Although a Warrior might not do itself too much damage if it collapsed the bridge I was also conscious that this might remove a lifeline for all people who lived beyond it. We would hardly be very popular with the locals if we ruined them. It

was a gamble but I decided we had to risk it. Driving painfully
slowly, they made it over both bridges. We got all my vehicles
across. Leaving the soft-skinned vehicles behind at the checkpoint just south of Maglaj, I took the armour directly into the
town down the main road. We positioned our vehicles around
the Joint Headquarters and I went inside to find Herzog
Sulejman there. Alois Gasparic was at the front lines about
a kilometre west of Maglaj.

Sulejman told me that the day before a fierce artillery barrage had hit Novi Seher, a small town about eight kilometres
south-west of Maglaj. A young girl had been very badly hurt.
But his forces had destroyed a T55 tank and had captured
another one. The Muslim forces had been resupplied with
Faggot, an ex-Soviet anti-tank weapon. He was pleased to
say that more people were returning to Maglaj now – there
were even some beginning to go back to the old town across
the bridge – because the front line to the east of Maglaj had
been pushed a few hundred yards further away from the
town. For my part I told Sulejman that I intended to start
patrolling Maglaj on a regular basis with armour. The intention in doing this was to try to deter shelling of the town by
our presence. We would also deliver humanitarian aid under
UNHCR auspices to the town, probably when we had armour
already there. However, if things were really bad I would
consider the use of armoured vehicles on their own to bring
aid into town; I planned to use FV 432s for this job.

I returned to Vitez quite quickly. The run from Maglaj in
armoured vehicles took about ninety minutes. At 5 p.m. that
evening during the daily operations conference I told everyone that armoured patrols of Maglaj were to be planned with
immediate effect, but no soft-skinned vehicles were allowed
into the town because of the risks.

But I still had the problem of getting Warriors to Tuzla. By
now I was beginning to wonder if we might just be able
to maintain a Tuzla humanitarian operation throughout the
winter. It all depended on keeping an all-weather route open
– or at least open for some periods. By 25 November we had
fully established our Forward Operating Base at Kladanj. Alan
Abraham with B Squadron, who had taken over from Martyn

Thomas by then, was doing a great job at converting his little factory into a 'home' – despite the fact that the Kladanj was frequently under shellfire. Scimitars are super little armoured vehicles but it was vital to get Warriors there as well, because of the better protection they offered, although we had not yet discovered a route that would withstand their weight. Therefore I decided to set up a Company-plus operation to try to get a decent route for our heaviest vehicles. Although it looked almost impossible I also wanted to see if there was any chance at all that we might negotiate our way directly up the main road from Sarajevo through Visoko, Olovo and then to Kladanj. Nobody seemed to have tried and so Brigadier Roddy Cordy-Simpson at HQ BHC and I thought it worthwhile to have a go. I felt that, even if we failed, there was a chance we might find some alternative route for Warrior – or at least one that could be adapted with some effort from the engineers. After a planning conference with Tim Park, my Second in Command, and Martyn Thomas, we agreed to start with a reconnaissance of a possible route starting in Visoko.

Tim Park, together with Martyn Thomas and A Company, left Vitez early on the morning of 26 November. Initially I could not go with them because late on the evening before Enver Hadzihasanovic, Commander 3rd Muslim Corps based in Zenica, had announced that he wished to come and see me in Vitez and this was my first opportunity to meet him. We had agreed to meet in Battalion Headquarters at 8 a.m. and, exactly on time, Hadzihasanovic arrived with two cars, accompanied by a number of bodyguards all of whom carried short Uzzi machine-pistols.

Enver Hadzihasanovic looked intelligent and professional. He was of medium height, with silvery hair and was smoking a cigarette in a holder as he got out of his car in front of the school. I introduced myself and then took him up to our makeshift Officers' Mess. Simon Ellis, the Operations officer, remained with me as I offered Hadzihasanovic first coffee, then – and rather wickedly at such an early hour – whisky. I thought perhaps I could get my own back, having been forced to drink so much slivovitz at most inappropriate times in Bosnia. In fact slivovitz is a vital part of visiting in Bosnia. Refusal to take a drink could easily cause offence and I endured an incredible amount of bad alcohol in the services of peace. The home-brewed variety of slivovitz was the one that worried me most. The stuff can be fatally poisonous and I was warned that many people had been instantly killed by drinking it. Thus that first sip was always a cautious one for me. Unsurprisingly perhaps, Hadzihasanovic accepted both the coffee and whisky. I explained what we hoped to achieve and asked him if he had any complaints about the way we were carrying out our tasks. He replied that he was very happy with the 'professional' manner with which we had started our time in Bosnia. He simply wanted to come and introduce himself. I ended the meeting by inviting him to have dinner with me in Vitez in the following week, which he accepted.

I left Vitez Camp in the middle of the morning and drove down to Visoko where I found a long column of A Company armoured vehicles lined up just off a flyover. Martyn Thomas was there but Tim Park had gone into Visoko. After a while Tim returned. Apparently he had met the local Muslim Commander, Kadir Kusic, who told him that it was not possible to go directly up the road to Olovo. The road was mined, destroyed and ran directly parallel and through the front lines. Nevertheless Tim tried anyway. He went to the front line and together with Sergeant Thornton, an interpreter, bravely walked across to the Serb positions. Amazingly nobody fired at the two of them and they managed to meet two Serb soldiers who were quite friendly. Tim explained that he was trying to find a route for armoured vehicles and obligingly the two Serbs showed him why it would be impossible. There were huge tank ditches and many mines blocking the way. Tim and Sergeant Thornton then walked back across the lines and returned to the flyover where I met them. I told Tim he was mad to have gone over the lines, but I admired his nerve. Tim briefed me quickly and then returned to Vitez because it was not normal for both of us to be away from the school at the same time.

I then took my Warrior into Visoko. The suburbs seem to

consist entirely of factory complexes, some of them modern. We were guided by a soldier through a series of concrete apartment blocks to Kusic's headquarters. It was on the second floor of one of those anonymous blocks that we met Kadir Kusic. He was bearded and had a humorous twinkle in his eye. After a few brief introductions, he offered to provide us with a guide to Breza. He thought that we might stand a better chance of getting through there by striking south through the lines before turning north again. I agreed to this and shortly afterwards our armoured column rumbled off to find a route around to Breza guided by a soldier from Kadir Kusic's unit.

As we approached Breza I noticed an ICRC vehicle going in the opposite direction to ourselves. It had had to stop because our column entirely blocked the road. Dismounting from Juliet I talked to Claire Podbielski and an interpreter. Claire had been visiting prisoners held by the Muslims in Breza and was trying to get back to Zenica when her way out had been entirely closed by our vehicles. As she was in a soft-skinned Toyota Land Cruiser, and Breza was receiving some incoming shellfire at the time, she was less than happy that her way was barred by UN soldiers – all of whom were far better protected than her interpreter and herself. She had a very good point and we cleared a path for her as soon as possible.

From Breza, which was just short of the front lines, we tried to go south to Ilijas but at a place called Podlugovi we came to front-line positions again. Here we had major difficulties. Try as he might, Martyn Thomas was totally unable to persuade the officer in charge there to move some of his mines so that we could pass. He insisted that he would do nothing without orders from his superior commander. Moving forward on foot I found Martyn persuading the man as hard as he could but there was no way that the officer was going to change his mind. I asked where his superior commander had his Headquarters and was told it was Breza. Martyn and I agreed that I should go and find this commander – especially as the overall Muslim Commander for the whole area, Kadir Kusic, had given us permission to try going across the lines. So I walked back down the long line of vehicles to Juliet. As I did so firing broke out to our right – small arms and mortars. Some of it seemed to be directed at us and so I used the leeside of our vehicles to provide cover as I went back. Certainly I did not want the column to remain there for too long. Remounting Juliet, I turned the vehicle around and went back to the place I had been told was the Head-quarters, a school building. I went inside to find the com-mander, whose name I did not get, but who was most unwilling to let us through his positions – regardless of the fact that Kusic had agreed it. As I was talking to him I heard a loud explosion outside the school. When I went outside I discovered that someone (we thought Muslims) had fired an RPG–7 anti-tank rocket at Juliet. The only thing that upset 'Tiny' Lawson, Juliet's gunner, and 'Gillie', her driver, was that the missile had struck a wall beside the vehicle and hurt a small girl, who had been rushed off by local people. They thought she would be all right but were very unhappy about the stupidity of what had happened.

I failed to get what I wanted from the local commander. It seemed to me incredible: if the Muslims were this intransigent – and we were trying to get a decent aid route through to a predominantly Muslim town, after all – what might the Serbs be like? I contacted Martyn on the radio and we decided to try striking north to Vares. Martyn turned the column around, with some fire still incoming, and returned up the route to Breza where I joined him. From Breza we took the road to Vares as the light faded. It was dark when we reached Vares but I went to the local Croat Headquarters in an old ski chalet some six kilometres the other side of the town and on the route we needed to take.

Rather decently the officers there offered to put some of us up for the night, although the majority of people had to sleep near their vehicles. Kate Adie of BBC News was with us and was also allocated a bedroom of her own. For my part I was to share my room with Martyn Thomas. However, I was very tired and so went to bed a few minutes before Martyn. Just after I had put out the light, the door opened. A Croat soldier walked in, set an alarm clock for the morning and then climbed into what was supposed to be Martyn's bed. I did nothing apart from chuckle and wait for Martyn to arrive, which he did a few minutes later. As he walked in I told Martyn that the man snoring in the bed opposite was a pirate. Martyn spent the night on the floor-space between both beds and the 'pirate' was still snoring gently when we departed the next morning.

We took breakfast, consisting of an ultra-sweet cup of tea, in the ski chalet. Luckily a refuelling vehicle we had requested the night before arrived shortly afterwards as all our armoured vehicles needed a resupply of fuel due to yesterday's detour. Jamie Sage had also come with the vehicle because I needed him to advise us on the strength of bridges we might encounter en route.

From Vares I asked Martyn to split his effort: Tudor Ellis and his platoon were to try one route to Olovo, whilst we tried another, due east. We were still trying to reconnect to the main road from Sarajevo to Tuzla. We had come to Vares on a good road from the south which had been no problem for armoured vehicles whatsoever, but now we needed to find a route from Vares to Kladanj. Bridges were a major difficulty. As Martyn and I travelled due east from the ski lodge we started to encounter some very dubious bridges indeed. Jamie Sage, unsurprisingly because he was a professional sapper, was constantly warning that we were well in excess of their capacity. We began to have a rule of thumb check: five wooden cross-struts which did not look rotten and over we would go. Jamie nearly had 'kittens'. Martyn Thomas led and at one stage took to judging bridges from the top of his Warrior. 'I think we've just disproved the laws of physics,' he reported back on the radio after one particularly suspect structure. But our luck ran out about five kilometres west of Olovo. There we came across the ultimate Warrior trap. It was rotten, had far too many holes in it and had only three cross-struts. And there was no way around it as we were in a ravine. Sadly we could go no further on that route. Neither did Tudor Ellis have too much luck. He was stuck on his route too. With some effort we turned the column around on a very narrow track.

On the map I had noticed a possible route high over the mountains. It went from Brdo to Mizanovici, Ligatici and thence to Solun. We tried it and slowly we worked our way high and tortuously through very small villages where Warriors scraped the walls and in one case demolished a wayside 'khasi'. I was quite surprised to reach a tarmac road leading into Olovo, but we did and we followed it towards Olovo from Solun. The road was good, the bridges on it strong enough but here we encountered a new problem. One of the bridges was far too narrow for Warrior. We couldn't go round it and despair began to take hold. Then Jamie Sage made a suggestion: put one track on the parapet and keep the other on the road over the bridge itself and drive across with the vehicle tipped on its side. This time I accepted Sapper advice. It would need brave and skilled driving with the driver receiving detailed directions from the ground, but it was worth a try – and it worked. Slowly all Warriors crossed the bridge with one track on the bridge parapet. I think the locals thought we were lunatics.

Next stop was Olovo and we were almost there when we found our way blocked by a Mercedes car. The owner of it proved highly reluctant to move it. Martyn Thomas and Captain David Sherlock, his Second in Command, grew threatening.

'Move it or we squash it,' Martyn shouted. There was still no reaction and so Second Lieutenant Gareth Wright jumped in while the owner was arguing and drove it to the side of the road. We passed and drove into Olovo. This town was another like Maglaj and the war is very much in evidence. However, no shelling was taking place when we entered it. We were directed to the Muslim Headquarters in the basement of the Town Hall. Together with Martyn I asked to see the commander.

'He's having lunch, but will see you in a few minutes,' we were told. That was unusual, I thought; normally commanders see us immediately. However, after a few minutes, the commander walked into the room.

'He's the guy in the Mercedes!' gasped Martyn. He was

right. Great start, I thought, and immediately adopted my most wheedling, apologetic manner.

'I am so sorry about the incident on the road . . . Forgive us, we didn't know who you were . . . We were desperate to get to see the commander in Olovo . . . We are only trying to help get aid through the area . . . We thought you were just trying to delay us . . . We had no way of contacting you in advance . . . I apologize for our very bad manners.' It worked. Although Fadil Karienc, the commander, was at first fairly unamused, he finally saw the funny side of it all. We got on very well after that. I explained that we were looking for a main road route to Tuzla that would be good for armoured vehicles (and incidentally aid). Fadil told us that it was impossible to get into Olovo from the south or to proceed north to Kladanj on the road. The only way to Kladanj was over a mountain road.

We had no alternative but to turn around again. The road he referred to was via Milankovici and I knew it. In my opinion the bridges on this way were very suspect and there were a lot of them. As we were so near, I decided that we would try anyway. Back we went on the same route we had come, including the difficult narrow bridge.

As we left the tarmac road towards Milankovici we had to cross a high concrete bridge. Jamie said it was very dangerous; later he properly classified it as a three-tonne-maximum bridge. Again though, Martyn had put his lead Warrior over before we could think too much about it all. The bridge held, although David Sherlock swore the struts were bending under the strain. But at this point I decided that we could release some of our vehicles. Martyn took the bulk of them back to Vitez whilst I continued the journey with Tudor Ellis's Platoon. Again there were a great number of bridges, particularly approaching Brateljevici. We risked them all and arrived in Kladanj in the late afternoon. I was absolutely delighted. There was a main-road route from Kladanj to Tuzla and clearly Warriors would be able to use it. All we needed to do now was to improve some of the bridges and get Warriors up to Kladanj.

B Squadron at Kladanj were making the very best of their

inadequate small factory. They had done all they could to improve its defences against incoming shellfire and to guard the place properly. Vehicle parking in a small area was a real problem and nobody had a decent place to sleep. But it was not meant to be a holiday camp; we required this as a vital staging post to Tuzla.

I decided to go on to Tuzla that night as two liaison officers, Bob Ryan and Mark Cooper, were living in Hotel Tuzla. They were acting as go-betweens from Alan Abraham's Squadron to the Commander of the Muslim 2nd Corps which had its headquarters in the town. Together with Alan Abraham, we used a Land Rover to drive along the main road. It was after dark when we left and so I saw no reason why we should not travel along the direct route, up what we were soon to call 'Bomb Alley'. This was a stretch of main road which wound itself north from Kladanj to a village called Stupari. We had already been attacked on it once when Martyn Thomas had taken the first aid to Tuzla. The problem was that for a distance of some eight kilometres or so the road was in full view of Serb positions. They could adjust their artillery and mortars at will and often direct-fire weapons like tanks were also used to take out vehicles. It was a very dangerous piece of road. Thus at speed and with no lights for the first part of the journey our two-Land-Rover convoy had us in Tuzla within forty-five minutes. I made a note to ensure that the Squadron or Company Group at Kladanj had proper night-viewing goggles for such driving.

We all booked into Hotel Tuzla where we stayed for fifteen Deutschmarks. Each of our rooms was very good; separate bathroom (joy) and satellite TV in a very respectable chamber. No wonder Bob Ryan and Mark Cooper looked so content with their lot. That evening we all had dinner with the European Community Monitoring Mission Team who were also based at the Hotel Tuzla. Sleep did not need much coaxing that night.

After breakfast the next morning, Bob Ryan and his very pretty interpreter, who happened to be the Mayor of Tuzla's daughter, took me to the Headquarters of Muslim 2nd Corps. Unfortunately the Commander, Zeliko Knez, was away but I was shown in to meet the Chief of Staff named Hazim Sadic. I had a long talk to him about what we hoped to do in Tuzla with regard to the delivery of humanitarian aid and asked for support from 2nd Corps. I was assured this would be forthcoming and we were most welcome in Tuzla.

But I had now been away from Vitez for over two days and felt I should get back, for which I borrowed a Land Rover from B Squadron for the sake of speed. We went the way we had come and I was delighted to discover that I had been able to return from Tuzla to Vitez in under four hours and thirty minutes! Although we had not found an all-weather main-road route to Tuzla as we wanted, nonetheless the new route was a substantial improvement on the old one. I felt that it might be possible to use it throughout the winter but I was not yet too optimistic on that one. The trip also confirmed in my mind that Kladanj should stay as an operating base – at least until we got somewhere in Tuzla. I left Tudor Ellis and his Platoon up in Kladanj with Alan Abraham. I was much happier now that we had Warrior with B Squadron as I felt they would be relatively invulnerable working on 'Bomb Alley'. Talking to Anders Levinson of UNHCR, I told him that I was a little concerned about humanitarian aid arrangements in Tuzla. The UNHCR warehouse up there was in fact being used by the Muslim Army. I explained that I felt the UNHCR and ourselves were delivering aid to Tuzla and then the Muslim Army was distributing it for us. This end-delivery problem was to bedevil UNHCR operations throughout our time in Bosnia. I do not blame the UNHCR – they just do not have enough people to supervise everything. Anders knew about the problem already and was trying to do something. Soon afterwards a proper UNHCR office in Tuzla was opened and it helped greatly to alleviate the problem.

I then had a feasibility study meeting with the company commanders. I wanted to make Tuzla itself into a Squadron or Company Base – provided we were able to sustain it during the winter, which I increasingly believed would be possible. That base would probably be on the airfield and the UNHCR warehouse could be there too. We might keep an offshoot from the Tuzla base at Kladanj but that might put a strain on our manpower and equipment. We also considered whether the Company at Gornji Vakuf might be reduced in number so that we could reinforce further forward. Jamie Sage and his Sappers were asked by me to do an extensive survey of the route to Tuzla and to assess what bridges required improvement in order to continue their use over the winter.

Tuzla had always been our primary humanitarian aid target from the very first reconnaissance. I was delighted, and a little surprised, to be honest, that we had been able to get there so quickly after our arrival. Establishing a base actually at Tuzla was going to take a little more time but essentially the Tuzla operation would soon be set up and running. I thought the Battalion Group had done exceptionally well to have achieved it. Personally I considered getting to Tuzla a major achievement.

CHAPTER 8

SETTLING DOWN FOR WINTER

A few chance remarks at one of my conferences by Company Sergeant Major Atherton about his company at Gornji Vakuf being the 'Forgotten Army' persuaded me that I ought to go there. His comments really hit home as I realized I had not paid much attention to Gornji Vakuf. In fact I had left it all to Alistair Rule to sort out and I felt rather guilty about that. B Company's Sergeant Major had implied that his Company had been rather overlooked; and, from my viewpoint, he was probably right. Together with Mike Winstanley and RSM Stevens I decided to visit them quickly and left Vitez bound for there early the next morning, on Sunday 29 November.

In good weather, the journey to Gornji Vakuf is wonderful and that day was bright and sunny. We drove west for six kilometres along a road which ran through rather untidy semi-industrial developments to a T-junction where there was a Croat checkpoint. Turning left at the checkpoint, the road then ran south, by-passing Novi Travnik to its east, and continued through the most beautiful valley. I noticed one particular stretch of country with woods and fields that reminded me of Sussex. Each village proclaimed its predominant loyalty by hanging Croat or Muslim flags. There were very few cultivated fields and the rugged, unspoilt quality of the land reminded me of Wales. Gradually the road became a large track as it wound higher and higher to the top of the valley where we discovered what looked like a holiday development of small chalets over an area of about a square kilometre. I presume they were once either ski or hunting lodges, but now many of them were filled with refugees who proclaimed their presence by masses of washing drying on the balconies.

Travelling to Gornji Vakuf down this route I became fully aware of how difficult it would be to divide Bosnia into ethnic cantons. Each village is either Croat or Muslim in nature, but within them the races are all very mixed up. There are Serbs living there as well. In times of trouble, then, it is fear that makes each village quickly put up checkpoints which owe no particular allegiance to any army – they are generated by local fears and controlled by local emotions, not any chain of command – making traversing such an area very difficult. Each checkpoint requires separate negotiation and often on every occasion that you want to go through it. However, on this day, after about an hour's journey, we reached the end of a ravine where a Muslim checkpoint marked the start of a short tarmac road journey to the base at Gornji Vakuf.

Alistair Rule's base was in what used to be a modern factory – and by Bosnian standards it was very modern. Apparently built by a Scandinavian firm, the factory was no more than a few years old, with recently installed equipment. It seemed to be an engineering works, but it had not been used since the start of the war and the Croats had taken it over as a training camp. One particular block that was separate from the main building had reputedly been used as a torture chamber. Certainly it looked like it as there was a lot of blood on the walls. However, there was a considerable amount of accommodation available there including hot water, showers and lavatories. All the troops were housed in the buildings, even if the conditions were not ideal. The base had an adequate fence around it, a building suitable for a guardroom and relatively good security compared with Vitez. However, it was also located only several hundred metres from the centre of Gornji Vakuf and sat beside Croat Headquarters which was in a large building on the high ground to its north. Both these factors were to bring the base directly into the firing line when serious trouble started in Gornji Vakuf later in January.

Alistair Rule was on very good form. He had been commanding B Company since I had taken over command and was a good friend. Tall, confident and with unruly red hair, he was always utterly reliable. I had been instrumental in recruiting Alistair because his elder brother, Douglas, had been at university with me and I had persuaded him to join the Regiment. Alistair had followed Douglas's example later. Alistair briefed me on progress to date and showed me the real estate. I was most impressed by what he had achieved. The place had been well sorted out already. We talked about local personalities and how Alistair was getting to know them. I decided that I did not really want to interfere there. In Gornji Vakuf, Alistair had to be the face the locals recognized, unless of course there were really great problems and my presence might help. Therefore I told Alistair that I did not intend to make it my business going around to meet them all the time and left that to him.

B Company in Gornji Vakuf had the task of keeping the routes to Vitez open and secure. We called it the 'Back Door Company' and they would offer help further up the line or provide protection for a quick exit. Obviously they also had to have a considerable presence in the local area of Prozor and Bugojno too and this was being achieved by confidence patrols. Alistair had three platoons of Warriors (a total of fourteen of them) and the Reconnaissance Platoon (eight Scimitars). Having talked it through with him I decided this was a little bit of a waste of assets. I felt there was not a full-time job for all Alistair's armoured vehicles and one platoon of Warriors should be redeployed to Vitez. I could use that platoon as the standby platoon exclusively, though this could be regularly rotated with another platoon from B Company to give them all a break from Gornji Vakuf. Lieutenant Alex Watts and his platoon redeployed to Vitez and became the standby platoon a few days later, but the distribution of the Warriors was radically to change again later in the tour.

On my return to Vitez I was met by Brigadier Andrew Cumming who had come to stay with the Battalion for a few days. Significantly he had nothing to say about the latest press reports to the effect that 'Whitehall' was concerned about the growth of some kind of 'cult of personality' around me. I had read about this in the newspaper articles faxed out to the PINFO office at Vitez. To start with it had worried me a little. I was concerned because people might believe it and I wondered if indeed I had unconsciously promoted such rubbish. In the end I decided that it was simply some journalist trying to sell his newspaper and I would ignore it. In fact nobody in the Army ever gave any indication of agreeing with such reports. If they did they certainly did not say so to my face.

From the start of the tour in Bosnia, I had been determined to face the press head on. I felt no reason to avoid the media, nor for that matter any reason to seek them out. The press in Bosnia was a fact of life: if an interview with me was requested, and I felt that I had the time and inclination, then I might agree to it. I never asked to be interviewed by anyone.

On Monday 30 November, I went to Maglaj with Brigadier Andrew in Juliet while Major Andrew MacDonald, Officer Commanding C Company, made a reconnaissance of the place. It took us ninety minutes to reach Maglaj and we drove straight into town via the main road. Brigadier Andrew and I went directly into the Joint Headquarters there to be met by Herzog Sulejman. Going down a set of stairs to the cellar Operations Room we could still hear the occasional burst of firing, but nothing more. Maglaj was much quieter than normal. Herzog confirmed to us that the place was relatively peaceful at the time. Having delivered a bottle of whisky (Famous Grouse) to a bad (because he drinks) Muslim (Herzog) we left shortly before lunch. In the early afternoon Andrew accompanied Alex Watts and the standby platoon to Turbe where they had a small contact as some light mortar fire struck the Warriors – there were no casualties.

General Sir Peter Inge, Chief of the General Staff (CGS) and as such professional head of the Army, arrived in Vitez on 1 December. His visit coincided with the inauguration of our new Operations Room, a large old classroom which we had converted well. Heavy beams had been positioned all around to support the ceiling and the room had been divided into various cells by a couple of partitions. The main operations desks were run by the watchkeeper who was normally an officer. Support desks included logistic and engineer operations. Maps were positioned in front of all desks so that operators could visualize as best they could what was happening on the ground and radio nets linked the Operations Room to troops who were deployed out from the base. This was a much better set-up than our original arrangement where we were all cramped into a very small room near the gymnasium. Tim Park, the Second in Command, had organized it all – and very professional it looked.

When the CGS had arrived we immediately took him to the Intelligence Cell where a briefing team, consisting of the Second in Command, Intelligence Officer and Operations Officer, took him through our concept of operations and recent events. After about forty-five minutes of this and a tour of the Operations Room, I took General Inge into Travnik and Vitez.

At this stage, accommodation for senior officers was very difficult and sometimes we had to move more junior personnel out of their bed spaces to give them proper facilities. The CGS stayed in the house occupied by the company commanders, but because of his very high rank we also placed a guard on that house overnight. In the evening the CGS visited the Sergeants' Mess for drinks and then he ate dinner with the officers. Again we took dinner in tents and again I had invited some local-force commanders, including Enver Hadzi-hasanovic (Commander 3rd Muslim Corps) and Dario Kord-ich (vice-president of the HVO based in Busovaca). Once more Corporal Keery, the soldier piper in our reinforcements from the Royal Irish Regiment, played his pipes for us. It was very much appreciated – especially later when Corporal Keery collapsed after having made the toast of 'Schlanter' once too often. For my part my head seemed to hurt a lot even before I went to bed.

It ached a good deal more though when I was pulled out of bed by David Sherlock and Tim Park at 6 a.m., in time to take the CGS on to Gornji Vakuf. I was a very 'unhappy' Commanding Officer all the way to Alistair Rule's base. The CGS received a quick briefing and tour of the camp there before he departed south for Split accompanied by Brigadier Andrew Cumming, leaving me to return to Vitez. The visit seemed to have been very successful and I felt we had given General Inge a fairly good 'feel' for what life out here was like.

There were still, however, some everyday operational problems to be ironed out. Although we now had very good communications from our Operations Room in Vitez to Split, and even to the UK and Germany, if necessary via a military satellite system, that was most certainly not the case with our links to Kiseljak. Right the way through our tour, we were never able to get this sorted out. I had been allocated a Dutch Communication Centre which was deployed with us permanently and they operated a high-frequency radio link and an INMARSAT telephone. However, the high-frequency radio rarely worked and when it did we were never able to get through to the right staff officers, and the INMARSAT was permanently 'clogged out' with fax messages. The result was that it sometimes took me over an hour and a half to get through to HQ BHC. And even when I did I was often unable to speak to the person I wanted. Command and control in such circumstances is obviously very difficult indeed. After all, it was HQ BHC, not HQ BRITFOR at Split, which was supposed to exercise day-to-day control over our activities and, although we were able to make normal decisions without reference to HQ BHC, we should really have had much better communications to our Tactical Headquarters when we needed assistance.

In order to understand our problems better staff officers from HQ BHC would often come down and spend the day with us. We would start their visit with a short operational briefing and then normally take them out into the field. On Thursday 3 December, Lieutenant-Colonel Mike Cornwall, the British Officer running the Operations Desk in HQ BHC, arrived with seven other UN officers. After the standard briefing they were split between Juliet and Romeo (the Second in Command's vehicle). I was going to Turbe anyway and so it made sense to take them along in the Warriors with the hatches up.

We drove directly to Turbe in about thirty-five minutes to do so and to my surprise there were even some people on the streets, as no shelling was taking place. I was in the middle of reporting this peaceful scene back to the Operations Room in Vitez over the radio when mortars or shells started landing around us. One was particularly close to Romeo and gave the visiting staff officers quite a shock. But nobody was hurt. As quite a lot of incoming fire was building up, I thought it safer to stay in the vehicles and not allow anyone to dismount. We returned to Vitez after about twenty minutes' observation of what was happening. In my view the Serbs were deliberately targeting our vehicles with indirect fire, which to my know-ledge was the first time it had happened in Turbe.

But the Serbs were not the only ones who happened to fire at us that day. A lorry carrying Croat soldiers passed by the school and an individual in the back fired about ten rounds of ammunition low over the school. Nobody was hurt. In another incident a civilian-aid convoy travelling near the gar-age was shot up by unknown gunmen. Both these incidents worried me because the attacks were so obvious. Were the Croats beginning to regret encouraging us to come to Vitez, I wondered? After lunch, together with Mike Cornwall and other HQ BHC staff officers, I went off to look for Mario Cerkez, the Croat Commander in Vitez. Eventually I tracked him down to the Café Grand in Novi Travnik and, over the customary glass of slivovitz, raised both matters gently. He didn't seem surprised at what had happened – an everyday event in this place, I supposed – however, I asked him to ensure that orders were given to all troops not to attack inter-national organizations, soldiers or property. He said he would do his best but I knew that nothing would probably happen. Mike Cornwall and I left shortly after that having declined, as courteously as possible, an offer from the café's owner of a couple of girls each.

As we arrived back at the school we learnt that a Danish soldier, out on a run from HQ BHC's location in Kiseljak, had been kidnapped, apparently by Croat soldiers. HQ BHC asked us if we could do something to help get the soldier back. The soldier had been taken quite close to Kiseljak and it was certainly not Mario Cerkez's area. We felt that Dario Kordich, based in Busovaca, might be able to help and so Captains Matthew Dundas-Whatley and Martin Forgrave drove down to see him. Apparently Kordich received them very well indeed, having thoroughly enjoyed the dinner night we had had when the CGS had visited. He listened carefully to what Martin and Matthew said had happened to the Danish soldier and promised he would do what he could. A few hours later the soldier was released unharmed by his captors close to where he had been taken. HQ BHC were most grateful and they believed our swift success was due to our influence with Kordich. It just showed how significant parties like dinner nights can be and how getting to know the local commanders had an important place in the search for peace.

During our tour in Bosnia, for six months in all, others were to come and go on much shorter trips. News teams seemed to do up to five weeks before they were replaced by 'fresh blood' or, perhaps more accurately, 're-cycled blood' because they kept coming back. In early December Kate Adie's post was being relieved by Martin Bell and she dropped in to say goodbye. I had got to know her quite well during her sojourn out here and I knew Martin from when he had come out to visit us in Fallingbostel. In the Army we had always been taught to be on guard whenever reporters were around as, like us, they are always on duty. But I found their company stimulating and relaxing. I thoroughly enjoyed being with them and, by the end of my time in Bosnia, I considered them good friends of mine. They still are. I have the highest regard for them, often asking and accepting their advice. On this occasion Kate seemed in a remarkably good mood. After Christmas I discovered why. She had just been told of her award of an OBE in the forthcoming New Year's Honours List. But she did warn me that I must take greater care of myself on operations, which I found very touching. I said I would do my best but could not change the way I was. Kate's remark prompted me to write letters to my family, just in case I was killed. I gave them to Colour Sergeant Black burn, the Chief Clerk, but I'm pleased to say that, at the end of the tour, he gave them back to me so that I could destroy them.

Martin Bell was more whimsical than Kate: this was his first time back after he had been wounded in Sarajevo and he was shortly to make a most powerful documentary for 'Panorama'.

Now we were established in our Forward Operating Base at Kladanj, the UNHCR began planning an aid route into Tuzla from Belgrade. We were asked if we would open a crossing point east of Tuzla and escort any such aid convoys across the lines. I was delighted that the UNHCR was being so dynamic and applauded their efforts. Amazingly quickly after this, I was told that the convoy was ready to go. Now all the UNHCR needed was the place where they could cross the lines and in many ways it was down to us to sort that out.

To start with I asked HQ BHC to ensure that the Serbs were informed that a crossing point needed to be opened. Here the ECMM proved invaluable to us. They had a team on the Tuzla side of the line as well as one on the Serb side. Additionally they had very good communications within their armoured Mercedes jeeps, which we were often to use in preference to our own.

From Kladanj Alan Abraham worked closely with the ECMM team in Hotel Tuzla to establish where on the line a crossing point would be possible. Initially he was given details of the authorized place and planned the operation in great detail, but then, at very short notice, he was told it was to be much further to the north. Apparently the UNHCR and ECMM representatives as well as the HQ BHC liaison officer, all based in Belgrade, had changed the entry point without informing Kiseljak. Alan and I discussed this change of plan over a very bad telephone line; he had managed to get through to Vitez from Hotel Tuzla on a local telephone line. No doubt, we felt, the people in Belgrade were doing their best, but it was terribly frustrating for us when we had to switch plans so drastically. I told Alan that he must not be rushed into a new plan to cross the lines. Everything had to be properly prepared and detailed reconnaissances needed to be made. After all, it was we who would have to cross the lines first and that was likely to be very dangerous.

A couple of days later Alan Abraham and B Squadron Group achieved the first line crossing in the Tuzla area. At 3.30 p.m. on 6 December, Alan ordered Tudor Ellis and his

Warrior Platoon to advance over the front lines. As Tudor led, he came under both small-arms and mortar fire. This was a very dangerous moment. The Serbs had main battle tanks and fire from them could have destroyed Tudor's Warriors, which are not designed to withstand heavy anti-tank fire. In Vitez we held our breath as we listened to what was happening on a very bad radio link. However, on the ground Alan Abraham decided to take the risk. Ignoring the incoming fire and not answering back, Alan ordered the group to push on until they encountered some front-line Serb positions. The gamble paid off and the risk was rewarded. The Serb soldiers were in fact very friendly and they maintained that they would not have fired on our vehicles if they had known we were coming. We had no way of knowing whether that was the truth or not, but the most important thing was that we had crossed the lines and had done so without taking casualties. Alan had ordered that fire could be returned if his soldiers had been attacked and their attackers properly spotted, but such firm identification had not occurred.

When Alan Abraham's squadron spent the night in Serb territory over the lines from Turbe with the Belgian Transport Company vehicles it was to escort back across the lines, another controversy arose. Alan was not too happy about the fact that the officer commanding the Dutch/Belgian convoy of humanitarian aid was insisting that he was in charge of everything to do with the line crossing. Alan argued that he had to be in command during the dangerous part of actually crossing the line. To non-military people this may seem petty, but it would be crazy for a man without experience or executive responsibility for the control of armoured protective vehicles to be in command. At this first line-crossing operation a rather public row broke out over this point – and Robert Fox of the *Daily Telegraph* picked it up and publicized it. Robert Fox's reporting backed Alan's actions and this caused considerable annoyance to the Dutch and Belgians, who, of course, normally read British newspapers. I had hoped the matter would blow over, and at first told Alan to sort it out at local level, but things remained unresolved. Eventually I had to talk to both the commanding officer of the Dutch/

Belgian Transport Battalion and Transport Operations in Kiseljak. After a few days of debate, we reached a compromise worthy of the United Nations: Alan would normally command for the actual crossing and would determine when it was safe to move but, the Dutch/Belgian convoy commander would have control of his convoy for the rest of the time. This suited us, as we were only concerned about the crossing itself. It was really much safer for Alan to have control during such a vital period.

One evening, on Saturday 5 December, I was invited to have dinner with Djemal Merdan, Deputy Commander 3rd Muslim Corps. Having driven over the mountain road to Zenica I met him in the Metallurgical Hotel, a monstrous concrete structure by the river in Zenica. Apparently the place is owned by the metal works which dominates the west bank of the River Bosna for two miles north of the city – thus the hotel's rather unattractive name. Merdan was sitting in the bar having a drink with a woman called Leila, who was to interpret for us. He soon suggested we went out of the hotel for dinner and we took his car to travel a circuitous route to the Café Horse which was only seventy metres from the hotel.

Over dinner we discussed the situation in the region at length. Merdan told me his command had lost four hundred and eighty soldiers killed since the war began. He raised the matter of a secret deal between the Serbs and Croats. He felt that both sides were talking to each other and trying to arrange a compromise between the two of them which would annihilate the Muslims. This was not the first time I had heard this particular theory but I was to hear it repeated again and again during the remainder of my tour. Merdan was coldly angry about this possibility. It was one of the few times I ever saw him visibly upset and he declared that if such a thing happened there would be a world war. There was nowhere for Muslims to go. Serbs had Serbia and Croats had Croatia but Muslims had no other state to which they could readily turn. They were not Muslims in the sense of many Middle Eastern states. They were South Slavs, just like the Serbs and Croats, and the only real difference between them was that they happened to have a different religion. In the past when faced with the choice of accepting Allah or dying, they had opted for life. Merdan was quite strict about not drinking but on this evening he joined me in drinking slivovitz; it was the only time I ever saw him touch alcohol. As the evening progressed Leila became more and more tired – she worked as a translator for Action Internationale Contre la Faim by day and so this was unsurprising. I returned to Vitez just after 11 p.m. having had a very interesting evening and having learnt a lot about the way the Muslims thought. It was clear that the Muslims felt very much alone in their struggles to survive. They had no particular desire to encourage support from more fundamentalist countries and yet they were beginning to think they had no other choice. Merdan was obviously beginning to despair of their ever getting effective help from the rest of Europe.

My Battalion area of operations was so huge that there were still some places I had not visited. Such was the case with Tescanj and I wanted to put that right. Of course I had a liaison officer for the area in Matthew Dundas-Whatley and so I asked him to be my guide, but there were no telephones up to the area and so he went on ahead of me to get a few interviews organized. Travelling in Juliet with my team, I also took the Discovery with me. It took about ninety-five minutes to travel past Zenica up to Zepce and then east to Novi Seher. Matthew met me outside this small town and suggested we left the Warrior there because a wheeled vehicle would be easier on the narrow roads. I agreed and we went on in the Discovery.

Strangely enough, the Commander of Muslim forces in Novi Seher was a Croat. His name was Ivitea Jozic and he used the title of Lieutenant-Colonel – although the Muslims still do not have rank in their Army. Jozic was a former Yugoslav Navy officer. He spoke very good English and was an expert on satellite navigation systems. We met in his small office off the square in the middle of town. As we talked over coffee, he told me that an offensive was taking place right at that moment and, as if to reinforce the point, artillery began to land on the town. However, he said that it was his forces who were doing the attacking – not the other way around.

General Sir Peter Inge, Chief of the General Staff, visits the Battalion at Fallingbostel. This was just at the time that final decisions on our deployment were being made.

Talking to Brigadier Andrew Cumming, commander of the British forces in Croatia and Bosnia, outside my office in the school we hired at Vitez.

This was my armoured vehicle – a Warrior nicknamed 'Juliet'. We always tried to use such vehicles in high-threat areas. Patrolling and 'being seen' was fundamental to success.

A soldier's view of Bosnia. They spent many hours in the backs of armoured vehicles – ready to leap out to provide intimate protection to convoys.

We were there to offer hands-on assistance right from the beginning. Here we deliver blankets to refugees from Jajce in Travnik on 31 October 1992.

Below: Talking to Bosnian Muslim soldiers in Travnik, 31 October 1992. They had been forced out of Jajce the day before.

Building a bomb shelter near the school we hired in Vitez. It was our main base in Bosnia. These shelters were rapidly built once the threat from artillery and mortars grew.

We soon had accommodation in place for over two-thirds of the Battalion Group. For the first five days after the main body of soldiers arrived, however, we had no electricity whatsoever. On 11 November a fierce storm had struck bringing live cabling down throughout Vitez, carrying away a good deal of canvas. Life was fairly miserable at this point.

RSM Stevens, myself, General Sir
John Waters and Captain Richard
Waltier inspect what had now
become 'Vitez Camp'.

A daily briefing for the Advance
Party in October 1992.

We were resupplied by a Main Supply Route that ran 240 kilometres from Split.

On reconnaissance: Juliet about to cross a three-tonne-weight-limit bridge near Milankovici – crossing bridges was always a tricky manoeuvre.

Below: Captain Nick Stansfield, General Philippe Morillon, General Nambia and myself on a tour of Vitez Camp on 10 November. This was my first meeting with the UN Commander and we joked at press comments that my Battalion Group were the first British troops to be under a French general since the First World War.

Below: Brigadier Roddy Cordy-Simpson, Alois Gasparic (Croat Commander Captain Nick Stansfield, Herzog Sulejman (Muslim Commander) and myself in discussion with the commanders in Maglaj about the outrage of a ceasefire agreement being broken, November 1992

The ever-present media:
I brief Kate Adie (BBC) and
Mark Laity (BBC).

Explaining to Kate Adie
that the Beaujolais
Nouveau donated by
the French Battalion
had a Sarajevo label,
20 November 1992.

An A Company patrol
halts just outside Olovo,
November 1992.

Morale-boosting visits: the Prime Minister John Major, at Redoubt Camp, talks to Richard Waltier the Adjutant, 22 December 1992.

Below: Baroness Chalker, Minister for Overseas Development, with Captain Martin Forgrave and Anders Levinson of the UNHCR. Captain Lee Smart and Captain Mark Weir in the background.

And a very different kind of morale-boost came from Jim Davidson at our Christmas festivities. He had had a good night in the Sergeant's Mess!

The offensive was apparently taking place west of Novi Seher in an area called the Black Mountain (a different 'Black Mountain' to the one we had encountered on our reconnaissance). He also told me that a few days before, the Serbs had captured two of his soldiers. They had been tortured: their skin was flayed before they had finally been beheaded. I was shocked by this story. Jozic told it in such a matter-of-fact way and yet, if true, it was absolutely appalling. Of course I would never really know whether it did happen or not.

From Novi Seher we travelled on to Tescanj. It took us quite a while to wind our way through the hills, by-passing Maglaj to its west before we began to approach Tescanj. The track was quite difficult at times, contouring around the side of hills and occasionally going through fairly muddy sections. We came across some magnificent, sweeping panoramas of rolling hills with very little sign of human habitation. In the sunlight, the countryside looked idyllic. Eventually we reached a Muslim checkpoint just to the south of Tescanj and, having passed through it with no difficulties whatsoever, we went on to the Town Hall.

Matthew guided me to the Mayor's office where a meeting was already taking place. Very kindly the Mayor, who introduced himself as Clanjak Muhamed, broke up that gathering and invited us into his office. However, he kept most of the people who had been at the previous meeting with him. They were introduced as representatives from Doboj and Teslic – both towns recently captured by the Serbs. Originally I had been tasked to get aid to Doboj but there was clearly little chance of that now. I introduced myself, explained that I was the Commander of the British Battalion based in Vitez and what we were trying to do in the area – particularly to get aid through to Tescanj and its surrounding villages. I asked for their help, particularly by instructing all officials that they were not to hinder us as we went about our business. My proposals were very well received and by return the Mayor explained that Tescanj and surrounding towns like Doboj and Teslic were having a very difficult time. They were short of essential supplies and were continually subject to aerial bombardment. Many citizens had been killed and there seemed very little that their armed forces could do to stop the Serb advance. I was sympathetic, but explained that I was not really in much of a position to stop it either. However, I did hope that the presence of UN personnel and vehicles might go some way to convincing those attacking to cease or at least diminish their shelling. I remember saying that at least our presence should not aggravate the situation and it might help.

The Mayor asked me if I would be prepared to speak on local television. Naturally, I had no objection to that; it would give my message on what we were trying to do an even wider audience – hopefully including the Serbs as well. Immediately after we had finished talking, the local press were invited in and I gave both television and radio interviews. I had already learnt that, by careful use of local media, the real facts of what we were trying to achieve could be put directly to the people and that whole statements or interviews would go out on the air without any cutting whatsoever. In Bosnia anything stated on the radio or television was believed implicitly by the vast majority of people who heard it, and this had its bad side too. Stories about alleged misbehaviour were accepted wholesale, a fact that was exploited in a fabrication aimed at trying to destroy General Lewis MacKenzie's reputation. Muslim propaganda suggested that General Mac-Kenzie had abducted three under-age Muslim girls. It was an absurd, pernicious lie, but, try as I might to quell such rubbish, I continued to hear this slander right until the end of my time in Bosnia.

With the interview over, Matthew and I travelled on even further north. From Tescanj to an area just to the south of Doboj the road was excellent . We were going to visit the Croat 110 (Usura) Brigade, which had an excellent reputation. It faced the Serb Army directly south of Doboj and was very much tied in with the Muslim command structure – indeed it would have been isolated if it did not, since all its resupplies had to come through Tescanj which was a Muslim town. In what used to be a rather large family house, now Brigade Headquarters, I met Jelec Anto, Deputy Commander 110 (Usura) Brigade. He was young, in his early twenties, but assured and confident enough too. We talked for a while over coffee and slivovitz. Clearly these people knew their business and I went away much impressed with what I had seen. Morale and confidence were very high amongst the Croat soldiers here. They seemed to lack for nothing, which suggested that relations with the Muslims in this part of Bosnia were excellent as all their military supplies had to come directly through BiH territory.

It took us quite a long time to get back to Vitez but when I arrived I received some very good news. The Rear Party in Fallingbostel had sent a signal: my sister Alison had just given birth to twin girls, Emily and Sophie. I went immediately into the Mess and 'wet' the babies' heads.

With a briefing team consisting of Tim Furphy, Simon Ellis and Chris Leyshon, I went down to Gornji Vakuf in Juliet when Malcolm Rifkind, the Secretary of State for Defence, visited. We had decided to brief Malcolm Rifkind there and then bring him into our area proper. Although we had left in good time, however, along the route there was a massive traffic jam of vehicles. We walked about eight hundred metres to the front of the queue to find local workmen were blasting the rock face beside the track in order to make it wider. Apparently nothing was going to move for an hour or more. So the briefers and I abandoned Juliet and our Land Rovers, having requested Alistair Rule to send a vehicle to pick us up from the far side of the road block, and we walked past the workmen and on until we saw two Land Rovers approaching from the direction of Gornji Vakuf. We were there in time for the Defence Secretary and even Juliet, commanded by Company Sergeant Major Lawson, arrived just before we needed to drive back to Vitez.

Brigadier Andrew Cumming had escorted Malcolm Rifkind up the route over the mountains that we called 'Triangle'. Accompanying the Defence Secretary were a host of supporting 'players' including Alastair Goodlad MP (Minister of State at the Foreign Office), Henry Bellingham MP, John Pitt-Brooke (Private Secretary to the Secretary of State), Ms Gill Samuel (Press Secretary Ministry of Defence), Bill Reeves (Assistant Under-Secretary Commitments), Brigadier David Jenkins (Director of Military Operations), and Major Bill

Cubitt (Military Assistant to the Chief of the General Staff).

Time being short, we briefed the Defence Secretary over a sandwich lunch with a package of Intelligence, Concept of Operations and Current Operations. Thereafter Alistair took Malcolm Rifkind on a brief tour of the Gornji Vakuf base. The press were everywhere but I suppose that was to be expected. When I met Malcolm Rifkind before in Germany I had liked him a lot and again I felt he was 'good news'. After a lot of posing for photographs by all the party as they got into Juliet, we returned to Vitez. With the air rushing past me in the turret, it grew colder and colder as we went. I was freezing and so, I think, was Malcolm Rifkind.

As we travelled, I heard over the radio from the Operations Room in Vitez that a vehicle from the International Rescue Committee (an American charity) had been struck by fire in Visoko. We were requested by HQ BHC to do something about it and so the Standby Platoon was despatched down there. But on arrival the Warriors were asked not to interfere and local Muslim forces extricated the vehicle's passengers from where they had taken cover. Their vehicle had been struck by twenty rounds of ammunition and it was amazing that they had not been hurt.

We were all very cold on arrival at Vitez and went straight into the Briefing Room where a cup of tea was waiting to warm us up. After a few minutes of unfreezing, I took Malcolm Rifkind to the gymnasium where a press conference had been set up. In answering questions, the Defence Secretary emphasized our right as British soldiers to reply to aggression with whatever weapons were appropriate and that included mortars and anti-tank weapons, if necessary.

In the late afternoon of that day, Tuesday 8 December, General Nambiar arrived at Vitez. He came with Lieutenant-Colonel Tom Gebirt, the Canadian Commanding Officer. Both of them had crossed the lines at Bugojno and were en route to Kiseljak. Malcolm Rifkind and General Nambiar chatted together for about thirty minutes and then General Nambiar departed. The rest of the evening flowed naturally enough with drinks in the Sergeants' Mess followed by dinner with the officers. The Secretary of State spent the night in Vitez and then departed early the next morning. It was a very long trip down to Split and he needed to get away early enough to ensure he could get back to London that day.

Later I decided that the Adjutant, Captain Richard Waltier, and RSM Stevens needed a break away from the school. They had been working very hard in the building for some weeks now and I was conscious that a change would do them good. I told them both to join me in my Discovery and all three of us then drove to Zenica. There I took them into the Horse Café, a place I came to know well over the months. The Horse Café was in the basement of a huge block of flats. Down a narrow flight of stairs, and with the bar by the entrance and a few columns stretching from ceiling to the floor to separate the tables, the room was about twelve metres square. Some large posters of girls decorated the walls and the whole place was always much too dark. At one of the tables, we ordered some drinks and avoided all talk of Bosnia. It was great to see Richard and RSM Stevens relaxing a little – even if we were all still in uniform and had our weapons with us. The waiters were quite used to seeing people in uniform at the café – it seemed to be the favourite meeting place for Muslim staff officers from the nearby Headquarters of the 3rd Corps. Some of the walls even had Muslim insignia painted on them.

On Friday 11 December, I went to Kiseljak where Brigadier Roddy Cordy-Simpson was due to meet Jean de Courten, Director of Operations ICRC. Iris Wittwer, newly appointed Head Delegate of ICRC in Zenica, and I had been invited to attend. The main subject for discussion was how to tackle the problems of displaced persons. The ICRC policy is to encourage people to remain in their homes and then to take aid to them, exactly as the UNHCR prefers to operate. The main reason for my attendance became clear when discussions switched to considering the escorting of detainees from detention centres in Central Bosnia to places of safety. Under the second part of our mandate, UNPROFOR was supposed to assist such detainee escorts if that be possible. We talked about how we would actually support such ICRC activities, bearing in mind that the ICRC never really want to be too closely associated with UNPROFOR activities, preferring to maintain their strictly neutral status. I could understand that approach and we devised a system whereby our escorts would be clearing the route in front of the ICRC convoy and protecting it from the back, but UNPROFOR vehicles would be well away from the ICRC column. Jean de Courten asked us to remain on standby for such an operation from now onwards as the ICRC felt there would soon be a need for such escorts. I told Iris Wittwer that she had only to ask and we would provide personnel and vehicles to help as quickly as possible. Jean de Courten left for Split and I spent a couple of hours in the Headquarters walking around the staff branches getting to know people.

The cultivation of our friendly relationships with local groups was still a key objective for us and considerable effort was made to keep this going. To this end Captain Jamie Balls had spent a lot of time fixing up a rugby match with Zenica. To his considerable credit, on Saturday 12 December a game took place between the Battalion Group and the Zenica Rugby Club. The venue was a large international stadium in the town and the local side really did all in its power to make it a truly memorable event. Advertisements and the programmes all billed the Battalion side as 'The British Army' and the match was classed 'international'. I really began to worry about it all as the proportions and importance of the fixture grew. The Zenica Rugby Club, Muslim to a man, recalled all its top players from the front lines and apparently played rugby to a very high standard. They told me that they had cultivated several top-class international players who were playing rugby in France at the moment. The Battalion Group team had done a few nights' training running around the gymnasium but nothing more. I dreaded the thought of a massive walk-over for Zenica.

A large number of Battalion Group supporters were taken by various means to the stadium and it was great to get so many soldiers away from Vitez, seemingly off-duty, and that alone made the event worthwhile. The weather was also fair and sunny. Within the stadium there was almost a carnival atmosphere. The Regimental Band played on the pitch. A bar was opened for the soldiers. On my arrival I was taken to meet a whole range of dignitaries, from Mayor of Zenica to Corps Commander. Just before the game started Enver Hadzihasanovic and I were escorted down to the pitch and we met both teams. Theirs seemed horrifically large to me; but then I was probably running scared at the time. I should have had more faith.

Having returned to the VIP box and after the Band played the European Anthem, the game started. Slightly to my surprise the teams were very well matched and it was a really good game. Some news teams, particularly local ones, filmed the event which went out on prime-time Bosnian television. Across on the other side of the stadium about a thousand local supporters cheered for their team – but also for ours when they felt like it. Merdan was there with his son and we talked during the game. In the end the result was tremendous: a truly politically inspired 17–16 points victory to them. Despite the disappointment of my team, it was exactly the sort of result I wanted.

We paid for the lion's share of the post-match party for over a hundred people in a very large room upstairs in the International Hotel. I sat with the VIPs at the top of a U-shaped table whilst each team sat down the wings. Staff from both UNHCR and ICRC were also present. During a relatively simple but ample cooked meal, the Regimental Band and a local group played. The Corps of Drums did a tremendous display of their victory beatings which went down very well. Speeches were made by them. Jamie Balls and I replied. Then gifts were exchanged. They were tremendously generous in the mementoes they handed out to all members of our team. This was very much a feature of Bosnian life and their tremendous generosity is one of my enduring memories of these people. I have lost count of the number of times I was offered food that was being saved for some special event like Christmas in Bosnian houses. I never wanted to take it but offence was easily caused if I refused. The business of accepting hospitality and gifts was very politically charged and in Bosnia it is a matter of honour to detain guests as long as possible. You are plied with cakes, meat, slivovitz and coffee, with hosts rarely taking no for an answer.

The best way I found to avoid drinking too much alcohol was not to touch my glass. If, by mistake, I drained it the glass would be refilled immediately.

Later that evening I had dinner with members of the ICRC including Jean-Paul Corboz, the ICRC delegate in Tuzla who was on a visit. We went to the Café Horse and had a most relaxing time. Jean-Paul Corboz looked rather like Peter Sellers with a military moustache and he had a great sense of humour. I really enjoyed the company of some wonderful people that evening and I found it very relaxing to get away from my duties for a few hours.

Trying to be even-handed, we had challenged the Croat team from the small town of Dolac to a game of soccer the next day, a Sunday. The match took place on a pitch between Novi Travnik and Travnik during the afternoon and again a lot of local support cheered vociferously for the Croats and we took some stalwart British soldiers down to watch. At half-time the Croat band from Travnik played music on amplifiers for us. This band was really a group of middle-aged 'swingers' who were quite good. The lead singer was particularly fine. Hospitality after the match was excellent and most generous. We lost this match too, but again the score of 4–3 was judiciously diplomatic.

Later that evening, Paddy Ashdown, leader of the Liberal Democrats, arrived for a visit. He had come via Gornji Vakuf where he had been briefed by Alistair Rule. In the Intelligence Section we briefed him on the situation. Having been a Royal Marine he was very much at ease with the way we did things and visibly enjoyed being with us. The feeling was mutual; he was good company and very easy to brief.

Brigadier Andrew Cumming stayed the night too. Earlier in the day Alan Abraham together with Andrew MacDonald, whose C Company was about to take over from B Squadron in Kledanj, had crossed the lines west of Tuzla. Whilst others escorted a UNHCR convoy from the Belgrade Company of the Dutch/Belgian Transport Battalion to and from Tuzla on what was now known as Operation Cabinet, Alan Abraham, Andrew MacDonald and Brigadier Andrew Cumming had used the opportunity to go and see the local Serb Brigade

Commander. They had been very well received and Brigadier Andrew explained our mission. He also pressed the Serbs not to open fire on convoys we were escorting north of Kledanj. This was the first time we had been able to talk directly to any Serb officers and it was significant. We needed to be able to talk to all sides if we were truly to act in a neutral capacity.

Brigadier Andrew joined Paddy Ashdown and the remainder of the officers for dinner in the Mess Tent. As ever the Master Chef, Warrant Officer 2 Straney, produced amazing results from his tented kitchen. This man, perhaps more than anyone else, had a tremendous effect on morale. The meals he and his chefs produced were reckoned to be the best in Bosnia and his later award of an MBE was richly deserved. Over dinner we had a really good discussion about what policy we should pursue in Bosnia. Paddy Ashdown argued strongly for more intervention; Brigadier Andrew and I were a little more cautious.

The next morning I asked Paddy if he would like to accompany me on a trip into Travnik. He willingly accepted and so I set him up in the back of Juliet: hatches were open – so he could see around – and he was on the intercom as well. We drove into Travnik taking the standby platoon with us. Travnik looked quiet and peaceful on that sunny day. Nothing was happening there and I thought it might help Paddy's understanding of our situation if he visited the front lines.

'Do you want to go to Turbe, Paddy?'

'Yes, please.'

'I'm not sure I should, you know. I suppose I could get into trouble for it.'

'You won't!'

'OK, then. I just hope everything will be all right!'

Matthew Dundas-Whatley quickly told the local-force headquarters that we intended to go to Turbe and we left Travnik for the short journey. As we approached Turbe I could hear no sounds of gunfire or shelling. The place seemed quiet and so we drove directly into the centre and stopped outside Leko's Headquarters. On dismounting from Juliet, some small-arms fire and an explosion occurred a street or two away, but then it fell quiet again. As ever Leko was most welcoming and I started by introducing Paddy Ashdown. Leko replied saying that he felt our constant patrolling of Turbe was having a great effect of lessening the shelling of the place. He was most enthusiastic about our presence and said some truly flattering things about my Battalion Group. I talked to Leko about my chances of getting across the lines and talking to the Serb Commanders. At first he seemed to suggest that it might be possible but in further discussion I realized that it would be very difficult as things stood. However, I had to get across the lines at Turbe, at least so that I could meet the other side.

The road out of Turbe is clearly visible from the high Vlassic Feature to its north and that day, being bright and sunny, visibility could not have been better. The Serb mortarmen sitting at the top of the mountain must have had a perfect view of our small convoy as it left Turbe. They judged our speed well and then dropped a mortar bomb down their barrel at a pre-arranged aiming point so that when the bomb landed some twenty seconds or more later it was exactly where our vehicles could be expected.

The first I knew about anything was a massive explosion just by the right side of Juliet. To start with I thought I had been blinded by the explosion as I saw white and seemed to feel the heat. I felt Juliet falter for only a second before Corporal Gill pushed his foot down hard on the accelerator. I opened each eye one at a time and then realized I was all right. Company Sergeant Major Lawson beside me said, 'Let's go, sir,' but we were going already. We drove on and kept going into Travnik. I checked with those in the back and all were fine. Paddy Ashdown was totally calm. Thank goodness we had Warrior. Again I silently thanked all those who had insisted that Warrior had to be deployed on Operation Grapple.

We motored straight through Travnik and I took Paddy to visit the Vitez UNHCR depot where he could see how we linked to humanitarian aid convoys. Then we went on to the ICRC offices in Zenica where I introduced Paddy to Iris Wittwer, the Head Delegate. Briefly I talked to Iris about the detainee escort operation which still had not happened, but was now scheduled for a few days later. Paddy Ashdown left Zenica directly for Kiseljak, bound ultimately for Sarajevo. A few days later he passed through again needing a lift down to Split and we arranged for Major John Donnelly, Officer Commanding Echelon, to accompany him. John was always in Split as part of his duties. We dubbed him 'The Black Swan' because he was always 'swanning' off either to Split or Tuzla.

By now we were firmly established in Central Bosnia. Both the Vitez and Gornji Vakuf bases were taking on features of permanence and being rapidly improved by great efforts from 42 Field Squadron. The route from Split up to Vitez and Zenica was working well – again thanks to massive Sapper efforts, especially in the mountains. Kledanj as a Forward Operating Base was working well and now it looked increasingly likely that we might be able to sustain humanitarian relief convoys to Tuzla throughout the winter. At least one convoy to Tuzla was departing daily. We were actively patrolling throughout our area and seemed to be well respected by all sides. I felt we had achieved a great deal.

CHAPTER 9

ON LINE CROSSINGS
AND CEASEFIRES

By now we were escorting as many as six to eight convoys of humanitarian aid a day for the UNHCR. We were managing to get to every destination that the UNHCR required. It also seemed that we might be able to sustain humanitarian relief to Tuzla throughout the winter. However, I thought it would be great if we could somehow shorten the aid route into Central Bosnia. Coming in from the east via Banja Luka across the Serbian lines was geographically the most sensible way to approach. I decided that I would do all in my power to try to open up this route, which was something the UNHCR itself wanted.

Therefore, my next objective was to get across the lines to the west of Turbe. I had heard that a Muslim officer called Beba Salko ran an Exchange Commission – negotiating the handing over of prisoners and bodies across the lines – for the Muslims from Travnik. Matthew Dundas-Whatley arranged a meeting for me with Beba. We drove into Travnik and stopped beside the local Red Cross office, which was in a ground-floor shop in a modern apartment block. Beba Salko worked from an office next door that had also been converted from a shop. He was most welcoming as we went in to meet him. Like most of the officers with whom we dealt, he had been in the Yugoslav National Army until the break-up of former Yugoslavia; I think he was probably an intelligence officer. As he spoke English well, there was no need for us to use an interpreter and Beba told me that he had crossed the lines thirty-four times since the war had started. His job was to talk to the Serbs and he met frequently with his Serbian counterpart. Without any telephone lines working across the lines, however, Beba had to use a radio and break into Serb nets when he needed to get a message through. In fact he was going across the lines later that day.

I asked Beba whether he thought it might be possible for me to accompany him. But on full consideration we thought that perhaps this might be premature and, in any case, he needed to warn off the Serbs. He thought that we should also get Serb approval to my crossing before we did it. Upon Beba's suggestion, I drafted a letter telling them what I wanted to do. We had it translated into Serbian, politely asking for me to be allowed to cross the lines and meet Serb commanders in two days' time, whilst Beba insisted on me eating a meat pasty and drinking two large glasses of slivovitz. He told me that during his meetings with the Serb Exchange Commission they had frequently complained to him about the war. They were sick of it and wanted it stopped by Christmas. I replied that in that case they had better get a move on as Christmas was in ten days' time. Taking my translated letter with him, Beba then departed for his line crossing. I wished him luck but privately thought we would be lucky if the Serbs agreed to me accompanying him across the front line.

Fortunately, though, I was wrong and on the next day Beba Salko contacted me to say that the Serb Exchange Commission had agreed to me accompanying him to their side on the following day. I was absolutely thrilled. Here was a chance to do what I had always wanted: to make direct contact with the Serbs in my area, and thereby make possible my long-term aim of opening up a crossing point at Turbe so that we could run UNHCR convoys directly into Central Bosnia from Zagreb via Banja Luka. Meeting the Bosnian Serbs was a first step and a vital one.

I decided that we should cross the lines in as military a way as possible. The Standby Platoon, commanded by Colour Sergeant Sheridan and consisting of four Warriors, was to move into Turbe at 10 a.m., an hour before we were due to cross the lines. A ceasefire in Turbe was supposed to take effect from 8 a.m. and Colour Sergeant Sheridan was to ascertain that the fighting had stopped before my party moved into the town. The Serbs had stipulated that no armoured vehicles were to cross over and so we were to use Land Rovers. If shelling was taking place, we would abort the task. Provided that Colour Sergeant Sheridan reported all was quiet, then a small convoy of Land Rovers would move into Turbe and cross the lines. The Warriors would remain on this side to oversee the position, although we realized that they would not be able to give us any real cover. The place where we were to meet the Serbs was about one thousand metres over the line and well out of sight from our side. Travelling in three Land Rovers my party was to consist of Matthew Dundas-Whatley, Nick Stansfield, RSM Stevens, and CSMs Lawson and Cusack.

During a tour of Northern Ireland in the mid-seventies the Battalion had arrested CSM Cusack, then a young hot-head in Belfast. Since that time he had joined the Royal Irish Regiment and risen rapidly through the ranks. He was now the senior Royal Irish Warrant Officer attached to my Battalion Group and was a superb soldier. He was very proud of having caused us trouble when he was young, but we had long ago forgiven him because he was such fun to have around. He was a Bisley shot and whenever he came out with me he always carried the British Army's latest sniper rifle – in the hope of making use of it.

In the event Colour Sergeant Sheridan was able to report that Turbe was remarkably quiet when he arrived. Our three Land Rovers remained at a Croat checkpoint on the western outskirts of Travnik, where we had been joined by Beba Salko in a civilian car. A journalist called Jim Hooper from *Jane's Defence Weekly* came with him in a jeep. Jim explained that he also had sought agreement from the Serbs to cross the lines and was going over to stay for a few days with them to interview the Commanders. The best of luck to him, I thought. I would not mind doing that myself. Beba's car had a huge white flag with a red cross painted on it. Our small convoy was parked behind him for a short while, just to reassure ourselves that things really were quiet, and then we

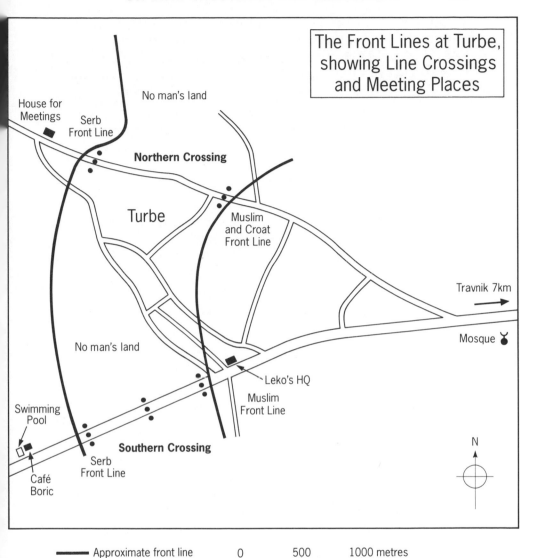

The Front Lines at Turbe, showing Line Crossings and Meeting Places

House for Meetings

No man's land

Serb Front Line

Northern Crossing

Turbe

Muslim and Croat Front Line

Travnik 7km

Mosque

No man's land

Leko's HQ

Muslim Front Line

Swimming Pool

Southern Crossing

Serb Front Line

Café Boric

N

———— Approximate front line

● ● ●   Mines

0   500   1000 metres

0   500   1000 yards

drove directly into the centre of Turbe. At 11 a.m. we were at the front line on the Komar road leading west from the town. Together with Beba we left the Muslim positions and advanced into no man's land. Two rows of Muslim mines stretched across the road. Beba demonstrated some superb mine-clearance drills: pushing them aside with his foot. Matthew and I helped him – considerably more cautiously. I couldn't help thinking that the Sappers would have a fit if they saw what we were doing. We reckoned there was little risk of anti-tampering devices being attached to the mines – especially as they belonged to Beba's own side. But the third line of mines were Serb ones. These were about five hundred metres into no man's land and were conspicuously observed by a section of Serb infantry watching from a fortified house fifty metres away to the right. The Serbs watched impassively even though we waved, maybe a little too enthusiastically. At any rate they did nothing and let us pass. It felt very strange to be going over the lines here and I was nervously excited. We could have been blown to bits at any time and that made the experience nerve-jangling.

We drove on for perhaps another five hundred metres until we came to what used to be a café. It had the word Boric emblazoned on its side and had clearly seen much better days. It was now in a fairly ruinous state, having received a considerable amount of incoming fire at some stage, with a lot of its windows broken and its walls pock-marked with bullets. Beside the café was a disused swimming pool.

A few Serb soldiers stood around the building. This was the first time I had been close to the Serbs since the previous September and I noticed how very different they seemed from both the Croats and Muslims. Most markedly, they all wore old Yugoslav National Army uniforms rather than combat clothing like the Croats and Muslims tended to wear. A side-cap was part of uniform – no hats for the Croats and Muslims was normal – and a lot of them had beards. However, they were welcoming enough and greeted Beba Salko as an old friend – which he was to a lot of them as they had been at school together. Beba was obviously a kind of postman too, as he brought a lot of mail which he distributed to the soldiers.

Inside the café were members of the Serb Exchange Commission led by Captain Milutin Gruicic, a middle-aged tired-looking man. Other members introduced themselves: Mladen Arezin, Rodogub Tryuga, Vaso Lukic, Mira Jokanovic and a woman whose name I didn't catch. We sat down at a long table with a white tablecloth on it. There was a silence. I decided I had better say something and opened up by pointing out what a vital task they all seemed to be doing. It was clear, I said, that everyone here wanted peace and obviously the sooner all sides realized war solved nothing the better. From my viewpoint, it was essential to meet all sides of the conflict in order to be fully effective as a neutral. I had to be able to come and talk to the Serb Commanders, particularly since I was sure that the areas held by the Serbs also needed humanitarian aid. Surely there must be a need for UNHCR operations across on this side of the lines too. As I went on the Serb Exchange Commission relaxed a little, which was more than I did in the freezing cold. There was no heating whatsoever and I was not wearing a pullover – a mistake I was very much regretting.

Gruicic said that he would try to arrange a meeting for me with his commanders who were away at the moment. I asked if I could attend all future meetings and Gruicic said he felt that would not be a problem. Beba then spent about thirty minutes or so locked in deep conversation with Gruicic on matters that seemed no real concern of mine. While he was doing this Matthew, Nick and I had tried to keep warm by stamping around at the other side of the room. After about two hours the meeting finally began to break up. It was agreed that the next meeting would be in seven days' time and I said I would like to be there too. As we left the café, people asked us to pose for photographs with them, which we did before getting back into our vehicles. Mercifully the drivers had the heaters on full.

We travelled back down the route we had come, again helping to replace the mines we had removed on the way to the café. Beba led us into Leko's Headquarters upon our return into Turbe and insisted that we join him for lunch. We were taken next door from the Headquarters to another café where we sat at a long table to await the meal. This café was freezing too. As soon as lunch was over, we left for Vitez. The ceasefire had held throughout the time we had been over the lines and in Turbe. I had hoped to be able to discuss the matter of a complete truce for the duration of the Christmas period but the Serbs we had met today were not the right people. Beba advised that maybe some higher-ranking officers would attend in a few days' time and they would be the ones to speak to about such a truce.

All in all, though, it had been a most successful day. We had managed to cross the lines west of Turbe for the first time; we had made contact with the Serbs; we had told them what we were trying to achieve and made clear what we were doing in the area; and we were now apparently welcome to attend all such meetings. Maybe we would be able to meet with Serb commanders next time to discuss a Christmas truce with them then. I felt we had done well.

Getting to Tuzla, my key objective for the tour, was still a problem, though, and we spent much time thinking about ways of easing the journey. One very sensible route would have been past Zenica to Zepce and thence from Zavidovici to Ribnica and Tuzla. There were reports that recently the Serbs had been forced to retreat a little in the area between Zavidovici and Ribnica. If they had retreated far enough then it could conceivably be possible for a good heavy-vehicle route to be opened up all the way to Tuzla from Central Bosnia. It was a long shot but might be worth the effort, at least to ascertain the facts.

Together with Matthew Dundas-Whatley, I travelled up to Zepce and Zavidovici. Everyone seemed to know Matthew, who was obviously doing a great job as liaison officer for the area. Over the space of a few hours we travelled around the various headquarters talking to the commanders there.

'Was there any chance that the Zavidovici to Ribnica road would be open soon?' I asked repeatedly.

It had been at Ribnica, approaching it from the south, that Bob Ryan's reconnaissance to Tuzla had been attacked on 7 November. Our optimism about these rumoured Muslim advances, however, was short-lived. All commanders we spoke to agreed that the Serbs were retreating north from the area, but Ribnica was still very much in Serb hands. Along the road between Zavidovici and Ribnica, for at least fifteen kilometres, the road was badly blocked by mines and anti-tank obstacles. The day was by no means a waste of time. It had enabled me to meet commanders I had not come across before and it also confirmed that any thought of using the Zavidovici–Ribnica route was out of the question for the moment.

By now I was getting to know many members of the media rather well. Robert Moore of ITN invited me to join the journalists in Kiseljak for dinner and I was more than happy to accept. I had a tremendously enjoyable evening, including a lively debate with Robert Fox of the *Daily Telegraph* on the philosophy of peacekeeping for UN forces. The next morning Brian Redhead talked to me over the INMARSAT telephone, in my first interview on Radio 4's 'Today' programme, predominantly about the conditions facing us in Central Bosnia. Later that same day Stuart Hall of Granada Television arrived in Vitez. He had come to do a Christmas programme for the north-west, and in its final form it was an excellent portrait of exactly what life was really like with the Battalion Group.

Throughout our time in Bosnia, HRH The Prince of Wales kept himself informed about what was happening to us. He is Colonel-in-Chief of the Cheshire Regiment and took a lively interest in our progress, normally by using the military satellite system. Whenever I had a conversation with the Colonel-in-Chief or his Equerry, I always passed on this fact to the Battalion. His interest in our welfare and the progress of our mission was a great inspiration for all of us. In early December the Colonel-in-Chief asked me if there was anything he could do to help. I told HRH that the one thing that would really help morale would be a telephone link available for the soldiers' use at Christmas. The Colonel-in-Chief together with the Army authorities must have made this a top priority because by 22 December ten satellite telephone lines had been established in Vitez. British Telecom donated them for our use for one month. These lines were open for twenty-four hours a day and, although calls were limited to ten minutes per person, you could make as many calls as you wished. It was a fabulous facility and we were most grateful to the Prince of Wales for his efforts on our behalf and to British Telecom for providing the equipment.

One of the greatest difficulties throughout my tour was

evenly dividing my time between the various factions in Central Bosnia. To start with the Muslims had accused me of siding with the Croats when we first arrived and were establishing ourselves at the school. All the contracts had been signed with the government of Vitez town which was Croat controlled. We had tried to employ a mixture of Croats, Muslims and Serbs to help with the administration of what was now quite a large base, but it was not easy, especially in the lower-paid manual jobs, because the only people who tended to arrive for job interviews were Croats in what was, after all, a predominantly Croat area. However, we were much more successful in employing a mixture of all three nationalities in the selection of our interpreters, and everyone knew it. But recently I had spent a lot of time with the Muslims, either with Merdan or in developing a relationship with Beba Salko in order to get across the lines. I gathered through various sources that the Croats felt I had not concentrated on them enough recently. It may seem a little silly but in Bosnia I was quickly learning that 'face' was very much about being recognized with a visit. Therefore I decided that I should spend a couple of days re-establishing links with the Croats. I started with Colonel Filipovitch, Commander of the Croats in Travnik. At the time, his Headquarters was in a rather dark building beside the main road which travelled east–west through Travnik. Filipovitch was another ex-YNA officer. Silver-haired and middle-aged, perhaps a little older than myself, he was a very civilized man who some said had been demoted to take command in Travnik. On Friday 18 December, I was received by him in his office, which, with his desk in front of a camp bed, clearly doubled as his place of work and sleep, much like my own arrangements at that time.

I admired Filipovitch, a decent sort of man who spoke softly and never changed his tone of voice. Quickly I realized that he had been a little hurt that I hadn't been to see him for a while. I apologized for that and told him that I had been concentrating on getting across the lines at Turbe. He told me that he too had an Exchange Commission Officer who worked with the Serbs. I spent some two hours talking with Filipovitch in his small office. As ever, we drank considerable quantities of slivovitz – a drink I was getting used to, although I never liked it much.

Having seen Filipovitch I next wanted to see Timomir Blaskic, Commander of the Central Bosnia Operational Zone for the Croats. The rumours suggested that Blaskic had replaced Filipovitch, who had been demoted to Travnik, but I never discovered whether this was true. Like so much in Bosnia, it was probably just gossip but I never wasted much time on such talk. When I first went to find him in Hotel Vitez, Blaskic wasn't there. Apparently he was in Kiseljak which was his alternative Headquarters. The next day he was back and so I returned to see him. Timomir was in a very good mood. We didn't talk too much about the problems in Central Bosnia but rather about our different backgrounds – particularly military training. We laughed about the contrasting pictures we had had of the potential threats posed by East and West in the days before Glasnost. Clearly the Yugoslav National Army had been preparing to fight in any direction – against NATO or against the Warsaw Pact. We also discussed that crazy day of 20 October when we had been on our reconnaissance and had spent the whole period trying to stop the fighting between the Croats and Muslims. He told me that we had really established our credentials with him that day. Obviously he thought we had been a little naive but he admired the way we had tackled the problem from a position of great ignorance. I had to agree with him about the ignorance bit. I told Timomir that I had never been so frightened in all my life as that day. He said he wasn't surprised – we had been very lucky to survive.

Another Croat area I needed to pay a little more attention to was Vares. Recently we had made a mistake there and I felt I needed to do something about it. One evening a sergeant had been returning from Tuzla with a small convoy of vehicles. It was after dark when a group of three unknown soldiers flagged him down. They pleaded with him for a lift as the weather was bad. The sergeant, being a decent sort, agreed, even though it was against UN orders, and the soldiers climbed aboard. In Vares the convoy was stopped by a detachment of Croat Military Police, at which the soldiers ran off.

The sergeant and the men under his command were detained and verbally abused. The Military Police maintained that the men who had run off were Serbs on a spying mission. The whole incident turned a little nasty and at one stage it looked as though some British soldiers might be shot. How the sergeant ever allowed the situation to develop like this – especially with the direct threats being made to his soldiers – was a mystery to me. I had my suspicions that it had been a 'set-up' but you can never tell in this place. Certainly offence had been caused. Timomir Blaskic had even mentioned it to me when I had seen him and I had promised I would go and see the local Croat Commander about it. Timomir had agreed that this might be a good idea.

Vares took about two and a half hours to get to by Land Rover. Once a ski resort, this pleasant town had been much modified for the Sarajevo Olympic Games and was as yet relatively untouched by the war. The place is Croat controlled, although it is rather an island in Muslim territory. I had been to the Croat Headquarters before, even spending the night there when I had been trying to find a main road route to Tuzla. The Ski Hotel Headquarters was through Vares on the Olovo Road. But I had not met Emil, the Commander, when I had spent the night there. With him present on this occasion, I introduced myself and thanked him wholeheartedly for his hospitality when I had last been there. Turning to the incident involving the sergeant and his men, I apologized profusely. It was a mistake made by a non-commissioned officer who should have known better, I explained. I tried to suggest that I felt there was something wrong about the whole incident and that the three soldiers who had begged a lift were most certainly not Serbs, but it soon became clear that I was not going to get to the bottom of it all. Emil must have known what really happened but I would never find out from him. The best thing was to take the blame and say sorry, and Emil was quick to accept my apology.

I then broached the subject of the bridges east of the Croat Headquarters on the road to Olovo and how they might be improved. We needed these bridges to be much better so that we could move our heavy armour (and aid vehicles) over them with confidence. After his extensive reconnaissance with 42 Field Squadron, Jamie Sage, the officer commanding, had advised me that about seven bridges needed to be rebuilt with stout timber supports. Emil agreed that the bridges were weak and that they probably did need improvement but he said he hadn't the authority to agree to something like that. Apparently he would need a written order from Blaskic before he could accede to my request. With an inward sigh, I realized that I would have to go back to Timomir. I parted with Emil on good terms having donated a couple of bottles of Scotch to raise Croat morale.

On my way back to the school I dropped in again on Timomir. I told him where I had just been and that I had apologized to Emil over the mistake we had made in Vares. I asked him for agreement to improve bridges east of Vares towards Olovo and he accepted my request. Timomir said he would issue orders to that effect and a few days later a written order authorizing us to improve the bridges was delivered to my Headquarters. Jamie Sage and his engineers completed the work very quickly, though I couldn't help feeling that the locals had a hell of a cheek. Here we were trying to improve the routes which they obviously had to use too and yet there was all this bureaucratic 'red tape' to go through in order to get agreement.

I was back with the Muslims that evening. Together with about a dozen officers I had been invited to a reception in our honour at the Travnik Logistics Centre. The party started at 5.30 p.m. and we made sure we were on time. It seemed very strange to be going into Travnik, which was still being shelled spasmodically, for a party. We went with mixed feelings about it, as we weren't sure about food we would receive – constantly alert as we were to the risk of food poisoning – and we weren't sure how we would all be able to communicate, as we had a shortage of interpreters. In the event, all went very well. The Logistics Centre was a large modern building in the centre of Travnik which seems to have been a department store at some time. As the Logistics Centre, it was now controlled by a man who called himself a Colonel and it seemed to be the main quartermasters' stores for the

Muslims in the area. All the Muslim Travnik leadership were lined up in the room to meet each of us as we walked in and Beba Salko was there also. A lady in her fifties who had been an English teacher – she said she had taught most of our own interpreters – translated for me. I was looked after by the Commander of the Logistics Centre and the food was excellent, despite the fact that I had to eat raw minced meat mixed together with egg which filled me with dread. The conversation obviously revolved around the war. A staff officer from the Headquarters in Sarajevo told me about how distrustful they all felt about the Croats. Again the suggestion was made that the Serbs and Croats were planning to ally against the Muslims. After a couple of hours, speeches ended the evening. Generously, they gave us a lot of mementoes. Thankfully, we had brought along a few bits of Regimental regalia which I presented by way of return. We seemed very popular with the Muslims and their pleasure at our presence in Bosnia seemed very genuine.

Saying goodnight to Beba, he reminded me that we were due to cross the lines again at Turbe the next day. This time there was likely to be no meeting but Beba Salko was going to try to find a body lost in the area between the lines northwest from Turbe.

Matthew Dundas-Whatley was with Beba by 8.30 the next morning. Using a local telephone from Beba's small office, Matthew briefed me that a line crossing was going ahead and so I gave out preparatory orders for it in the Intelligence Cell. This time though I decided to allow a press vehicle to accompany us as Martin Waters, our new PINFO officer, had been pleading to allow at least one camera team to come with us. A ceasefire had supposedly been in place since 8 a.m. but there had been several reported breaches of it by 9.30. However, I decided that the line crossing could go ahead despite that and Paul Gill, commanding the Standby Platoon, went into Turbe to take up protective positions at the front line.

Turbe was not as peaceful as the first time we crossed over a few days before. Automatic fire occasionally punctured the otherwise relative quiet of the ruined town. This time we took another route across the lines by taking a fork in the road some three hundred metres short of the town's centre and moving north-west on the road to the Vlassic Feature. This route took us through the northern edge of Turbe. No house seemed to have escaped extensive damage. The road was littered with bits and pieces. Abandoned and destroyed vehicles did much to add to the general look of destruction.

Paul Gill had positioned two of his Warriors about one thousand metres up this road at the last Muslim trench positions. At the front line, there was a small delay whilst Beba Salko checked something out with the Muslim soldiers. I used the opportunity to talk to the Muslim soldiers manning positions there. They were very well dug in and had made extensive use of cellars to protect themselves. Nobody seemed particularly downhearted. In these well-prepared positions, they seemed determined to hold the line and again I had the impression that these defenders were not about to give up. An ITN news team asked if I could give them a short interview and whilst I was telling them that a ceasefire had been established, a machine-gun opened up very close to us. Although my heart jumped convulsively, I managed to stay outwardly calm. Later I was to receive an order, down the chain of command from HQ UKLF, that, in future, I was to wear a helmet and flak jacket when line crossing. The irony was that the reason I was not wearing them was because I felt ashamed to do so when so many people around me in the Muslim forces had nothing, especially Beba Salko. My soldiers all wore their helmets and flak jackets though.

Like much of the southerly route across the lines at Turbe, there were mines on the road that needed clearing before we could leave Bosnian Muslim lines. Having learnt mine clearing Bosnian-style on the last occasion, it didn't take us long to move them with our hands or feet. There was some loose firing around but nothing directed towards us. The road went slightly uphill, littered with a considerable number of wrecked vehicles which we had to drive around. Beba Salko warned us to keep on the tarmac as there were a lot of anti-personnel mines in the verges. We drove up this rather exposed road for about half a mile before we reached another barricade. This was the front line of the Serb forces. Just beyond a small wooden pole stretched across the road was a large house on the right of the road. A few vehicles were parked on the road alongside it and outside the house were members of the Serb Exchange Commission. Beba immediately went off with a few men to try to locate the body which was the primary purpose of the line crossing. I talked to the same members of the Exchange Commission I had met a few days before.

They told me that their authorities had instructed them to inform me that I would need authority from Pale, Serb Army Headquarters, before senior Serb Commanders could meet me. They suggested I asked HQ BHC to pass the request on to Pale. Later I was to do so but to no avail.

Jim Hooper, the journalist from *Jane's Defence Weekly*, was also there. He had spent the last few days with the Serbs and I agreed to his request to come back across the lines with us. Jim told me that he had met Lieutenant-Colonel Janko Trivic, Commander of the Serb 122 Brigade, at Vitovlje. As we had previously agreed before he left, Jim had mentioned my wish to meet Trivic when he had interviewed him. Trivic had suggested I first get agreement from General Mladic through General Morillon's Headquarters at Kiseljak, which I was already trying to do. Jim also informed me that he had seen the remains of the BBC armoured Land Rover in which Timomir Tunokovic had been killed in the Karaula at the end of October. Apparently the vehicle had a hole through it caused by an armour-piercing shell of some kind and all its tyres had gone. It was on blocks. Colonel Trivic had offered to return it to the BBC. Later I relayed this to Martin Bell, but I agreed with him that there was no point and the BBC did not want it again after what had happened.

There was quite a thick mist around us that day and it did little to help Beba Salko find the body he had come for. Beba returned after about thirty minutes saying that they could see very little and the search was a waste of time in the conditions. Our business across the lines thus ended, we returned to Turbe. Once again we had lunch with Commander Leko in his Headquarters there. It consisted of small pieces of spicy sausage baked in a bread bun and was remarkably good. The whole dish was called *cevapcici*. Naturally we also had the ubiquitous slivovitz and Turkish coffee. I recalled the Standby Platoon as we left Turbe.

Since I had arrived in Bosnia, I had been sleeping on a camp bed in my office. This was fine but I could never get away for a break from work. Brigadier Andrew Cumming had suggested frequently that I should get a house of my own and eventually I did just that. Mike Winstanley took over a place right beside the PINFO building. It was close but not too close to the school and had the security of being near the PINFO contingent. Unfortunately it had no heating, I had to rely on electric fires from a variable electric supply, and the water, when it ran, was never hot. But at least it was a place in which to get away from the affairs of the Battalion and I was grateful for that. From now on, VIP guests could also stay there too and indeed an increasing number of people were beginning to pass through.

Orlando Fraser was one such migrant visitor. An eccentric even in his mid-twenties, Orlando had started an appeal called 'Bosnia Winter Appeal' and he wanted to get a convoy of humanitarian aid right to the north of Tuzla. I liked this bearded rogue greatly and had helped him all I could. Together with his cousin Willie Sterling, he had organized their convoy from the UK and had taken it all the way to a destination in Northern Bosnia. At various times we had helped where we could, particularly on the way to and from Tuzla, but on his return Orlando had had a very bad accident on the road between Kekanj and Zenica. In the early evening he had hit what we called a 'Bosnian motor-bike' – a vehicle with only one main light showing – and in this case it was the nearside light. Thus at night Orlando had been unable to see that a large vehicle was approaching him. Orlando and Willie's car was a write-off. Willie was OK, but not so Orlando. The first I heard about it all was when I was told he had been admitted to Zenica Hospital. Not being a great fan of the Bosnian Medical Service, I asked the medics to check it out. They returned with Orlando in an ambulance. Zenica Hospital had not diagnosed that one of his lungs was punctured and had collapsed. He could have died and had to spend the next ten days or so courtesy of the British Army's Medical Surgical Team in Vitez before being moved by ambulance down to Split and thence to England. But Orlando had achieved what he set out to do by getting over £110,000 worth of aid well beyond Tuzla.

In fact the situation in Tuzla was greatly improving. We were now in a good position to establish a permanent base on the town's airfield. Martyn Thomas and A Company were to set up the first base there just after Christmas. Kekanj base was to close down as he did so. I decided that each company would complete six weeks on Tuzla duties before being rotated back to Vitez, that is except for B Company which would remain in Gornji Vakuf. The Tuzla Company was to have three armoured infantry platoons of Warrior and a Scimitar troop. It was to be a semi-independent command because of the difficulties of commanding it from one hundred and eighty kilometres distance. Quite rightly, all the company commanders were keen to get there and I don't blame them for that.

Whilst reviewing how we tackled the Tuzla operation, it was also an opportune moment to revise how we used liaison officers. In particular the route to Tuzla seemed to need someone to look after it. Having discussed the matter with the Company Commanders, I decided that Captain John Ellis, who until now had been part of the PINFO team, should take on responsibility for liaising in the Visoko, Breza, Vares and Olovo areas.

John had not really been to that part of the country before and so I took him up there a few days later. Taking two Land Rovers with us and a party of about eight personnel in all, we called in at the various headquarters I knew en route, finally making towards Olovo to meet Fadil Karienc, the Muslim Commander. As we approached Olovo in our Land Rovers, we met two ICRC vehicles outside the town. They were stopped where the road ran through a ravine just before the ground opened out a little on the way into Olovo. Claire Podbielski and Claire Graber, an ICRC nurse, together with their interpreters, had halted because Olovo, which was about a kilometre away, was being shelled. An explosion could be heard every few minutes. We stopped and talked with the two women. Claire Podbielski wanted to visit the local authorities in the same building as us and Claire Graber needed to go to the hospital. But the hospital was apparently one of the most dangerous places in Olovo – it was a frequent target for shelling.

Olovo – meaning 'lead' in English, and named after the product of the mines nearby – is not a town well known internationally but it has had a very hard time during the war. It sits surrounded by hills, from some of which the Serbs have excellent views of the town which most surely helps their gunners. As a result Olovo is like a shooting gallery with those firing on the place having perfect views of their targets. Most of the original inhabitants had fled or been killed. Now, not including soldiers, only about one thousand people, mainly displaced persons, were living in the place. There was no water or electricity except in the Muslim Headquarters and the hospital, which had its own generators. Unsurprisingly, the majority of the buildings were extensively damaged by shelling and people only moved around the streets on the run from shelter to shelter. The dreadful civilian living conditions were much as I imagined those to be in Sarajevo, which I had not visited.

After a while, the shelling from the hills seemed to lessen in frequency and I went ahead into town to see what the situation was like. I left RSM Stevens behind with the other vehicle and the ICRC landcruisers.

It took no more than a couple of minutes to drive into the town. Towards the centre, I turned right across a bridge to an old spa hotel, which was the Muslim Headquarters. As we drove through the deserted streets of this shattered town, we heard some shells land on the hills to the north. At the hotel I spoke over the radio to RSM Stevens.

'Don't move yet,' I said.

'But the Red Cross want to go.'

'Don't let them.'

'Too late. One vehicle has gone.'

The RSM had succeeded in persuading Claire Graber not

to go into danger, but Claire Podbielski's Land Cruiser was already on its way into town. A couple of minutes later, this first ICRC vehicle was at the hotel. We parked our vehicles beside the hotel on what we considered to be the lee side from the shelling and went into the building. This relatively modern structure now had all its important offices in the cellars. When we arrived there was no electricity but it came on after a few minutes. The ICRC delegation went off to talk to the civilian authorities whilst John Ellis and I looked for the town's Commander. We couldn't find him and had to content ourselves with a meeting with his deputy, Refik Herja. I introduced John to him and we talked about the general situation for a while. Clearly Olovo was once again under pressure – indeed we could hear more shells landing outside as we spoke. I knew RSM Stevens would have ensured that all soldiers were well under cover and so was not worried unduly about those left on the road. After about forty-five minutes our conversation began to dry up and it was time to go. The ICRC delegation was ready to go too. They left before us and drove out of town. In the field the ICRC much prefers to operate on its own, strictly maintaining its neutrality. The two Claires had gone by the time our vehicles returned to the original spot where we had stopped outside Olovo.

A couple of days later Claire Podbielski secured the release of sixty Serbs who were held prisoner in Visoko. It had taken her a great deal of time to negotiate with the local Muslim commander and she had spent many hours in the prison, right on the front lines, frequently under fire herself, interviewing the prisoners. Once the interviews were concluded Claire put all her efforts into getting an agreement from those in authority for their release. Once released, the prisoners would be supervised and escorted to safety by the ICRC. As a result of Claire's success, we provided our first detainee escort for the ICRC on Wednesday 23 December, in accordance with our UN mandate. The ex-prisoners from Visoko were destined for the coast at Ploce from where they would go by ship to Montenegro. An escort from my Battalion Group stayed with them as they travelled through our area until we handed over to the Spanish Battalion on the inter-Battalion Group boundary.

Having left Olovo, I was glad to get back to Vitez relatively early that day as I had to leave for Redoubt, the Royal Engineers' mountain camp, early the next morning. The Prime Minister, John Major, was flying out on a visit to British troops in Croatia and Bosnia. Brigadier Roddy Cordy-Simpson drove to Vitez and then together we drove south through Gornji Vakuf, Prozor and on to Route Triangle through the mountains. We were quite fast by comparison with a selection of Warriors and Scimitars which had had to leave very early that day from Gornji Vakuf. The mountains were relatively benign that day and we made it to Redoubt within three and a half hours of leaving Vitez in the Discovery.

The decision for us to go to Redoubt with a selection of soldiers from the Battalion Group was not mine. Naturally I would have preferred for the Prime Minister to visit Vitez but, for security reasons, it had been decided that Redoubt was as far as he should come. Later, in conversation, I realized the Prime Minister himself was not too happy about that either. It just goes to show that nobody is totally master of his own destiny.

Mr Major arrived slightly late, which was not surprising as he had had to travel overland up the route from Split. We gave him a short briefing and then he took a walk down to meet the soldiers standing beside their vehicles. Having insisted on talking to everyone who was there, John Major then distributed some Christmas presents to the men – a selection of the latest music tapes, which went down very well. Mr Major had my full sympathies, since I know what a tiring journey he had had to get here, and he showed signs of tiredness towards the end of the morning walk-about. He finished his visit by addressing the troops and thanked them for all they had done.

As we walked back to his vehicle, the Prime Minister told me to ignore anyone who suggested I should not appear on television. He said that I should appear as much as possible. Actually, in spite of press speculation, nobody within the Army had said anything of the sort. I never once asked to appear on television or be interviewed by anyone – my appearances were always in response to requests. However, I did take the speculation a little to heart and thought perhaps I would try to be a little less 'high profile'. But I didn't spend too long worrying about it as I had other things on my mind, particularly trying once more to meet the Serb Commanders west of Turbe.

HQ BHC at Kiseljak had recently informed me that they were having little success in getting me permission to meet these commanders. They were going to continue to press for it but felt they were unlikely to have much joy. At local level, I decided that I would keep trying regardless. Perhaps more pressing than meeting anyone right at this time was my desire to try to get the Serbs to stop shelling Turbe, Travnik and, for that matter, any other town under threat. From Vitez it was always possible to hear the pounding Turbe and Travnik were taking from artillery and mortars. Every time it happened, I felt angry and even more determined to stop it. I was particularly outraged at the bombing of Travnik, which had remained thus far just like any normal town and was still full of families.

We crossed the lines at Turbe for the third time on Christmas Eve. As was now normal practice, a ceasefire was supposedly imposed from 8 a.m.. My main contact with Beba Salko was Matthew Dundas-Whatley again. He had spent many hours in the Exchange Commission office. The relationship between my liaison officers and their local contacts was always crucial to the success of our tour in Bosnia and I never forgot it. I had some excellent officers doing that job and Matthew performed it brilliantly.

In order to bind ourselves into the system of line crossings so that nobody could exclude us, I wholeheartedly agreed a suggestion, I think from Matthew, that we make it our role to 'supervise' local ceasefires during such events. This was most certainly a role we could do as UN soldiers.

On this occasion Beba had asked if we could move earlier than previously, as he wanted to use the time to find the body of the dead soldier he had failed to locate a few days before. Again the Standby Platoon went into Turbe first and

then we followed. Briefly pausing at Sulejman Leko's Headquarters, we then drove into the northern outskirts of Turbe
up some narrow roads and tracks into a small village. It was
really cold and the ground was covered with snow. Ice made
movement along the tracks treacherous. Our vehicles slid all
over the place. In a small village at the Muslim front line, we
got out of our vehicles. From here on we needed to proceed
on foot.

It was not our job to recover bodies from the field, but I
felt, for the sake of 'face' and goodwill, we ought to help. It
would certainly do our relationships with either side no harm
whatsoever; hopefully they would see that we were a positive
influence on events and thus accept us more readily.

But there was great tension in the air as we walked forward.
The occasional shot could still be heard and there was always
the threat from mines and booby traps. There were reputedly
many mines in the area. Beba Salko and his assistant produced their large white flag with a red cross on it and we all
went with them into no man's land. We walked uphill in
single file. We were on what used to be farm fields; there
were tracks, fences, hedges and the occasional house. Walking
was quite hard work simply because we had to keep our wits
about us – as well as our footing, since the ground was terribly
slippery. On the hard tracks there seemed to be less of a
threat from anti-personnel mines, although we did find two
tripwires and several dug-in anti-tank mines across our path.
Only the very tops of the mines showed. This worried us, as
obviously some mines could easily be covered by snow. The
trip wires were linked to off-route mines. When we crossed
fields, we all tried to walk in each other's footsteps as this
diminished the risk of standing on an anti-personnel mine.
Periodically Beba Salko would shout out his name and what
was happening so that anyone within earshot knew what we
were doing.

After twenty-five minutes or so, someone shouted that the
body had been located. Down a small slope, a man was lying
face down on the ground. He was sprawled out beside a fence.
A Kalashnikov assault rifle was beside his body and he seemed
to have been killed by shots to the chest and head. He was

wearing normal Serb military uniform including a side-cap and what seemed to be very large boots. The man himself was very big. Nobody seemed particularly upset about him; we just wanted to get the job done and leave this highly dangerous area. In keeping with normal practice, though, we had to pull the body over before we tried to recover it properly in case the corpse was booby-trapped. I asked RSM Stevens to organize it, but it was easier said than done. Using rifle slings clipped together, the RSM had the greatest difficulty turning the man's body, which was absolutely frozen to the ground. It took the collective pulling power of both the RSM and 'Tiny' Lawson — large men by any account — to get movement. We had a body bag with us and, with a certain amount of effort, managed to get the large body into it. But the zip would not do up and the bag itself was not strong enough to allow us to carry the body properly. We had to use a blanket and a branch underneath for support. On top of these difficulties, despite the man's body being frozen for a couple of weeks, the smell was pretty bad too. We were lucky though in having some strong soldiers with us, as we then had to carry the body about five hundred metres into the main Serb lines.

As we passed a wrecked house close to the spot where we found the body, I noticed a teddy bear lying on the ground. It looked brand new and, apart from a little bit of frost, could have come straight from a shop. Having seen a Serb soldier pick it up first, I was not worried that it had been booby trapped and so picked it up myself. I carried it with me as obviously the child to whom it belonged had long since gone. Later back in Vitez, CSM Arthur, who was running our community relations, suggested that he knew a very good home for the bear. I was reluctant to give it to him for a child, knowing the appalling circumstances in which I had found it, but I relented when he said how delighted the child he had in mind would be to receive it.

Carrying the man's body took some effort but we made it to the Serb positions after twenty minutes' hard work. It was with considerable relief that those carrying the body handed it over to his own friends. We then walked back the half mile to the Muslim positions and thence drove back to Leko's Headquarters where we were forced to undergo a Christmas dinner – which was wonderful gesture from Leko and the other Muslims in his command. The meal consisted largely of goat's cheese, mutton and excellent roast potatoes.

But our work across the lines was not over. We had not yet formally met the Serb Exchange Commission. After about ninety minutes we re-crossed the lines on the southern route to the Café Boric. We moved the same mines as last time again and went on to the café, watched over by Warriors of the Standby Platoon which had to remain on the Muslim front lines. The format of our meeting was much the same as the first in this building, except for two things. Firstly, I had brought a paraffin heater with me this time: at least it took some of the edge off the cold in the place. Secondly, to my delight, the Deputy Commander of the Serb 19 Brigade from Donji Vakuf was there. His name was Major Mico Poletan.

We talked whilst standing up in the room, but no one minded. Major Poletan wore formal uniform including a leather belt and side-cap. He had a lined, weather-beaten face and seemed a seasoned soldier. I explained our tasks and, rather more quickly than I should in Bosnia, asked straightfor- wardly if the shelling of towns on the front lines such as Travnik, Turbe, Bugojno, Tescanj and Maglaj could be stopped over the Christmas period. Was it possible for a truce to start immediately and extend from then until after the Serb Christ- mas on 8 January, I asked. It should not really be a problem, I argued, as everyone had supposedly signed a general ceasefire recently. All we needed was local restraint from aggressive action. Major Poletan replied that the Serbs did not shell civ- ilians and that they would cease firing if everybody else did. I replied that I would pass on that message to everyone involved and therefore could I again ask for his reassurance that the Serbs would do nothing aggressive towards populated areas in that period. Poletan agreed.

We were carrying a Regimental plaque which I presented to Major Poletan – as well as a bottle of Scotch. Beba Salko agreed to inform both the Muslim and Croat Commanders about what we had negotiated and, on behalf of both the Muslims and Croats, accepted that hostilities should cease forthwith. John Simpson of BBC News was with us and parts of the meeting were filmed, which was very helpful. The media in Bosnia sometimes served the useful purpose of being present to record agreements – there were sometimes no other records. Being held accountable in the forum of world opinion can occasionally be a powerful means of persuasion and agreements made on camera are more difficult to break.

In the event the agreement we made that day seemed to work. We did not record any breaches of it in the Travnik and Turbe areas until a couple of days after the New Year and even then the shelling was 'light' with no casualties. We had achieved far more than I could have hoped for. Major Poletan was the first 'official' contact I had had with the Serbian command structure in the Turbe area. And we had achieved this just in time for Christmas, which, despite our surroundings, we intended to celebrate in the traditional regimental way.

CHAPTER 10

A WHITE CHRISTMAS

In the Cheshire Regiment, Christmas Day always starts with a tradition called 'Gunfire' – but this gunfire comes from the barrel of a bottle rather than a cannon. At 6.30 a.m. in Vitez Camp all members of the Officers' and Sergeants' Messes assembled in the cookhouse tent. Serenaded with Christmas music by the Band, we then went round each tent or room with a hot toddy for each soldier.

In the time-honoured tradition, Christmas away from home is the soldiers' day. It is the one time in the year when the officers and sergeants serve their men. Of course it may be considered by some to be a little silly, but actually the officers, sergeants and soldiers all thoroughly enjoy the 'play acting' it involves. It is harmless stuff and emphasizes that Christmas Day is special.

As Commanding Officer, I should also have visited all detachments of the Battalion Group on this day, but unfortunately there was no way that RSM Stevens and I could get to Kledanj and back in time. We did drive to Gornji Vakuf immediately after the distribution of hot toddies was over to spend an hour or so going around talking to the boys in the base. We were back by late morning, in time for Padre Tyrone Hilary's Christmas Service in the gymnasium. I read the lesson, fairly badly as I recall.

Prior to serving the soldiers their Christmas lunch, the sergeants and the officers met for drinks in the newly acquired Officers' Mess, a nearby discotheque which had been converted. Far more suitable than I had ever envisaged, it made

an excellent Officers' Mess. All ranks in the Battalion now
had places for relaxation. We had one satellite TV dish for
the Services' Sound and Vision Corporation's Armed Forces
Channel and that was fixed up in the Junior Ranks Club.

After about forty-five minutes of chatting, both sergeants
and officers formed up as a large squad to march to the cook-
house tent. Led by the Band and under command of the
junior Sergeants' Mess member, this motley crew arrived to
serve Christmas lunch to the Battalion Group – in two sittings,
due to a lack of space. Whilst the Band played as loudly as
possible in the corner – trying to compete with the tremendous noise of the assembled diners – the officers and sergeants
queued for food and then took it around the tables. Previously
some beer, two cans per man, had been placed on the tables,
although there was little evidence of it by the time we arrived.
Normally the first course is reasonably civilized but thereafter
things can quickly become a bun fight, literally. Christmas in
Bosnia was no exception. After about an hour or so of may-
hem, the first sitting was pushed out of the tents and quickly
the second sitting was installed. A repeat serving then
took place.

Late afternoon and evening were recovery periods for most
people. I had ordered that patrols on Christmas Day were to
be minimized, but we had to be on call. With no humanitarian
aid convoys planned and the area quiet, however, there was
really no demand for our services. Most people tried to relax,
write letters and, most importantly of all, telephone home
using the excellent British Telecom Satellite System that had
been installed a few days before. Together with Mr Straney's
excellent food, this facility did more for morale than
anything else.

Fighting broke out between the officers and sergeants the
next day, but again it was perfectly normal for this time of
year. The 'Fight for the Key to the Khyber Pass' is now a
traditional regimental activity which dates from the 1930s. A
large wooden key was presented to the Battalion in India by
a group of visiting sergeants and this so-called 'Key to the
Khyber Pass' should, by rights, stay in the Sergeants' Mess.
But each year at a specially arranged time the officers and

sergeants meet to decide the matter. We had previously agreed that Boxing Day at lunch time would be appropriate and we met in the Sergeants' Mess. At 12.30 p.m. the Key arrived preceded by a drummer. It was positioned on a far wall of the Mess and thereafter the 'fight' could start at any time. It was not long in coming and a phalanx of junior officers launched themselves towards the far wall. But, as ever, the sergeants were too wily for them. It would have been impossible to get near the Key in any case because the sergeants guarding it far outnumbered the predatory officers, but nonetheless our 'forlorn hopes' repeatedly tried our best. For my part I thought I had broken my nose on Sergeant Disley's head. I hadn't but it felt like it. Padre Tyrone Hilary, along with some others, only just kept their dignity when they were foolish enough to join in the scrum. Amazingly, nobody was hurt at the end of the allotted hour and, surprise, surprise, the sergeants kept possession of the Key for another year. We were not to repeat the glory of three years earlier when, against all odds and precedent, the Sergeants' Mess did lose the Key: that year an officer broke in through the fanlight of their Mess and, having shinned along a pole, removed the Key from its position high on the wall, before escaping across the roof. Childish though these high jinks may sound, especially when recorded in cold print, this harmless, spontaneous release of energy and humour does much to maintain the spirit of a regiment and it is invaluable for dissipating some of the nervous tension that was inevitably felt throughout the camp.

Meanwhile, and on a much more serious note, whilst we were fighting for the Key in Vitez, C Company in Tuzla was escorting aid across the front lines. A UNHCR convoy from Belgrade needed access to Tuzla and Andrew MacDonald's Company deployed to help them. Whilst waiting at the rendezvous prior to crossing the lines, three mortar rounds landed in the village of Kalesja. Lieutenant Justin Freeland, keeping a lookout in the turret of his Scimitar, felt a blow to his arm. A piece of shrapnel had wounded him above the elbow. Apparently Justin was terribly phlegmatic: 'I think it's gone in,' he reportedly said whilst sitting in his turret.

I was told about Justin's injury soon after the end of the 'Fight for the Key'. Despite his accident, the line crossing operation continued and Justin was driven by ambulance down to the Mobile Surgical Team in Vitez, where Lieutenant-Colonel George Attard, Royal Army Medical Corps, then operated. Justin's wound was not too bad and he was not in severe pain, though he had to spend the next ten days or so in our small hospital – Orlando Fraser and he kept each other company. The medical opinion was that Justin had to go back to the UK to be fully checked out and, much to his dismay, he had to comply. However, I am pleased to say he came back to the Battalion Group fully fit before the end of our tour.

Andrew MacDonald, who was commanding in Tuzla at the time, had formally written to me prior to this incident asking if he could deploy mortars and Milan weapons on line crossings. The matter of deploying support weapons was something that my company commanders still felt very strongly about. They believed that the very act of deploying the weapons on to the ground would be a deterrent and, if a target was identified, they might also be useful. I understood this viewpoint but by now was firmly in agreement with Brigadier Roddy Cordy-Simpson. I felt they would have little if any impact and most certainly would escalate the seriousness of the situation – possibly in other areas of Bosnia where the UN troops did not have as much protection as we had. However, I would probably have argued along the same lines as my company commanders if I had been in their position. Ultimately, of course, the decision was out of our hands because UN Rules of Engagement forbade the deployment of such weapons, making their use illegal under international law.

Aside from these events and considerations, the Christmas festivities continued. We played football against the local Vitez team and lost. Jim Davidson, the comedian, arrived in Vitez to do a one-man show for us and that was really well received by the boys. John Donnelly organized a stage in the Garage and Jim entertained us for over an hour. Afterwards, by way of return, he was very well entertained in the Sergeants' Mess by an old friend. CSM Percival and Jim Davidson had known each other from a previous visit to the Battalion in Belize eight years before. Then CSM Percival had 'saved' Jim from a knife-wielding Belizean who had taken exception to certain jokes told in a bar in Punta Gorda. Jim had ended up running down the road pursued by the knifeman in turn chased by CSM Percival – who eventually calmed the situation down.

The snow and ice were very bad the next morning, on Monday 28 December, when Jim left to travel south with a severe headache, having spent the night in the Sergeants' Mess. That day three vehicles had accidents as a result of the weather – Jim Davidson's vehicle being one of them. Luckily, nobody was seriously hurt in any of the incidents – although it looked for a while that John Ellis, travelling with Jim, might have to delay his R & R because of injury. The accident which was potentially the most disastrous was a Warrior over-turning. In winter, a Warrior can rapidly take on all the attri-butes of a bobsleigh, with the metal tracks providing no grip on the ice and the driver almost completely unable to combat the forces of gravity and momentum. All in all, three Warriors were to somersault on ice during our tour and we were extremely lucky with these accidents. Soldiers travelling in the back of Warriors are always meant to be strapped into their seats, but in practice they rarely are. When a Warrior somersaults the effect is like shaking dice, throwing the sol-diers inside all over the place and into collision with some very sharp objects. It was amazing that we only sustained minor injuries in such accidents.

Initially our only alternative to using the normal slippery tracks was to fix studs into the rubber pads on tracks, but they were worn down almost immediately by the severe road surfaces of Bosnia. Captain Bill Irving and Artificer Sergeant Major Craig had devised a short chain that fitted across the tracks at intervals which seemed to be better but, in truth, we were never able to devise a way of keeping the Warriors adequately stable in the winter conditions. Once the road surfaces were covered with impacted snow, which soon turned to ice, they were absolutely treacherous. The weather also had considerable effect on how long a member of the

Battalion was away on his R & R, as in bad weather the trip
to and from Split could take as long as three days.

The Battalion Group had started R & R – 'rest and relaxation' that consisted of two weeks' leave back in either Germany or the UK – at the beginning of December. Right from
the start, to their considerable credit, senior officers in the
Army had insisted on each man in the Battalion being entitled
to a break from the theatre of operations, and a scheme was
devised whereby each of us was taken down to Split and
thereafter flown out of theatre. This effectively deprived the
Battalion Group of in excess of seventy members at any given
time, with each individual absent for about seventeen days,
including travel time. This permanent short-fall of about ten
per cent of the company, many of them key players, had
quite an impact on operational planning. But there were
always others who could substitute and everyone thoroughly
benefited from the break afforded by R & R. The advantages
totally outweighed the difficulties overall, and never was
R & R more appreciated than at Christmas.

In the middle of this Christmas period, I received a telephone call from Brigadier Andrew Cumming in which he
gently reminded me that I should have followed up initial
contacts made with the Serbs east of Tuzla by himself and
Alan Abraham some two weeks before. He implied that
maybe, just maybe, such a contact might have stopped the
Serbs shooting at us and thus Justin Freeland might not have
been injured. This criticism hurt and I felt it a little unfair. I
had seen no evidence that the Serbs would withhold fire from
us to date and, in any case, I had a growing feeling that the
people who did fire at us were doing so simply because they
felt like it. They were not under the control of anyone when
it came to fire discipline.

But Brigadier Andrew was right, at least in part. I realized
that I had been concentrating too much on the threat apparently posed to Turbe and Travnik. I accepted the rebuke and
agreed to do something as soon as possible. Immediately afterwards I telephoned Andrew MacDonald and asked him to
keep trying to get a second meeting with the Serb Commander, if that were possible.

In discussion with Brigadier Andrew I also talked about 'hardening' our bases against possible artillery fire. Vitez Camp was only fourteen thousand metres from the Serb artillery on the Vlassic Feature. Captain David Sherlock, a keen bird watcher, used to set up his telescope on a tripod and watch Serb ski patrols on top of the high mountain. If we could see them clearly, they could certainly observe us too. Again I had not classified the hardening of Vitez Camp as a top priority – we had so many – but after talking with Brigadier Andrew I decided to do so and 42 Field Squadron's main efforts were switched from building accommodation to the fortification of what we had already. The Engineer Squadron was requested to strengthen the Operations Room and the area of the hospital within the school, as well as to build a number of bomb shelters outside around the camp. Infantry soldiers from the Company which was performing general duties in the camp were seconded to help in construction and very rapidly I saw great improvements. Old freight containers filled with rubble and placed all the way around the school fortified the building. We even stacked these containers up so that the protection reached the top floor of the school. Inside the Operations Room and the hospital, reinforcing beams of wood were positioned and glass was protected with wooden planks, much as we had seen done in Bosnian towns. In the event of a severe attack, the top floor of the school would be sacrificed and the falling roof would thus provide additional protection to the bottom floor. Shelters erected outside looked like mini-castles and were designed to withstand a direct hit with a 155mm shell. The Sappers worked enormously hard anyway but their efforts to provide us with protection were prodigious. Later the Dutch/Belgian Transport Battalion also made outside shelters similar to ours but unfortunately with little success, to start with at least: their first bomb shelter collapsed under its own weight.

The turn of the year produced a strange atmosphere, at least I thought so. We were just getting fully established in Central and indeed in Northern Bosnia because Martyn Thomas had now set up the Tuzla Company Base at the airfield. Our organization was complete on the ground and we were within an estimated six weeks of completing the hard accommodation; thus ending the requirement for some of our soldiers to live under canvas. In operational terms, we were escorting as many convoys as the UNHCR wanted, wherever they were required. The routes through the mountains were very difficult, but workable. A weekly UNHCR convoy run from Belgrade to Tuzla was now fully established with a crossing point over the lines near Kalesja. Even the front lines to our west seemed quieter and we had succeeded in getting over them and meeting at least some Serb officers. A genuine ceasefire seemed to be working at this time, so some towns like Travnik were not being bombarded.

However, matters were by no means settled. HQ BRITFOR was continually reviewing plans for our withdrawal from Bosnia. All the time I was being asked to assess how long it would take me to pull out under specific circumstances, what equipment we might have to abandon and what route we would withdraw along. I argued quite strongly that we should not withdraw, even if the Serbs did advance through Travnik, but I was convinced they would not. I found this discussion a little disconcerting. I knew it was my principal job to get on with the day-to-day running of my area but I found this withdrawal planning dispiriting, even though it was only a contingency operation. Neither was I sure how such orders would be received by my soldiers. They were deeply committed to their job of saving lives and I knew that asking them to up sticks and leave people in such need would be something that would make them extremely unhappy.

Contingency planning was something I tried to keep from the Companies, who had enough problems. Attacks on our vehicles were becoming common and, in these hostile conditions, it was no time to question whether the Battalion's contribution was worthwhile. Just north of Kladanj, 4 Troop were moving along the road to Tuzla on Wednesday 30 December when a massive amount of direct and indirect fire came at them. As well as Bofors guns (normally anti-aircraft weapons), mortar shells landed amongst the vehicles. The Troop managed to keep going and there were no casualties, but such attacks on us north of Kladanj were now becoming daily occurrences. I felt it would not be long before luck turned against us.

Brigadier Andrew's suggestion that we get across and talk to the Serb Commanders in the area was certainly one way of lessening the problem. If the Serbs would recognize that we were not 'legitimate' targets, then perhaps they would order their forces to withhold fire. But I was by no means certain that Serb units, or indeed Croat or Muslim units, for that matter, obeyed the orders of their superior commanders. And so we also considered our alternatives using the weapons at our disposal. Pre-positioning Scimitars and Warriors in over-watch positions before running convoys through a danger area, a picketing operation, was one plan, but the ranges at which we might have to engage were considerable, as we were about to discover.

Martyn Thomas, having taken over from Andrew Mac-Donald in Tuzla, was particularly worried about an A Company column commanded by David Sherlock which was due to run up to Tuzla from Kledanj twenty-four hours after 4 Troop was attacked. Martyn told me over the INMARSAT telephone that he would use Mike Dooley's Platoon to run the route in advance of the column. Having checked the dangerous part of the route, Mike would then leave vehicles at appropriate points in a picket line as the column ran through. This was all text-book British Army procedure, developed and much used in India and normally highly effective. The problem in Bosnia was that the ranges we were likely to be engaged at were well in excess of two thousand metres, the maximum range of the 30mm Rarden cannon and the Hughes chain-gun – unless the fall of shots can be observed. He told me also that the chances of getting across the lines to speak to Serb Commanders in the near future looked good and so I said I would get up to Tuzla two days later.

In fulfilment of my promise to Brigadier Andrew about speaking to the Serbs in the Tuzla area, I drove there on New Year's Day together with Richard Waltier, Tim Furphy, Nick Costello (interpreter), Tyrone Hilary and CSM Lawson with my Warrior team. As far as I was concerned, there were three

main points to the visit. Firstly, I wanted to have a good look
at the accommodation occupied by A Company within the
airfield. Secondly, I wanted to meet the Commander of 2nd
Muslim Corps whose Headquarters was in the centre of Tuzla.
And finally, I wanted to use the opportunity afforded by our
operations to escort aid into Tuzla from Belgrade (known as
Operation Cabinet) to see the Serb Commanders on the far
side. The game plan was to establish regular meetings with
them, perhaps occurring simultaneously with each Operation
Cabinet crossing.

The road from Vares to Olovo passes through a large hole
in the mountains that is a truly amazing piece of natural
architecture. It never ceased to impress me. The tunnel
stretched for about three hundred metres and jinked backwards and forwards following natural fault lines in the rock.
It was also very dark and on this occasion the caverns were
full of ice stalactites which reached from the twenty-metre-
high ceiling of the cave almost to the floor. On the other side
of the tunnel, though, travelling became very difficult. Right
in the centre of our journey through the mountains, after
about two and half hours, the weather became appallingly
severe. Around us, through the heavy snowfall, we could just
make out the huge coniferous trees that were weighed under
by enormous quantities of snow and the fast-flowing streams
that were totally iced up. Our Warriors started sliding badly
on the road and several of the vehicles found it impossible to
move at all. Our snowchains helped a lot but still were not
good enough on packed ice. Progress was very slow as, of
necessity, we had to help a lot of local transport that was
blocking the route. Travelling on frozen snow packed on to ice
on routes that were perched in cliff-faces, with thousand-foot
drops into ravines that were nothing to us but swirling masses
of snow, was a highly dangerous endeavour and it reminded
me forcibly of how lucky we had been not to have had a fatal
traffic accident on the tour so far. In fact we never did have
one throughout the six months, much to my surprise and
relief.

On our arrival at the airfield, Martyn Thomas rather
proudly showed me the facilities he had established. I was

impressed. The place was ideal and he had adapted it very well to our purposes. The soldiers were accommodated in barrack rooms which were acceptable if not very warm. Lavatory and washing facilities were adequate by the standards we had come to expect in Vitez. The cookhouse had a decent kitchen and a good dining room in which A Company had a huge television with a satellite dish. The Warriors had an old hangar as a garage in which maintenance could be carried out. Finally the Operations Room as well as the officers' and senior ranks' accommodation were all in one block. With very little work, Tuzla airfield had become a very acceptable company base, and one of which Martyn could be justifiably proud.

But it was also a good opportunity for myself and those with me to have a little luxury too. I decided that we would all book into Hotel Tuzla where, for twenty-three Deutschmarks a night (much increased since our last visit), we could each have our own room, including bath and satellite television. Hotel Tuzla, once obviously a proud example of socialist planning, is a large modern building with a huge marble entrance hall that seemed the height of opulence to us after Vitez school's rather basic architecture. True, the baths and sinks had no plugs but a squash ball soon overcame that problem. And the minor inconvenience of MTV being the only channel my television seemed able to pick up was soon forgotten as I luxuriated in my hot bath.

We all met in the dining room and there had dinner together with a few journalists, with Anna Pukas of the *Daily Mail* and Simon Israel of Independent Radio amongst them. They were already up in Tuzla having been there for several days filing their reports. I knew that Jean-Paul Corboz, head ICRC delegate in Tuzla, lived permanently in the hotel. We had instantly liked one another when we had met a few weeks earlier and I was delighted to meet him for a drink and later be invited to join a small gathering in his room.

At this informal party, there were a few journalists, one of whom demanded to know what I was going to do about Serbian Rape Camps, as I represented the UN. Throughout my time in Bosnia, I do not recall one occasion when I had to deal directly with this very serious matter. Of course I had been briefed and read with horror about Serbian Rape Camps. Some of them were reportedly close to Tuzla, but across the lines and thus not accessible to us. I had also been briefed by the ICRC and UNHCR on the subject. Many of the victims of rape were in Zenica and Tuzla, having been forced out of Serb-controlled areas into Central Bosnia. Although I was sure that the crime of rape was not simply restricted to the Serbs and had heard of rapes being carried out by Croats and Muslims, nobody in my Battalion Group witnessed such things to my knowledge. I promised the American journalist that British soldiers would do everything in their power to intervene in a rape situation if they came across one, but we had not seen much evidence of the crime so far. If we did then she could rest assured that we would not be passive bystanders.

The next morning we made a very early start to the day. While we were all eating breakfast in Martyn Thomas's cook-house at 7 a.m. at the airfield, the ECMM team arrived. I had met Tom Colebourne-Malpas, the leader of the team, during my last visit to Tuzla. He was an ex-Irish Guards officer who was on contract to ECMM for a year and he was doing a great job according to reports I had heard. Tom was vital to Operation Cabinet as it was only through his contacts with another ECMM team on the far side that we had any form of command and control and it was from them that we would receive the word as to when it was safe to cross over the lines. It was also through the ECMM's good graces that we could talk to the Serbs on the other side.

But Tom had bad news for me. The Serbs were most reluctant to let me go over the lines. Operation Cabinet could go ahead as planned, but the Commanding Officer of the British Battalion could not. Martyn Thomas, Tom and I talked the matter over. On the one hand I could just go as part of the operation and ignore their advice, but on the other hand we were still in the early stages of getting Operation Cabinet established as standard practice and nobody wanted to jeopardize it. Tom advised against pushing our luck and I agreed. Martyn Thomas would carry on commanding the crossing and I would return to Tuzla where I could usefully visit the UNMOs as well as Headquarters 2nd Muslim Corps.

Returning to Hotel Tuzla, I called in to see the Senior UNMO. There had been growing bad feeling between the UNMO organization and my Company Commanders in Tuzla and I wanted to straighten this out. There seemed to be some problems about who was in command in the Tuzla area for the UN. I had to assert that my Company Commander was the ultimate UN authority and I wanted this to be understood. After a somewhat one-way conversation, we reached an understanding that this was indeed the case.

Amongst other things, I asked why the Airfield Monitoring Team lived in Hotel Tuzla rather than with my Company which now had a base on the airfield itself. Apparently the UNMO Airfield Monitoring Team arrived at the Control Tower and did a normal day — nine to five — before retiring each night to Hotel Tuzla. The answer I received was hardly reassuring. The team received $US80 a day for living expenses in a hotel but would get nothing if they lived with my Company. It cost the team only $US26 a day to live in Hotel Tuzla. I never found out whether the Air Field Monitoring Team subsequently moved to the airfield or not.

While I had been making my visit to the senior UNMO in Tuzla, Operation Cabinet had proceeded as planned. Martyn had crossed from Kalesja and had met the UNHCR convoy. He had taken Captain Nick Costello with him as interpreter. A dark, good-looking young man, Nick was superb at his job. He was first and foremost an infantry officer and so understood how we operated completely and was much more than just an interpreter. He would offer opinions and advice as we were negotiating and it was always very sensible. Both he and his predecessor, Captain Nick Stansfield, were first-rate officers. In June 1993 Nick Costello was awarded a Queen's Gallantry Medal for his work in Bosnia — a medal that could not have been more thoroughly deserved.

Once over the lines with Martyn Thomas, Nick had asked if he might be left behind with Corporal Clark to try to persuade the Serb officers that they should see me. Martyn agreed in the knowledge that the UNHCR convoy he was escorting into Tuzla was planned to return back into Serb-controlled territory later in the day and so Nick could be recovered within hours. However, things went slightly awry when the UNHCR convoy failed to unload at the depot in Tuzla in time to make it back across the lines by day. It was too dangerous to go back by night, so the convoy leader decided that he would stay overnight in Tuzla, leaving Nick and Corporal Clark stranded on the other side of the lines without any means of me being able to contact them. Although it gave both Martyn and me considerable cause for concern, we were somewhat reassured by Tom Colebourne-Malpas who stated that both Nick and Corporal Clark would be with the ECMM team over there. Next day we learnt that they spent the night in a first-class hotel at Zvornik and had a great evening into the bargain. The Serbs could not have been nicer to them. But nonetheless I was very worried: I did not like Nick and Corporal Clark being so isolated from us.

Early the next morning word came through from the ECMM team across the lines that Nick Costello had persuaded the Serb Commanders to see me. Nick always seemed to get on very well with all local-force commanders. He had a knack of gaining their confidence very quickly and obviously it had worked again. Acting quite fast we left Hotel Tuzla at 8 a.m. and thirty minutes later picked up Martyn Thomas with the Tuzla liaison officers, Bob Ryan and Mark Cooper, at the airfield. We drove east towards Kalesja which, consisting of almost entirely of ruins covered in a blanket of dazzling snow, looked like a scene from Dr Zhivago. Tom Colebourne-Malpas was positioned at the destroyed town in his Mercedes jeep. He took a few minutes to establish contact with the other ECMM team on the far side of the lines but then told me the crossing could go ahead. The Serbs had passed the word around their front lines to hold fire as we crossed over. From Kalesja we drove down a snow-covered road which turned ninety degrees left before winding its way eastwards again. We crossed a narrow bridge, where I was told Tudor Ellis had come under fire when Alan Abraham had first forced a crossing there. After driving about eight hundred metres further, we made our way up a short slope to a house. There we saw the other ECMM team – and Nick Costello with Corporal Clark. Jumping out to have words with Nick, I fell flat on my backside and slid down the slope of the road in that highly ungainly position. It was quite difficult to recover my dignity but I tried.

Rather too heatedly, I said sharply to Nick that I had had a lousy night worrying about him and I was 'bloody angry' with him. Nick played me absolutely rightly. He was sorry but felt he was perfectly safe. By the way, had I hurt myself when I slipped down the road? Unable to muster any further indignation at Nick, I was mollified. He had after all negotiated an audience with the Serb Commanders.

Nick then briefed me on what he had arranged. We were to travel to the Serb Brigade Headquarters at Sekovici, which was where Brigadier Andrew Cumming and Alan Abraham had met the Commander a few weeks before. Whilst we were away, both ECMM teams would remain in place to keep the crossing point open for our return.

By now the snow was beginning to fall quite thickly and I started to worry about whether we would get through to Sekovici, which was about twenty-five kilometres away. My worries increased as we drove down the road past Serb positions, which looked deserted but for the smoke from their fires. We passed a T–55 tank that looked as if it had been abandoned. Driving on, we travelled through deep, virgin snow as we went in a column of three vehicles: my Discovery, my normal Land Rover which was fitted up with radios, and the liaison officers' Land Rover. Nick Costello had joined Martyn Thomas and myself in the Discovery. I had been to Caparde and Sekovici the September before when we had tried to complete our reconnaissance from Serbia. I never thought I would see them again but here we were. Both places were recognizable despite the deep snow.

Nick Costello had been to Sekovici with Brigadier Andrew and so was able to take us directly to the Brigade Headquarters. To my surprise, we had been allowed to travel there without an escort and had not been stopped at any checkpoint. This seemed a sign of Serb confidence and confirmation that they were well in control of the country over here.

Parking by the curb in Sekovici, which seemed very much a large village built alongside the main road, we dismounted from our vehicles and walked about one hundred metres up to the front of a school. Inside, Nick spoke to some soldiers. The Brigade Commander wasn't there. Why didn't we go on to Corps Headquarters at Vlasenica? We asked if we needed an escort, but they just told us to drive on, and that a warning of our arrival would be signalled ahead.

I could not believe this unexpected openness nor the lack of customary suspicion and conscientiousness. Quickly we retraced our steps to the three vehicles where we briefed everyone and then departed in a southerly direction. Soon we were passing the checkpoint at Tisca, which was the furthermost point we had reached on the reconnaissance the year before. Still there were obituary notices on the wall of the guardhouse This time we wanted to turn east from the checkpoint and we were not even stopped. Nobody questioned what we were doing and so we drove on – for one hundred and fifty metres or so, that is. Suddenly there was a shout that the liaison officers' Land Rover had disappeared. The vehicle had developed a problem and, though it caught us up, it could only crawl along. At Tisca we had to stop and wait for it to ensure it followed us and did not take the wrong turning.

Eighteen kilometres further on from Sekovici, we approached Vlasenica. At the checkpoint guarding the town, manned by benevolent Serb soldiers, we were not even stopped as we drove directly along the main street. At what seemed to be the first major junction, we came across a military jeep. Three officers were waiting for us and alighted as we approached them.

By now the snow was getting heavy, and my worries about its effect on our return journey were growing. However, having come this far, we were committed. Colonel Skocogic Milutin was the large imposing man who greeted me first in the driving snow. He introduced himself as the Deputy Corps Commander of the Drina Corps. He was well over six feet in height, well built, but lean and with a moustache. The two other officers were introduced too but we failed to get their names. Milutin did not waste much time and told us to follow him in our vehicles. After a short while, we drove into a disused factory; obviously we were not to be allowed to see the Corps Headquarters.

Following Milutin we climbed some stairs to what was plainly the old boardroom of the factory. There we sat around a table and Milutin asked rather pointedly what we wanted. He listened politely as I talked, occasionally interjecting with intelligent counter-arguments. He was obviously a man well in control, who knew his business.

I started by saying that our convoys were being repeatedly attacked by both direct and indirect fire from Serb positions north of Kladanj. Milutin accepted that this did occasionally happen but suggested that it could be avoided if we were to give him advance notice of when our convoys were travelling. I replied this was likely to be very difficult, if not impossible, as the weather conditions made arrival times unpredictable. In any case, the only way we had of getting information through to him would be via Kiseljak and Pale. We agreed that our convoys should identify themselves with their four-way flashing indicators when transiting through dangerous parts of their route. (We tried this later but it did not seem to make much difference.)

Next we discussed the possibility of a liaison officer or team being placed in the Headquarters of the Drina Corps at Vlasenica. HQ BRITFOR had several United Kingdom liaison officer teams on standby for deployment over the lines and, provided Brigadier Andrew Cumming agreed, this seemed a perfect opportunity for them. They were supposed to have excellent communications which included a mobile INMARSAT telephone system − although this high-tech equipment never worked without the vehicle being stationary and even then was fairly unreliable. But at the time we thought these teams had near perfect communications. Milutin said that he thought the idea was well worth pursuing, but it had to gain approval from Headquarters at Pale first. I said we would put the proposal to Pale via HQ BHC. (We did this later but never had a response.)

Finally I asked if there was any possibility of there being

a weekly liaison meeting between the British UN company commander from Tuzla and an appropriate Serb officer. I suggested it would make sense for this to occur while Operation Cabinet was in progress. Milutin again thought this was not a bad idea and we even discussed where the meeting might take place and who might represent the Serbs. He said that a staff officer from Zvornik might be made available and the meetings could take place there also. Again though, Headquarters of the Serb Army at Pale would have to be consulted before anything like this could occur. (And again, we later made an approach via HQ BHC but never heard anything further.)

Our meeting with Milutin ended after a very cold forty-five minutes. All my conferences with Serb Army officers seemed to take place in freezing rooms – perhaps they were trying to tell me something. We parted formally with handshakes and salutes. I thanked Colonel Milutin for receiving us and hoped that we would meet again soon. He replied in much the same way.

Outside the snow was now very deep and I wondered just how we were going to get through to Kalesja. It was already close to midday. In fact the Discovery and Land Rovers, except for the liaison officer's vehicle, had performed very well in the conditions. The problem, however, was how other traffic coped on the road. On several occasions our way was blocked by civilian vehicles which just could not move. One such blockage was remedied by a Serb tank pulling a bus out of a ditch. To my relief (and surprise) we did make it back to Kalesja by mid afternoon. There Nick Costello had a quick conversation with the Serb soldiers manning the front lines before we reversed our original route over. The ECMM teams had stayed in position throughout and we had much to thank them for.

At the airfield, Martyn and I had a quick debrief on what we had achieved. There was nothing concrete of course, but at least we had met a high-level officer, had been able to put our points across, had suggested some changes and these had apparently been well received. However, attacks on our convoys up the route from Kladanj did not subsequently diminish

– even when we made ourselves better targets by putting on our four-way flashers. Neither did we ever get liaison officers at Headquarters of the Drina Corps or regular meetings with the Serbs whilst Operation Cabinet was taking place. But at least we had tried to make progress. I was also able to report back to Brigadier Andrew Cumming that, rather late admittedly, I had followed up his original meeting with the Bosnian Serbs east of Tuzla.

CHAPTER 11

THE BATTLE FOR GORNJI VAKUF

We were now into January 1993 and events in the area of Novi Travnik and Gornji Vakuf were soon to take almost all my attention. In many ways the importance of improving our relationship with the Serbs was shortly to take second place, at least in my mind, to trying to stem the marked deterioration in the Croat–Muslim alliance. To start with, there was a minor incident close to Vitez, but the subsequent flare-up in Gornji Vakuf was a full-scale battle. For my part, I had to react to what was happening. It would have been much better if I could have been in a position to have influenced events before they occurred but in reality the distrust between the two sides had been deepening for many weeks. For much of the rest of my time in Bosnia I felt like a forest-fire fighter who rushes around simply trying to extinguish flames as they break out, containing the worst damage without a hope of tackling the heart of the blaze. But just at the point where I needed to put all my energies into negotiating with the local-force commanders, I had my first real trouble with the press.

It was very embarrassing and hardly helped my relationship with General Morillon. Anna Pukas wrote an article in the 7 January edition of the *Daily Mail* with the banner headline: 'This town ain't big enough for both of us, Colonel Bob'. According to Anna, General Morillon had banned me from going to Sarajevo because we were, apparently, the most successful UN troops. At the time, Battalion Group APCs were escorting firewood into Sarajevo and providing an escort service for technicians trying to keep essential services going around the city. A so-called 'senior British officer' was quoted as saying:

'We shouldn't be taking fuel into Sarajevo. It is strictly out of our area. We regard ourselves as being sucked into the Sarajevo operation. It was the UN Command that gave us this task because the French, Egyptians and Ukrainians who are in Sarajevo can't manage it.'

Unsurprisingly, the newspaper article was not well received by General Morillon and his staff, not to mention the other nations. It looked very much like I was the 'senior British officer' quoted and the reaction was not long in coming.

The first I knew about it was when I received a telephone call from HQ BHC saying that General Morillon was very angry about what had been written. Someone faxed through a copy of the article and I nearly died when I read it. Who could blame General Morillon? I would have felt just the same in his place and it certainly looked like I could have been the source of the article. I managed to get through to Pyers Tucker, a British officer and General Morillon's Military Assistant, on the INMARSAT telephone and asked him to present my absolute apologies to the General. I was very sorry about what had been written and was most certainly not the 'senior British officer' apparently quoted. Pyers agreed to pass on my apologies which I followed up with a formal letter.

Neither Brigadier Andrew Cumming nor Brigadier Roddy Cordy-Simpson was amused either. I told them that I had said nothing of the sort but they felt that the source, or at least the feelings expressed in the article, had come from officers in Vitez. For example, one of them said, too many members of the press were allowed access to the Officers' Mess and anything could be picked up there. I suppose that was right and I had no way of knowing what loose talk in the Mess may have given rise to the article. Thus, although I may not necessarily be to blame, there was no way that I could escape apparent responsibility. I was terribly uncomfortable about the matter myself and never did find out what had really happened. Anna Pukas was very upset too. There was no way she had meant to do any damage and I accepted that. She had nothing but praise for the way we were performing. However, I did not waste my time asking her for the source of her information. I knew she could not give it to me. Under the circumstances, General Morillon would not have been out of line in demanding my removal as Commanding Officer. It was generous of him to accept my apology and I always remembered that fact from then onwards.

But matters far more important than unfortunate newspaper articles suddenly took everyone's attention. The day after the *Daily Mail* article appeared, a Vice President of Bosnia was assassinated at Sarajevo airport. At the time he was with the Commanding Officer of the French Battalion and was actually in a French APC when he was shot by a Serb soldier. I can understand how such an event happened in the middle of the night. There was great confusion, the trip was unscheduled, nobody knew what was going on and the French Commanding Officer was doing his best to sort out the situation. Colour Sergeant Oram, then on escort duties in Sarajevo and with two APCs, was at the airport shortly before the event. He had been told by the French Commanding Officer to leave the area and had done so reluctantly. He told me afterwards that he felt he should have stayed but had obeyed orders. In the aftermath of the incident, there were grossly unfair calls by the Bosnian Government for General Morillon's resignation. That was absurd.

By then, though, real trouble between the Croats and Muslims was brewing. It started in Novi Travnik on 10 January when I received a local telephone call from my liaison officer for the area, Martin Forgrave. There had been bad feeling in the town followed by some firing. A Muslim had been shot at a Croat checkpoint. After that, hostages had been taken by both sides, Martin told me. He felt we could probably help by brokering a hostage release and asked that I join him in Novi Travnik, a twenty-minute journey away.

I took Mark Weir, the Regimental Medical Officer, with me when I left Vitez. It seemed a sensible precaution as Mark could then examine all the hostages to ascertain if they had been mistreated. I met Martin Forgrave in the early evening light outside a café in Novi Travnik. Inside was Lendo, still Commander of Muslim Forces in Novi Travnik, despite the fact that the Croats considered him a war criminal. I had not seen him for three months. We greeted each other as friends and I remembered the last time we had met was when I took a Croat hostage called Illya from him. Talking with Lendo, he seemed amenable to exchanging his hostages and said he held three Croats. I asked Mark Weir to take a look at the three men and whilst he did so I had a drink with Lendo. Things were a little tense and so conversation was not easy and I was grateful to get away once Mark returned. The three hostages were fine and had not been ill-treated.

Leaving Lendo, we then travelled across a very quiet town to the Hotel Novi Travnik where, in an upstairs bedroom, we met Malabasic, Croat Commander in Novi Travnik, whom I had never met before. Malabasic seemed philosophical and all in all rather a decent sort of man. But beside him sat a very young Major who gave quite the reverse impression. Although I missed his name, I assumed he was a Croatian rather than Bosnian Croat officer; the difference being the Bosnian Croats are HVO whilst forces from Croatia are HV, although he did not wear the insignia on his uniform that would have confirmed this suspicion. Others suggested the young Major was HV and there was no doubt that he was a fanatic. The Muslims were asking for trouble and they would get it, he informed me. His unit had apparently moved into the area over the last few days and would not allow anything to happen to Croats in Novi Travnik. Malabasic looked vaguely embarrassed by the man's presence and I felt for him. But after a while it was agreed that a hostage swap made sense and, once again, Mark was despatched to check on the state of the four prisoners the Croats held. He returned about twenty minutes later and declared they were fit enough. One had received slight injuries, in a car crash, we were told, but apart from that everything was fine. I had already assured Malabasic that the Bosnian Croat hostages were in good condition when we had examined them and so I sent Martin Forgrave back to Lendo with the message that those held by the Croats were fine too. After a few more minutes Martin telephoned to say that Lendo accepted our word and an exchange could now take place.

Malabasic escorted us to another hotel room where there were the four men. They complained that a few of their weapons had been taken as well as a little cash. Malabasic said he would get these back and I had to accept his word – as did the hostages. We took them with us and drove back to Lendo's café. There we gave up the Muslim hostages whilst the Croat ones were driven by Martin and his crew back to Hotel Novi Travnik. I thought our work for the evening was done when we returned to Vitez but I was wrong.

Whilst we had been locked in negotiations in Novi Travnik, Lieutenant Monty Woolley, 9/12 Lancers, had opened fire against Serb positions north of Kladanj en route for Tuzla. Monty was escorting a Danish UNHCR convoy through 'bomb alley' whilst working with A Company when he was engaged by both small-arms and mortar fire. This was the fifth time in four days my Battalion had come under fire and the second time that day that we had been attacked on this stretch of road. Monty had, of course, made some preparations before committing his convoy. He had placed some of his troop in static over-watch positions on the hills above the road so that if fire was directed at him they might be able to return it immediately. In the event, they did. A total of fourteen rounds of high-explosive shells, three armour-piercing discarding Sabot shells and ninety-seven rounds of 7·62mm machine-gun ammunition were shot at a firing point that Monty declared to be 2·4 kilometres away. Although this was almost out of range, Monty later promised me that he hit with ten out of seventeen shells and he could see the strike from the machine-gun ammunition. All the Rules of Engagement given to us by the UN had been applied. The convoy was under effective fire, its four-way flashers were working, UN flags were flying and the range to the firing point was just acceptable. We had no idea what impact Monty's return of fire had on those attacking him, except to say that they had stopped – and so too did attacks on our vehicles along 'bomb alley' for some days.

It was at this point in the tour, just as things were hotting up, that two out of four of my company commanders were replaced, as had been scheduled from the beginning of the operation. Alistair Rule in Gornji Vakuf was being relieved by Alun Jones, a Royal Irish officer who was to command B Company for the rest of our tour. And Philip Jennings was to substitute for Andrew MacDonald in command of C Company. Those handover days were probably some of the most turbulent ones of our tour. We were also aware of the growing international frustration on the broader front as the Geneva Talks looked set for failure and the possibility of the UN imposing a 'No Fly' zone over Bosnia was increasing. Consequently, the British Government's concern that we might come under severe threat reached its height at this point and the need to be able to extricate ourselves swiftly from Bosnia, if necessary by force of arms, was further discussed. The United Kingdom announced that the aircraft carrier HMS *Ark Royal*, armed with light guns, was to stand off the Dalmatian coast. Within Bosnia, Sarajevo seethed as it was repeatedly struck by indirect fire from the hills around the city and seemed impossible to calm down in the aftermath of the assassination of the Bosnian Vice President. Tomaslavgrad received one hundred and forty incoming shells fired from Serb positions to the north – some of which landed on Malcolm Wood's National Support Element Headquarters, with no casualties to us, thankfully. And, to cap it all, the situation seriously deteriorated within our own area. The tension, shootings and hostage-taking in Novi Travnik had been a warning; now the real problems were about to begin in Gornji Vakuf.

It was on 12 January that a full-scale battle between the Croats and Muslims developed in and around the town of Gornji Vakuf. This flare-up just happened spontaneously, and we never discovered its cause. Our base there was only some two hundred metres from the town, which was the scene of some vicious fighting. Alistair Rule's handover to Alun Jones was delayed as the battle raged all round them. Small-arms fire, mortars, shells and even rockets were landing. It was a very intense battle. Speaking to Alistair on the INMARSAT telephone, we agreed that I would need to go down there as soon as possible – which meant the following day, as I did not want to risk travelling by night.

As my escort on the road to Gornji Vakuf, I took Lieutenant Alex Watts with his Standby Platoon vehicles. I went in Juliet. Travelling through a small village called Lisac a very large dog, looking like an outsized labrador, ran after Juliet but misjudged our speed and hit the track. It was awful. I ordered Corporal Gill to stop and, looking back, thought the dog had been killed. But, just as we were about to leave, someone told me over the intercom that the dog was moving. The dog seemed to have a broken back and so I had no choice but to ask RSM Stevens in the rear compartment if he would dismount and put the dog out of its misery. The RSM looked as horrified as I felt but jumped down from the Warrior to do so. I followed him, very conscious that I would not like to have carried out this order myself. As I walked down the road, I saw RSM Stevens aim his rifle and I heard the shot. The deed was done and so I turned and started walking back to Juliet, only to see, to my horror, the dog bounding past me up the road, writhing in agony. I was immediately angry with the RSM and shouted at him for such bad shooting. But RSM Stevens answered that he had shot the dog straight through the head. Immediately we chased after it and a second round ended the poor beast's misery. Despite being soldiers and thus, I suppose, prepared for such things, we were all upset by what had happened. For several minutes on our onward journey to Gornji Vakuf we were all silent.

As we approached the end of a gorge, just prior to reaching the tarmac road which leads into the base, we heard severe sounds of battle. Loud explosions and small-arms fire seemed to be constant. We discovered that the Croats were in possession of the checkpoint at the entrance to the gorge – normally this checkpoint was controlled by the Muslims. There were mortar shells landing in the hills to the north-east and some woods were on fire up there as well. The battle also seemed to be raging through Bistrica, a village adjacent to the checkpoint. I ordered all Warriors to close down hatches.

By doing so everyone was under armoured protection but the penalty was that our vision was very greatly restricted. Closing down always gave the very best guarantee of safety yet it severely restricted our ability to appraise the situation about us. A compromise was to have the driver's hatch in an umbrella-like position and for the commander in the turret to keep low whilst his gunner was fully under cover watching his arcs through his sights from inside the turret. I had always ordered that the decision on when to close down must be left to the commander on the ground and that rule was to apply throughout our time in Bosnia.

We patrolled aggressively, totally closed down with our weapons ready to fire and our turrets traversing to select potential targets, from the checkpoint into the Gornji Vakuf base. We also moved fast along the road so that we did not provide anyone with an easy shot. Entering the base I could see just how close the battle could be to B Company. Croat Headquarters was behind our camp and would presumably be a prime target for the Muslim forces. But as we drove into our camp all seemed to be quiet in Gornji Vakuf.

Alistair looked calm and totally in control when I walked into his Operations Room. He briefed me quickly on what he thought was happening. Basically, it seemed that the Croats were trying to take the town from their position in the hills. The Muslims had their strength within the town and were resisting as much as possible. The majority of mortar, artillery and rocket fire was from Croat positions on the road to Prozor.

Just as Alistair finished briefing me, a soldier rushed in and asked him if he would agree to a local ambulance being escorted through Gornji Vakuf. Apparently an ambulance containing three women – two Muslims and one Croat – needed to get to hospital urgently. Alistair and I consulted quickly and agreed that we should do something. Alex Watts and his Standby Platoon who had come with me were normally from B Company and thus knew the area, and so Alistair asked if he could use them as all his soldiers were fully occupied. Naturally, I agreed to release them back under command of Alistair. Alex was with us in the Operations Room and Alistair briefed him quickly to take the ambulance well out on the road to Prozor before he let it go.

I went off to find a cup of coffee upstairs in the Mess leaving Alistair in the Operations Room whilst Alex Watts rushed off to organize his mercy mission. A few minutes later Colour

Sergeant Williams, the Intelligence SNCO at Gornji Vakuf, walked into the Mess. He came up to me and whispered that a soldier had been shot – nobody knew how badly he was injured. An ambulance and extra Warriors were already prepared to go. I rushed out to the front gate. There I startled two medics as I jumped into their wheeled ambulance which was just about to leave the base. Within thirty seconds we were in the town.

There we saw a Warrior slewed off the road, half over a bridge. There was considerable mortar and small-arms fire around. The rear door was open and inside I could see soldiers trying to get through the tunnel which links the passenger compartment at the back of the vehicle to the driver's seat at the front. This was standard operational procedure for extricating a driver from his seat under fire. Jumping out of the ambulance, I confirmed that it was indeed the driver that had been hit. How long had they been trying to get him out, I asked. Even a few minutes was too long if we were to save his life, I thought. I ordered that we would have to risk taking him out by the front hatch in the open. Nobody held back and the crew immediately got out and rushed around to the front. Whilst I stood on the ground three very brave soldiers, Corporal Dodgson and Privates Dobson and Huxley, climbed up on to the front of the vehicle, opened the hatch and then hauled the driver out of his seat. As gently as we could, we lowered him to the ground and carried him to a nearby patch of grass. The battle still raged around us but nobody cared about that. The driver was Lance-Corporal Wayne Edwards and he looked in a bad way. It seemed as if he had gone already but we had to try to revive him.

Nobody on the ground could identify where the bullet had struck but that didn't matter to start with as he was not breathing at all. Private Dobson, gave exhaled-air resuscitation whilst Corporal Dodgson tried to get his heart beating. Major Tracy Clark, the doctor at Gornji Vakuf, tried hard to find a vein in which to insert a drip, but she was unable to do it. We kept working on Lance-Corporal Edwards for several minutes despite the fact that there was no sign of life. When it seemed hopeless to continue, I suggested to Tracy that we could do no more and should get out of the place as we were at considerable risk working in the open with so much firing around us. We carried Lance-Corporal Edwards to the wheeled ambulance and it rushed back to the base with Tracy still trying to save his life. Very sadly, it seems we had no chance from the start. Although we did not know it at the time, Wayne Edwards had most probably died instantly when a bullet hit him in the right cheek. As I arrived back at Gornji Vakuf, Tracy approached me as I walked towards the Medical Room. Quietly she told me the news. It was just after 11 a.m.

I continued into the Medical Room itself where Lance-Corporal Edwards had been laid on the examination bed. Standing beside him I felt overwhelmed with guilt. I had brought him down here this morning from Vitez with the Standby Platoon. I had agreed to escort the ambulance through Gornji Vakuf. But, most of all, I was the Commanding Officer responsible for the safety of all members of the Battalion. I had failed completely. Utterly wretched and upset, I felt ill. I wept a little as I stayed with Lance-Corporal Edwards's body for what must have been a few minutes before Tracy came back. Carefully she guided me away. Someone, probably a medic, gave me a cup of tea. I pulled myself together. When I was a Company Commander in Northern Ireland I had lost soldiers and thus had experienced this tremendous feeling of despair and emptiness before. Yet I knew very well that I had to come round quickly so that I could lead effectively, as well as show an example to the remainder of the Battalion. Nonetheless I needed a few minutes to gather my thoughts and standing beside Wayne Edwards as he lay there was probably the best place for that.

I went back to the Operations Room. Alistair Rule was there and I could see it had hit him hard too. We talked briefly. Together we went to look for 5 Platoon and met Alex Watts and Sergeant Senior, 5 Platoon's Sergeant, in the corridor. Obviously both Alex and Sergeant Senior were blaming themselves. We all felt that if only we had done something different then it could have been avoided. But life is not like that. After a few minutes trying to reassure them, Alistair and I went upstairs as local commanders were arriving for a pre-planned ceasefire meeting in the Officers' Mess.

Later I was to learn what had happened in detail. Alex Watts had positioned the civilian ambulance between his Warrior and that commanded by Corporal Furniss and driven by Lance-Corporal Edwards. Normally Lance-Corporal Edwards was the vehicle's commander but on that trip had decided to drive himself. As Alex left the base, Gornji Vakuf was relatively quiet; there were no sounds of fighting, with the battle at that point restricted to the Bistrica area to the north. Because of this and in order to have the best visibility possible, Alex ordered drivers to have their hatches in the umbrella – slightly open – position. Under the same circumstances I might have made that decision too. But while approaching the bridge in the centre of Gornji Vakuf, a shot had struck Alex's vehicle which was leading the three-vehicle convoy. Alex was in the process of ordering both his and the second Warrior to close down when Lance-Corporal Edwards's vehicle, travelling behind the ambulance, slewed off the road. It was obvious something was badly wrong and probably the driver had been hit. Alex had immediately ordered a proper casualty evacuation to be carried out, although nobody could have known what had really happened to Lance-Corporal Edwards until we pulled him out of his driver's seat.

After my return from Bosnia, in September 1993, I was reminded by Sergeant Smith, the Orderly Room Clerk, of a chilling premonition I had had about this tragedy. Apparently I had said to the clerks, on the morning of 13 January, in the Orderly Room, 'Today's going to be a really bad one. I can feel it.' My intuition was sadly correct.

The death of Lance-Corporal Edwards once again demonstrated the sheer courage of the soldiers I had the honour to command. Not one of them had paused to consider how dangerous the situation was when we had been trying to save Wayne Edwards's life. All those who were needed had done their duty without regard for the explosions and shots all around them. It is very common these days to hear older people saying that 'soldiers are not as tough as they used to

be', but they are wrong. There is no doubt that modern soldiers are different to those of previous generations. Young
men nowadays prefer computers and video games to football
in the streets. They have never worn a hard shoe like an
Army boot until they join up and in some ways they may
indeed be less physically robust than their predecessors. But
when it comes to courage, there is no difference. Officers like
myself are sustained by the realization that they cannot show
fear. Soldiers have no such incentive and therefore their fear
can be the greater in my view. And I define courage as the
overcoming of fear, not absence of fear. A man who knows no
fear cannot be courageous — he has nothing to be courageous
about. In my view, the soldiers I led in Bosnia are the best
in the world.

CHAPTER 12

UNEASY TRUCE

Before the death of Lance-Corporal Edwards on Wednesday 13 January, Alistair had called a meeting of local commanders to try to get both sides to stop fighting. The meeting had to go ahead as scheduled and they started to arrive at the base during the late morning. Despite the vicious war they were conducting outside our camp, the local commanders greeted each other correctly, if not with warmth. As ever in civil wars, men who had probably known each other all their lives had been thrown into a bloody feud and I wondered, yet again, how these people could possibly countenance killing what amounted to old friends.

We sat upstairs in the Officers' Mess around the large dining table there. I opened the meeting by announcing that one of my soldiers had been killed by somebody under one or other of their commands. It was a disgrace. As I was sure that no orders to attack UN troops had been given by either Croat or Muslim Commanders, I suggested that whoever had killed Lance-Corporal Edwards was not only a murderer according to us but he should also be considered a murderer by his own authorities. I said that the whole matter would be considered very serious internationally and I wanted the murderer identified and brought to justice. Everyone around the table expressed regret at what had happened. However, the most important thing right at this stage was to stop all fighting immediately.

After a considerable amount of accusations and counter-accusations, both local commanders agreed that an artillery ceasefire would come into effect immediately and a small-arms ceasefire should work from forty-five minutes after that. The Commanders rushed off to arrange matters and things seemed hopeful. Alistair and I were more optimistic than we should have been at this stage and I returned to Vitez with the Standby Platoon. I had arranged to go and see Enver Hadzihasanovic, Commander 3rd Muslim Corps in Zenica, because I wanted to hear his assessment of what was happening in Gornji Vakuf and elsewhere. I visited Vitez Camp briefly before rushing on into Zenica, which was a thirty-minute journey beyond the school.

In a building that once belonged to the steel works, I paid my first visit to Enver Hadzihasanovic's office. It was well decorated, equipped and lit, and, in short, it looked rather more like the office of a senior officer than most of the dark, poky quarters I had seen at other local-force headquarters. Enver was most welcoming and offered me coffee; slivovitz was produced anyway. Over these refreshments, Enver gave me his theory of what was happening. He felt that prior to the fall of Jajce the Croats had started to make trouble in Prozor, taking Muslim eyes off Jajce so that it fell to the Serbs more easily. The trouble in Gornji Vakuf was an extension of that. This time, the Croats wanted Turbe to fall to the Serbs. Enver was convinced that there was a secret deal between Croats and Serbs to the detriment of the Muslims. In my view, this theory was beginning to gain credibility, particularly because Serb actions seemed to quieten down when Croat forces were attacking the Muslims.

Later that evening I went to the Junior Ranks' Club and sat down with the Standby Platoon (5 platoon) who were very depressed about the death of Wayne Edwards. Over a few beers, the boys told me they wanted to put Wayne's name on one of their Warriors, which I agreed. They also suggested that we should offer a reward for information leading to the arrest of his murderer, which I said might prove more difficult but I liked the idea in principle. Soldiers deal with death as part of their job but the death of someone they know well is especially hard to bear, as it is for anyone, and 5 Platoon needed a time to reflect and mourn. Of course they would have done their duty and gone out on patrol immediately if I had wanted it, but in Bosnia there was the opportunity to let them reflect for a while. It is good to do it. After all, it could have been any one of them and they knew it. An officer who does not understand the value of this period of mourning runs the risk of losing the respect of his soldiers. A soldier imagines his own death when a friend is killed and he also sees how an officer responds, should he one day be as unlucky. Officers should take care here. But in this case, Alex Watts was doing a superb job with his Platoon. After sitting with Alex Watts and his boys for an hour or so, I went back to my house and fell asleep in a chair. I awoke some five hours later, freezing cold, and fully dressed but for one boot that I had kicked off.

Messages of sympathy came flooding into Vitez from all over the world. I wrote to and then telephoned Wayne Edwards's mother in Wales. She was terribly sad and yet this amazingly strong and kind woman was able to offer me words of comfort and encouragement too. Within B Company I agreed that the hand-over between Alistair Rule and Alun Jones should take place despite all the current problems. I told Alistair to get up to Vitez, from where we would arrange his transportation down to Split.

In Gornji Vakuf, the 'ceasefire' was not holding at all. Both sides had representatives constantly present at our base and Alun Jones did all he could to try to stop the fighting. Merdan, Deputy Commander of 3rd Muslim Corps was there at all times. B Company Warriors patrolled through the area trying, by use of a number of monitors, to get the guns and mortars to stop firing. They recovered a Croat body, with the face mutilated. Having spoken to Alex Watts I decided to release his 5 Platoon back to its parent Company. B Company were under severe pressure and therefore I ordered the companies in Vitez to produce a Standby Platoon. It seemed to me that there was not much more we could do to stop the fighting; it would probably have to start to run out of steam before we could have a real effect on the course of it.

I made daily visits to Gornji Vakuf in Juliet. If anything, the situation seemed to be getting worse. The checkpoint at the end of the gorge was now burnt out and deserted, and as I moved from there to the base I could see that Bistrica was in total ruins. Practically every house was burning. The road itself was blocked by falling telegraph poles and wires; we drove round them. Nobody was on the streets, yet the sounds of battle were everywhere. Standing at a shelter in Gornji Vakuf, I watched the battle on the hills around and began to worry enormously. I felt terribly responsible for the soldiers in Gornji Vakuf and it seemed that I was impotent to protect them. I had never heard anything as intensive as the battle that was raging around me. Yet I still had a feeling of detachment.

'RSM, can you hear that?' I said. 'It sounds like rocket launchers firing from down the valley. Do you know, I've never heard rocket launchers firing before?'

'I think you're right, sir.'

'Interesting, isn't it?'

'Take cover!' The rockets started landing around us.

At the spot where Wayne Edwards had been killed, 5 Platoon laid a wreath. I was present as they did so, on Saturday 16 January. Two Warriors drove across the bridge and positioned themselves alongside each other. Another two did a neutral turn and backed up to the bridge. A few people dismounted but most stayed in the shelter of the rear compartments of the vehicles whilst Padre Tyrone Hilary held a short commemoration service. Shots continued for a few minutes into the service but then stopped. One of our interpreters said that he had heard distant shouting from the town: 'No shooting, no shooting.' I suppose someone had some decency up there. Merdan and the local Croat liaison officer attended the short ceremony as 5 Platoon laid a big wreath inscribed with the word 'ED' at the spot where Lance-Corporal Edwards died.

With international concern for our safety growing, Brigadier Andrew Cumming visited Vitez to discuss the situation. Nobody was sure how things would develop. It seems that the British could either considerably upscale our commitment, withdraw altogether, continue operations as they were or indeed institute a peace plan – if one could be cobbled

together. Everything was in confusion, but for now we were
to continue operations as they stood. On Sunday 17 January,
General Sir John Waters also arrived in Vitez. As Commander
in Chief United Kingdom Land Forces based at Wilton near
Salisbury he was responsible for overall direction of Operation
Grapple. We showed him as much of the Battalion Group as
we could, as well as taking him on a visit of Leko's Head-
quarters in Turbe, during which some mortars landed outside.
Although the Commander in Chief wanted to go to Gornji
Vakuf, time would not allow it as he had to return to Split
via the Kiseljak route – transit through the town of Gornji
Vakuf being impossible for soft-skinned vehicles at the time.
I had finally been struck with Bosnian 'belly' at this time,
and may not have been at my best during this particular visit.

Gornji Vakuf was just not quietening down and the reason
for this was now becoming much clearer to us. The Croats
had apparently decided that, in view of the Vance–Owen
Plan's intention to make Gornji Vakuf part of a Croat canton,
they should have total control over the place immediately.
They had demanded the unconditional surrender of all
Muslim forces in the town. It looked like the trouble between
Muslims and Croats we had first encountered in October 1992,
and which had rumbled on intermittently since, was now
getting out of control. As Gornji Vakuf itself was largely
Muslim, this ultimatum was hardly reasonable, especially as
the Vance–Owen Plan had not been agreed to by the Bosnian
Government. The Croat tactics as to how they were to capture
the town were fairly straightforward. Surrounding villages,
such as Bistrica, would be pounded unmercifully so that
nobody could continue to live there. From the Prozor road,
mortars, artillery and rockets rained down on Muslim positions, while the attack on Gornji Vakuf itself was taking place
from the south with T–55 tanks. Systematically, these tanks
were taking out each house in their path. For their part,
the Muslims seemed to have very little indirect fire weapons
beyond a few mortars. They certainly had no tanks available
to them. Yet, despite the apparent imbalance of military hardware in favour of the Croats, the town remained in
Muslim hands.

Shellfire and small-arms fire hit our base frequently. The Croat Headquarters beside the camp was under constant fire. First Alistair and then Alun had organized our defences. Warriors were dug into hull-down positions (only their turrets showing) around the perimeter, and the number of sentries was doubled. One morning, while Alun Jones was conducting yet another fruitless meeting with local commanders, a sniper's shot came straight through the sill of a window, hitting the chair of the Muslim representative, and then ricocheting around the room. It was a tracer round that still had the remnants of burning phosphorus on it but, mercifully, it eventually fell to the floor harmlessly. Mortar and artillery rounds frequently landed within the perimeter too, which further motivated Alan and his soldiers in their feverish work to improved the base's inadequate protection.

On Thursday 21 January, Ambassador Bousseaus, from the ECMM, arrived in Gornji Vakuf. He had spoken to the highest levels of both the Bosnian Government and the Croats in Mostar. They had ordered an immediate ceasefire and Ambassador Bousseaus had come to try to implement it at local level. Alun Jones and I quickly deferred to him. Whilst Alun organized Warriors to escort the various local commanders into the Gornji Vakuf base, the Ambassador started a meeting to stop the fighting once and for all.

Colonel Siljeg, the Commander from Tomaslavgrad, who I had met before, represented the Croats in these meetings. He was also the overall Croat Commander for the operation. A man called Selmo Cikotic, a staff officer from 3rd Muslim Corps who was in his late twenties and spoke English, represented the Muslims. It had been Selmo's chair that had been struck by the tracer round a couple of days before. He had been in our base ever since.

In accordance with high-level instructions, both sides agreed to a ceasefire in no more than a few minutes. It seemed to have dawned on Siljeg by this time that taking Gornji Vakuf was not going to be as easy as he had at first thought and so a ceasefire might be a good idea. Both Siljeg and Selmo agreed that a 5 p.m. cessation of hostilities might be workable and they were escorted off by Alun Jones's Warriors to fix it locally.

Shortly after 5 p.m. the meeting reconvened, although there was still quite a lot of firing to be heard. Ambassador Bousseaus turned to me and asked if I would mind going into Gornji Vakuf to monitor and, if necessary, try to stop the firing by my presence. I agreed to do it, taking Juliet and two other Warriors with me. We drove into Gornji Vakuf, crossing the bridge where Wayne Edwards's wreath was still positioned. At a T-junction in the centre of Gornji Vakuf, a house was burning fiercely. Turning left there, we drove through the southern suburbs of the town. The place looked liked World War Three had been fought there. Everywhere was in ruins and lots of houses were on fire. It was nerve-racking being in the place as we could have been engaged by either tanks or anti-tank rounds at any minute. I knew there was a minefield across the road at the south edge of town and as we approached it we were engaged with small-arms fire, several rounds going over the top of the Warrior. I ordered everyone to close down properly. Turning on the road was difficult despite the Warrior's ability to rotate in its own length. At one point, the back end of Juliet nearly slid off the road into what was probably a part of the minefield, though I couldn't really see properly as by then it was dark. Slowly we drove back through town to the T-junction where I had left one Warrior. We then drove out of Gornji Vakuf to the north and, at the outer extremities of the town, turned again. Whilst we were turning a number of shots were fired at us, but we did not identify the firing points and thus did not fire back. Then I heard over the radio that two ECMM armoured jeeps needed an escort through the minefield south of the town. We returned there and helped them negotiate a safe passage with the local forces, who were unsurprisingly rather reluctant to move their mines. But then after they had complied with our request, we drove back to the base.

As I walked into the building at about 7.30 p.m. I was ambushed again, this time by the press. On being asked what was happening, I told the journalists that we were hoping for yet another ceasefire. It was now nine days after Lance-

Corporal Edwards had been murdered and local commanders had agreed ceasefires on practically every day since then. I said that Gornji Vakuf was relatively quiet although there was still some spasmodic firing. It was far too soon to say that the shooting was over. At 8 p.m. I reported back to Ambassador Bousseaus, who suggested we break for dinner before writing and signing the latest ceasefire agreement. But then Colonel Siljeg received a message: two of his soldiers had just been shot by snipers, he declared, and he could stay no longer. For my part, I learnt that General Morillon was going to visit Vitez early next morning and so decided to go back that night. The Ambassador made vague plans for another meeting with local commanders the next day and the meeting broke up.

It was good to see General Morillon when he arrived shortly after 9 a.m. on Friday 22 January. After we briefed him in our Intelligence Cell, he was naturally eager to go to Gornji Vakuf and so we did not waste time. I went with the General in his armoured car. General Morillon is quite a character. He smoked cheroot cigars constantly and frequently listened to his beloved classical music on the car's music system as he travelled around. His driver was a large Macedonian Sergeant Major from the Foreign Legion who spoke Serbo-Croat well and who obviously adored his General. The General and the driver made a good team and I enjoyed the journey.

At Gornji Vakuf, Alun Jones and Ambassador Bousseaus were waiting for us. Alan reported that the last ceasefire had worked in a desultory fashion through the night until about 7 a.m. but then all hell had been let loose again. The Croats had now recommenced their attacks with a serious thrust into the town from the south. As he spoke, the base was being rocked by the sounds of heavy-artillery shells landing nearby. General Morillon said he wanted to meet both local commanders himself and so Alun sent messages for them to come as soon as possible.

Since they would not come without an escort, the local-force commanders took some time to arrive, as we had to send Warriors through the battle zone to collect them. After about seventy-five minutes, a quorum had assembled upstairs in the Officers' Mess. Colonel Siljeg and the local Croat

Commander, Zenko, were there and Selmo Cikotic with Pia Agiuc, the local Muslim Commander, were present also. The talks were fairly fruitless, with Siljeg remaining at his most intransigent.

'All Muslims must surrender unconditionally. Provided they lay down their arms, they will be allowed to leave Gornji Vakuf.'

We offered to take up positions between the forces and man roadblocks in the town, if necessary. The Muslims seemed prepared to do most things to stop the fighting but, clearly, Siljeg was not going to compromise on his demands. He said he would agree to nothing and would go back to his 'authorities' for consultation. As we were speaking, a small-arms round penetrated the Medical Centre's window downstairs. There was little more that General Morillon could do. He wished Ambassador Bousseaus and Alun Jones the best of luck. The Ambassador left for Mostar as we departed. On our way back to Vitez, I asked the General if there was any way he personally could bring top-level pressure on to the Croats and Muslims so that local commanders were absolutely forced to stop the fighting. At the moment it seemed as if Colonel Siljeg could do what he wanted. General Morillon agreed and promised he would do all he could. He dropped me off on the road just outside the school.

'Bob, tell your soldiers, I have come and seen them,' General Morillon reassured me. 'I am satisfied with what I have seen.'

'Thank you, General.'

Later that afternoon I spent my time in meetings with Enver Hadzihasanovic, Commander 3rd Muslim Corps, and Timomir Blaskic, Croat Commander for Central Bosnia. I was trying to find a way at a higher level to get pressure on to local commanders. In Gornji Vakuf, Alun had organized another fruitless meeting. The fighting and killing continued unabated. Alun Jones asked me if I could go back there tomorrow as he had scheduled another meeting at midday. By this time it was absolutely clear to me that my main point of effort had to be Gornji Vakuf until some form of stability was restored to the situation, and so, wondering what new approach we might try this time, I departed for Gornji Vakuf early the next morning in Juliet.

Selmo Cikotic was there, he was staying in the base permanently now as it was safer. However, Colonel Siljeg did not arrive until much later, since we had had to pick him up from well south of Gornji Vakuf and had needed to bring him to the base through a minefield.

Gornji Vakuf was certainly no longer a healthy place in which to live. The Croats were continuing their systematic destruction of houses by tank fire. Mortars, artillery and rockets were raining down on the town and on the surrounding villages. The Croats seemed hellbent on ethnically cleansing, by fire, as many Muslims as possible. Bistrica was struck by multi-barrelled rocket fire twice whilst I was in the base. Three mortar rounds also landed inside the base's perimeter.

When we finally sat down to talk, Siljeg remained unbending. He demanded that the Muslims centralize their weapons under his – and possibly our – control. It was now conceded that the Muslim soldiers would be allowed to stay in Gornji Vakuf but he wanted some of them handed over for 'war crimes'. By way of reply, I said that was unconditional surrender and for the first time in this series of negotiations I told Siljeg:

'Colonel Siljeg, the world will note who is doing the attacking and it is not the Muslims. And it will note whose attacks are killing the most civilians.'

The number of ceasefires we had agreed and which had not taken place was growing farcical. I suggested that both sides just stop shooting – no ceasefire, simply stop shooting at each other. All forces could stay in place but stop the slaughter. Once more, both sides agreed that from 6 p.m. that day a 'truce' would operate. It would continue until the results of the next meeting we had scheduled were known. In the meantime B Company was to continue to patrol Gornji Vakuf, using four-way flashers at night so that they could be identified as UN vehicles. All sides were to try to get high-level instructions to end the fighting by the next meeting, which was to take place at midday the next day. For our part, we would do our best to bring to the meeting any person either side wanted to be present. I went back to Vitez taking Selmo Cikotic with me. He could then go to Zenica and receive fresh instructions from his authorities.

I felt the next day, Sunday, 24 January, was probably the last effort we could make to stop the fighting. To be honest, I believed we had very little chance of success when I woke up in my house but we had to try. After breakfast I telephoned HQ BRITFOR in Split. I wanted to discuss the matter with Brigadier Andrew Cumming but he was not available. Instead I gave a verbal message to the Watchkeeper on duty that I felt there to be little prospect of our obtaining a ceasefire in Gornji Vakuf without something dramatic happening. I suggested that Colonel Siljeg seemed set on battle for and capture of Gornji Vakuf. I explained that ethnic cleansing was now being carried out by multi-barrelled rocket-launcher strikes on villages. Tanks were destroying towns and villages systematically.

Of course HQ BRITFOR and indeed HQ BHC knew all this already from our situation reports. In reality, I think I was at the end of my tether and just needed some support or help. I could think of nothing more that I could do to sort out the situation. Of course I got total support from Brigadier Andrew. Apparently when he arrived a few minutes after my verbal report to the Watchkeeper he took immediate action by drafting a signal to HQ UKLF at Wilton. The signal suggested that matters now needed absolutely top-level help. It seems that in the UK everything possible was done and the contents of what Brigadier Andrew had reported reached Lord Owen in Geneva. There, I gather, Lord Owen talked immediately to Mate Boban, leader of the HVO, though of course at the time I did not know what was going on in Geneva. In Central Bosnia I was preparing for what I considered to be our last chance to get peace in Gornji Vakuf.

En route to pick up what I thought might be a high-level Muslim delegation from Zenica, I called in at the ICRC offices. Talking to Iris Wittwer, the head delegate, we discussed whether representation from the ICRC would be appropriate at these 'last chance' negotiations in Gornji Vakuf. Denis Cretenet, another delegate and a good friend, had already spent several days trying to operate in the town from our base there. Iris decided that both she and Denis would go down to Gornji Vakuf. I was grateful to them for that as they were always helpful when it came to advice about prisoners and prisoner exchanges.

At Headquarters of 3rd Muslim Corps, I had a brief interview with Enver Hadzihasanovic who told me that he didn't have much hope of a peaceful resolution in Gornji Vakuf either. Again, I gave a lift to Selmo Cikotic, who had been provided with all the necessary instructions and authority. Under the circumstances I do not blame the Muslims for not sending a higher-level delegation. First Merdan and then Selmo had been living in our Gornji Vakuf base for twelve days so that a Muslim representative was on call at any time. It was not the Muslims that were causing the problems in Gornji Vakuf. They were more than willing to compromise every time.

As I drove back over the mountains to Vitez, I noticed that the whole area seemed to be much more tense. Roadblocks were fully operational, with more soldiers around than usual, and all of them carrying their personal weapons with them. At Vitez I picked up an escort of two other Warriors and was joined by two ICRC cars containing Iris Wittwer and Denis Cretenet who were travelling to Gornji Vakuf with us. By midday we had arrived and some time later the Warriors bringing Colonel Siljeg in from south of the town drove into the camp and we were able to start our meeting.

The two sides sat opposite each other at the table, with Iris and Denis at the far end, and me at the head with an interpreter beside me. I opened the meeting by welcoming everyone present and saying that I believed this was probably the last chance we all had to get a peaceful resolution to the crisis. I asked Iris if she would like to say anything and she made an appeal for both sides to comply with the Geneva Convention in all its forms. To start with it looked like Siljeg was not going to bend at all and I began to think we were finished. But just then I was told by a runner that Brigadier Andrew Cumming wanted to speak to me on the INMARSAT telephone. I told the runner that I was in the middle of a meeting and would he ask the Brigadier if I could telephone later. The runner told me that the Brigadier insisted on speaking to me. He would not have said that unless something important had come up and so I handed over the meeting's chairmanship to Alun Jones and, having excused myself, went down to the Operations Room on the floor below.

Brigadier Andrew told me about the actions he had taken earlier and he had received a message back that Mate Boban had personally ordered an immediate cessation of hostilities by his forces. The Muslim chain of command was being informed of this at the moment and this might, just might, have an impact on the way Colonel Siljeg behaved. I was really grateful. He had done everything he could to support me. Thanking him for this superb piece of news, I then returned to the meeting.

Taking back the chairmanship from Alun Jones, I informed everyone about what Mate Boban had ordered. Turning to Colonel Siljeg I asked him if he would accept my word that this had happened. He did so with hardly a demur, which made me think that perhaps he already had an inkling about events outside the theatre. Maybe it was part of some game plan, I really did not know and I had no time to speculate. It seemed that there was some chance now and so I went straight into the guidelines for a ceasefire.

Firstly, the ceasefire was to be established by 6 p.m. that evening – although there should be a realistic expectation by all sides that some breaches may occur as not everyone will either receive or possibly accept it. Secondly, Gornji Vakuf was to be patrolled by UNPROFOR (as B Company was, in fact, already doing) and the routes through the town were to be opened as soon as possible. Thirdly, withdrawal of all forces normally positioned outside the area was to take place, if possible within twenty-four hours. Fourthly, alleged war crimes should be investigated by the side accused of the crime and a report of that investigation sent to the ICRC with a copy going to UNPROFOR as well. Finally, both sides were to provide full lists of people they had detained to the ICRC by midday in two days' time.

It did not take long for everyone to agree these basic prin-

ciples and the meeting soon broke up. Selmo Cikotic had
been instructed by his Commander to remain in Gornji Vakuf
for the foreseeable future and so there was no need for me
to take him back to Vitez. Things seemed more hopeful than
for many a day and I was quietly confident that we stood
some chance of getting a real ceasefire this time. All seemed
to have hinged on that signal to Lord Owen – but who could
tell what might happen in this crazy country. Once back at
the school, I checked with Alun Jones who reported Gornji
Vakuf to be relatively quiet, with just the occasional shot
being heard. Perhaps we had eventually reached some form
of solution. It was still a little early to be sure.

However, in Vitez we were beginning to receive extremely
worrying reports from other parts of Central Bosnia. The
Croats reported that two of their soldiers had been killed at
Kacuni near Busovaca. Barricades were up, manned by both
sides. I was sceptical about whether anyone had died, because
so many such reports were gross exaggerations, until I
received a telephone call from Djemal Merdan to confirm that
the two Croat soldiers had been killed. He asked us to help
by taking back the two bodies from his soldiers to their own
side. With the verification of this report, it seemed that the
whole of Central Bosnia could explode now and we had only
just managed to contain the small town of Gornji Vakuf. I
agreed to do to escort the bodies back, but with a sinking
feeling in my stomach. More trouble was bound to flare up
between the Croats and Muslims, and this time possibly in
the valley between Vitez and Kiseljak. The whole of Central
Bosnia could be in flames very quickly if the forces of both
sides were to start attacking one another around Vitez.

CHAPTER 13

CENTRAL BOSNIA IN FLAMES

My worst fears for the spread of the fighting in Central Bosnia were soon realized. Gornji Vakuf had been a preliminary bout in the struggle between Croats and Muslims in the Vitez–Kiseljak valley and we were going to be cut off from our supply routes in the process. As ever in Bosnia, the situation blew up very suddenly. The first we knew that the conflict had reached a new level of intensity was when we received a patrol report by Sergeant Smith.

The Platoon Sergeant of 8 Platoon, Sergeant Michael Smith, had been ordered to patrol to Kacuni on the road to Kiseljak. Reports suggested that on a bridge on this road a logging truck was blocking the traffic completely. Sergeant Smith did not know which side had erected the blockade, but, approaching from Vitez, he was flagged down by Dutch sentries outside the Headquarters of the Dutch/Belgian Transport Battalion in Busovaca. The sentries warned Sergeant Smith that there had been a lot of firing further up the road and so he decided that both drivers and gunners in his two Warriors must be battened down under complete protection before he went any further. He then drove on towards Kacuni.

About one hundred metres short of the bridge, Sergeant Smith noticed a truck in military colouring. It was stationary but, as the lead Warrior passed, it slipped in between the first and second Warrior commanded by Corporal Willett. The road was not quite wide enough for Sergeant Smith to pull over and let the truck pass. At the bridge a truck filled with logs was positioned diagonally across the road. Three or four houses at the far side of the bridge were burning and he could hear shots.

It was getting dark as the lead Warrior approached the truck but Sergeant Smith had been ordered to try and open the route. He attempted to nudge the truck off the bridge using his vehicle as a ram. But the truck's air brakes were on and it just would not move, despite being pushed by thirty tonnes of metal. Suddenly a mortar round landed five metres to the right of the Warrior.

The Croat truck was still between the two Warriors but quickly, from a nearby house, three soldiers dashed to it and jumped in the rear. All three vehicles reversed and the truck finally pulled into the side to let Sergeant Smith's Warrior past it. The armoured vehicles did neutral turns to reverse their direction of travel, but the truck had to do a three-point turn. As the Warriors withdrew more mortar rounds landed nearby. The Croat truck could not move as fast as the Warriors under fire and, as it started to drive behind them, it was struck by mortar fire, killing two Croat soldiers, although Sergeant Smith did not realize this at the time. The Muslims in Kacuni then took possession of the truck and its crew, including the two dead soldiers. In fact, this was the incident that Merdan had telephoned me about.

We were now cut off from HQ BHC at Kiseljak as the road through Kacuni was the main route there. I was very unhappy about this and was determined to re-open the road as soon as possible. Philip Jennings was given the task of getting the road open again. Immediately he took a patrol out and tried to get through, but had no joy. The Muslims manning the checkpoint at Kacuni were adamant: nobody was to pass. Whilst Philip was on the ground still trying to get the truck off the bridge, I went to see the regional commanders and reached agreement with them that all UN, UNHCR and ICRC vehicles should be allowed to pass through the area. In particular, I spoke to Enver Hadzihasanovic, 3rd Muslim Corps Commander, who agreed that we should man a checkpoint at Kacuni rather than his own soldiers.

A few hours later, Philip Jennings and I together with some escort Warriors went down the road towards Kiseljak. At the

River Lasva junction, I noticed that the bridge itself was being very well defended by at least thirty Croat soldiers. There were wires everywhere and the bridge was mined. Through Busovaca there were a few Croat roadblocks but we were not stopped. The front lines between the two sides was a stretch of territory which ran between Busovaca and Kacuni. We closed down our vehicles as we left Busovaca and drove into the area. Croat soldiers were manning defensive positions, particularly around the small Croat factory/barracks about a kilometre outside Busovaca, which was very well fortified. The area was terribly tense – we could feel it. Further away we could also hear a great deal of firing and occasionally artillery or mortar fire landing in the villages north of the road. We watched it for a while before proceeding further. The odd indirect-fire round was landing in the vicinity of Kacuni too.

Cautiously we moved on to approach Kacuni where the two Croat soldiers had died. Observing the bridge before we went near it, we could see that there was a Muslim defensive position just behind but there was no evidence of mines or booby traps on the truck with logs. The truck was stuck firmly across the bridge at an angle. I was not surprised that Sergeant Smith had been unable to move it. Deliberately, I moved forward in Juliet and stopped directly before the truck. I dismounted from the armoured vehicle together with RSM Stevens. CSM Lawson stayed in command of Juliet. Walking up to the truck we inspected it carefully, and found no mines. I knew the Muslim soldiers were watching us from their positions eighty metres away. I wanted them to see who we were and made quite an obvious show of inspecting the truck. They said and did nothing. Next I ordered CSM Lawson to move the Warrior up to the roadblock and try pushing the truck. I knew we were likely to have little success but wanted to show determination to those watching. Under CSM Lawson's command, Juliet edged up and made contact with the logging truck. It did not move an inch but the Muslim soldiers did. They started shouting at us.

Just at that moment some mortar rounds started landing about one hundred and fifty metres away on the left. RSM

Stevens and I ran into what looked like a looted café just over the bridge. Whilst sheltering there I took off my binoculars to adjust my flak jacket. Just as I was doing so some Muslim soldiers came into the house. They indicated that we should cross the street to the other side where their defensive position was located. RSM Stevens and I followed them, leaving my binoculars behind never to be seen again.

Over the road I talked with the position's Commander. His soldiers were nervously excited. I told him, using Nick Costello as interpreter, that Enver Hadzihasanovic had agreed we could pass. I also stated that his Corps Commander had agreed that our Warriors could replace the log truck and we would man a barricade here. The Commander let us pass but was adamant that the log truck would have to be repositioned after that. As we were debating this point, one of his particularly nervous soldiers mistakenly placed his finger on the trigger of his Kalashnikov assault rifle. The weapon fired a burst directly into the area around our feet. The toe-cap of one of Nick Costello's boots was seared by a ricocheting round. It gave us a tremendous shock, as at first everyone thought we were under direct attack. The Commander was clearly very annoyed with his soldier and he started kicking him. Nick, Lance-Corporal Higginson and I were simply relieved that it hadn't been worse. In fact I was later to discover that a small piece of chipped stone had hit me in the leg, but it was hardly a serious wound.

I returned the conversation to the matter in hand. The road needed to be opened I told the Commander and Enver Hadzihasanovic had agreed that we could man a checkpoint here. Did the Commander not accept orders, I asked. Apparently not, from the reply I received. I was still talking to the Commander when a UN armoured Land Rover arrived from the direction of Kiseljak. Inside was Brigadier Roddy Cordy-Simpson. He had mentioned to me earlier that he might try coming up from Kiseljak.

Talking over a fence by the road I suggested that we should take cover in the Muslim defensive position as there was quite a lot of loose fire around. Brigadier Roddy and his escorts jumped over the fence and joined us behind the house. He

too tried to get the Commander to accept that we should man
a checkpoint here. We suggested he check with his authorities
and he agreed that we could superimpose a checkpoint on
his but would not accept that it should be the only one. The
Commander eventually agreed to consult with his authorities
and we waited until he received an answer. After ninety
minutes of waiting, it was clear that any answer was not
going to be swift. Brigadier Roddy and I discussed the problem
together. I would finish my patrol and then go to Headquarters of 3rd Muslim Corps in Zenica whilst he tried to see
Blaskic again. We agreed that we would go for a ceasefire for
the following morning at 6 a.m. I stayed on for a few minutes
after Brigadier Roddy had left before I decided we would
continue our patrol towards Kiseljak.

Past Kacuni we could see great evidence of recent destruction. Philip's Warrior broke down and so I left him on the
outskirts of Kacuni. A lot of houses had been burnt and there
were many wrecked vehicles littering the sides of the road.
At a number of checkpoints, the soldiers manning them were
obviously very worried. Although they were not particularly
keen on letting us through, they always did so after a short
discussion. Eventually we reached the small hotel which the
media had made their main base. From here is was only a
couple of miles into Kiseljak and that was a clear road. Kate
Adie was there. I told her about the situation back down the
road and advised that it was best to stay near Kiseljak for the
moment. She made us all some tea before we turned around
to go back to Vitez.

The return route was not as easy. The soldiers manning a
Croat checkpoint tried to bar our passage. But after a while
they relented. We carried on to Kacuni where we met up
with a couple of Warriors that Philip had arranged to stay
with the Muslim checkpoint. Talking with Philip, we decided
that it might be too dangerous to leave them here overnight
and he gave instructions that they were to return to Vitez
with us. As if to reinforce our decision, mortar fire started
again straight away. However, we did leave the vehicles at
the Headquarters of the Dutch/Belgian Transport Battalion
instead. Lieutenant-Colonel Jan de Boer, the Commander

there, and I thought it sensible under the circumstances to give the Dutch and Belgians a bit of support if they required it.

At the Lasva checkpoint, I turned right as if to go down the valley route into Zenica. But about a mile down the road where we knew a cliff above the route had been brought down in an attempt to block passage, the narrow defile had been blocked by three large vehicles and mines. The block looked unmanned but I was certain it was under observation from some dug-in positions on the hills behind. It was too risky to hang around there and so we turned around and I went back to the mountain-road checkpoint. Going over the mountain to Zenica was not a problem. To start with I visited Iris Wittwer in ICRC, then I went to the UNHCR offices where I spoke to José de la Mota before I finally went to the Head-quarters of 3rd Muslim Corps.

Neither Enver Hadzihasanovic nor Merdan was there and so I spoke to staff officers. I complained that on this occasion the Muslims had really started the trouble by killing two Croat soldiers. More than that, the Commander on the ground at Kacuni was not obeying instructions to allow us to establish and man the checkpoint. I was rather more rueful about the negligent discharge fired by the Muslim soldier but nonetheless did complain about it in a roundabout way – suggesting that, in the British Army, a soldier would be sent to the Guard-room for twenty-eight days' detention for such conduct. With the Commanders away, they were unable to respond to any of my points, but I also asked them to try to get a proper ceasefire agreed for the following morning at 6 a.m. and I returned to Vitez across the mountains.

Reviewing the day, on Monday 26 January, I considered the dreadful mess the road from Vitez to Kiseljak was in and that, although we could still get through in armoured vehicles if we wanted to, we had no safe and reliable access along that route in order to do our job. Getting the road open thus became a high priority. It was to be Philip Jennings's major problem.

Philip left early the next morning with a platoon of War-riors to Kacuni with the intention of substituting a couple of armoured vehicles for the log truck and thus getting the road open. But after two and a half hours of fruitless negotiation with the local commander he was still being frustrated in this aim. Over the radio he informed the Operations Room that the situation seemed impossible. The Muslim Commander at Kacuni was simply not prepared to change a thing.

In some irritation, I used my local telephone and rang Muslim Headquarters in Zenica. I asked to speak to Djemo Merdan and was put through to him quite quickly. I complained to Djemo that his Commander had agreed that the road to Kiseljak should be opened and that we could man a checkpoint there in place of the Muslims. Yet we were being frustrated in our attempts to do so by the local soldiers. I felt that, this time at least, the Muslims had been responsible for causing much of the trouble by killing two Croat soldiers. Did the Bosnian Muslims really want a full-scale war in the Kiseljak valley? It seemed to me that they were going about it the right way if they did. It was simply not good enough and something must be done.

Merdan agreed, apologized and said he was ready to come with me himself to sort the problem out. He explained that it was impossible for his Headquarters to speak to local commanders as the telephones to the area were not working. They did not use radios to Kacuni, he explained. I accepted Djemo's offer to come with me and despatched my Land Rover to pick him up from Zenica. He arrived at the school some ninety minutes later looking tired out. We greeted each other warmly; I had always trusted him and, in truth, I never had any reason to go back on that feeling throughout my time in Bosnia. Djemo was placed in the back of Juliet and we drove down to Kacuni.

There I met Philip who explained that the local Commander had remained intransigent. Not wasting any time, I asked Djemo Merdan to talk to him. A heated discussion took place between the two men, at the end of which Djemo turned to me and stated that our vehicles could replace the truck. We agreed that a Warrior would sit on the bridge whilst another back-up vehicle would be free to patrol up and down the road in the local area. Only UN, UNHCR, ICRC, other inter-national-aid vehicles and ambulances should be allowed to pass through the roadblock. This I agreed to for the moment as I simply wanted the road opened again. After a long wait, the vehicle's air brakes were de-activated and the truck backed out of position and one of Philip's Warriors substituted for it.

Talking with Djemo, I suggested that perhaps he may wish to travel on with us to meet up with Brigadier Roddy Cordy-Simpson so that he could put the Muslim position to General Morillon's Chief of Staff. After all, I told him, Brigadier Cordy-Simpson had only heard Timomir Blaskic's side of the story. Readily he agreed to this and we started down the road to Kiseljak.

Shortly afterwards, as we were passing some Croat positions to our north, a high-velocity shot went close over my head and CSM Lawson's. Rapidly we swung the turret using power traverse towards the direction from where we thought the shot had come. We could not identify a firing point but neither did we stop. Over the radio to the Operations Room, I reported that we had been engaged with 'non-effective' fire and were continuing to Kiseljak.

HQ BHC was in a hotel built especially for the Winter Olympic Games that had been held in Sarajevo in the early 1980s, but it was clearly a very badly constructed building. The place was also in a frightful mess. The UN Headquarters had only been there three months but had occupied the building in a hurry. Wires, boxes, Portakabins and even vehicles were everywhere. There simply was not enough space for this major operational headquarters, but it was the best that could be found at short notice. At the entrance to the UN Headquarters, I noticed a large column of UN vehicles. Most were not British but an officer told me they needed to get through the Vitez–Kiseljak valley, along the route we had just come. CSM Lawson suggested that he and RSM Stevens should escort them back along the road, which made sense to me as I could always summon or beg a lift home to Vitez later. I agreed and watched as the two warrant officers rapidly organized their new charges for a convoy through to Vitez. Turning away, I then took Djemo up the short hill into the UN Headquarters.

Down four flights of stairs to the Operations floor, I brought Djemo to Brigadier Roddy Cordy-Simpson's office. I introduced Merdan to Roddy who was quick to suggest that it made great sense to get Timomir Blaskic there as well. Timomir had two headquarters where he could regularly be found; one was at Hotel Vitez and the other was at the Croat Barracks in Kiseljak. He was in Kiseljak at the moment and a message was sent asking him if he could join us.

After Timomir arrived, Brigadier Roddy chaired a small meeting in the Conference Room close to his office. He opened by strongly stating that the present fighting was lunacy and in nobody's interests. Surely, he suggested, the matters in dispute, whatever they were, could be quickly resolved. Djemo and Timomir began talking to one another and it seemed as if progress was being made when a message came for Blaskic. He read it and told us that seven Croat soldiers had been killed at a prisoner exchange with the Muslims. He had to go immediately to check on the matter, which ended the meeting. It was agreed, however, that we should all meet again the next day.

We were thus finished far earlier than I had anticipated. I sent a message to Vitez asking for the Operations Room to send an escort for me, but to speed up proceedings requested that maybe a vehicle from Kiseljak take us some of the way back – at least until we met my own vehicles coming from the opposite direction. Although this sounded like a good idea, HQ BHC did not in fact have standby vehicles and so we remained where we were until Sergeant Edwards arrived from Battalion Headquarters with two Warriors. Together with Djemo Merdan, I jumped into the first vehicle and returned to Vitez, dropping Merdan off along the way to be escorted over the mountain road to Zenica by CSM Lawson.

Early the next morning RSM Stevens picked Merdan up from Zenica and he joined me at the school to travel back along the Kiseljak road in Juliet. Two Warriors were still positioned blocking the bridge at Kacuni. Obviously, with the battle still raging around them, they were closed down. As we passed by, three mortar rounds landed and there was some sniper fire at us. But it was nothing too serious in the circumstances of the time. All of us were now much less worried by such firing as we learnt to live with what we had at first considered so outrageous. The rest of the journey to Kiseljak was uneventful.

This time the meeting, again chaired by Brigadier Roddy, reached a conclusion fairly swiftly and a ceasefire was agreed. For my part, I accepted that the British Battalion would continue to man a roadblock at Kacuni. However, I also wanted the valley road to Zenica opened up. The three trucks and mines were still in position in the defile and so the only way into Zenica was over the mountain road. This was a dangerous route at the best of times, but now in midwinter with the snow and ice it was lethal. All the international agencies seemed to be concentrated in Zenica – not just the UNHCR and ICRC – and so this had a direct impact on their operations too. Blaskic was not prepared to do anything about this though. He argued that this Croat roadblock was vital in order to protect Croats in the area of Busovaca. Eventually we broke from the meeting with agreement of sorts but neither Brigadier Roddy nor I felt it had been tied up properly. We believed that neither side was prepared to commit itself wholeheartedly to a solution.

I took Djemo Merdan all the way back to Zenica and then returned to Vitez. Later that evening, Baroness Chalker, Minister for Overseas Development, arrived. With her were Gilbert Greenall and Doug Houston. We briefed Lady Chalker on our role and how we carried it out in the Intelligence Section and after that she had dinner with all the officers. I rather liked her straightforward, no-nonsense approach. She departed early the next morning for Gornji Vakuf having had a 'candlelit' breakfast in my house as there was still a power-cut.

For my part, I was to attend a two-day seminar held in Kiseljak. General Morillon wanted to get all the UN commanding officers in Bosnia together so that we could discuss a unified approach to our problems. I travelled down in Juliet but as I passed the Headquarters of the Dutch/Belgian Transport Battalion I picked up Jan de Boer. He followed my Warrior in his armoured Mercedes jeep along the route. We passed through C Company's roadblock at Kacuni and we detected no firing whatsoever en route. By 9 a.m. General Morillon opened his seminar.

The General explained that he wanted everyone to get to know one another but more importantly to use the opportunity to understand the problems each of us was up against and how we were attempting to solve them. Victor Andreev, the UN's Russian Civil Affairs Advisor, spoke next. He concentrated on the political environment in which we were operating and explained exactly where we stood with regard to the proposed Vance–Owen Peace Plan. Thereafter, each Commanding Officer in turn gave a five-minute talk about his Battalion's area and their problems. I felt very sorry for the Ukrainian and Egyptian officers as they had to have absolutely everything translated for them by interpreters sitting alongside. It cannot have been easy for them. Thankfully General Morillon had organized some French wine at lunchtime which made a very welcome contrast to the food, which was at its Kiseljak worst.

However, whilst we were debating academic matters in Kiseljak, on the ground things were taking a turn very much for the worst. Brigadier Roddy pulled me out of the seminar and briefed me on reports of intense fighting in Busovaca and that the whole of the valley between Kiseljak and Vitez was involved in a full-scale battle. I had to get back as I just could not sit there talking theory whilst a war was breaking out in my Battalion's area. Brigadier Roddy agreed and gave permission for me to leave. Jan de Boer came too.

The problem was that we had no transport back as Juliet had been returned to Vitez once I had been dropped off that morning. However, the Operations Staff at Kiseljak organized a Danish APC to take us back through the valley and I sent a message to Vitez asking for a couple of Warriors to meet me halfway.

The Danish M–113 APC bumped its way down the road towards Vitez but about six miles from Kacuni it ground to a halt. The Commander, a young Corporal, knelt down from his turret position and informed Jan and me that we were at a Croat checkpoint. The checkpoint Commander was refusing to let us pass. I told the Corporal that we had to pass but he said the Croats were adamant that we should not. Opening the back door, both Jan and I got out and talked to the Croat soldiers. I explained as best I could, since we had no interpreter, that both Jan and I had to go through, back to our Battalions. We were going to go through the barricade and they must not try to stop us. I also tried to explain that Timomir Blaskic had given his authority for all UN vehicles to pass. They could not be stopped at all. After that both Jan and I remounted into the APC and I told the Danish Corporal to get going. After a couple of false starts as the Croats wrestled with their dilemma, the Corporal drove over a small section of the roadblock and we continued along the road. Both Jan de Boer and I looked at each other wondering what mess an RPG–7 anti-tank rocket might make of the back door – he smiled when I showed him my fingers were crossed. Just as we were approaching Kacuni, the Danish Corporal brought his vehicle to a stop. I was very pleased to discover that we had not come across another checkpoint Commander we would have to brow-beat, but the friendly face of Lieutenant Richard Rochester. Jan and I gladly transferred to Richard's Warrior, but not before I had checked that the Danish Corporal was happy about going back to Kiseljak on his own – he seemed to be very glad to get rid of us.

The next few days were ones of great tension in the Kiseljak valley. The situation at Kacuni continued to be highly dangerous with intermittent shelling around our vehicles at the bridge. Clear orders were given that personnel manning the Kacuni checkpoint were to remain under hard cover at all times and that the vehicles were to be closed down for the entire duration of their duty there. I made a further trip down the valley in Juliet and ended up at Fojnica Junction where I met Robert Fox of the *Daily Telegraph*, who very kindly gave us lunch at his hotel. We were mortared, two rounds landing fifty metres to our right, between Kacuni and Busovaca on the return journey. I also visited Zenica where I briefed the UNHCR and ICRC on what was happening.

Coming back over the mountain road, I was approaching a Croat checkpoint at the lowest point in the road when I saw a UNHCR convoy being systematically robbed by soldiers. I stopped Juliet immediately, jumped down and angrily demanded to know what was happening. The 'local' convoy commander could only smile and wave his hands in some form of apology. I knew that his was an impossible position, but I was very angry with the Croat soldiers and told them in no uncertain terms to get off the vehicles as well as put everything back. They were a little reluctant at first and I was very glad to note that RSM Stevens had dismounted behind me. He stood close to me and looked suitably aggressive whilst I ranted and raved. It worked. The aid taken off the convoy was put back and I told the convoy commander to get going over the mountain into the UNHCR depot at Zenica. We stayed at the checkpoint until the convoy was well away from it.

But convoys of soft-skinned vehicles were still unable to move through the Vitez–Kiseljak Corridor. It was really only military vehicles, some soft-skinned admittedly, which were able to use that route. The road was still at the centre of the hostilities, but both Brigadier Roddy in Kiseljak and I in Vitez were determined to get it back to normal as soon as possible. Moreover the valley route to Zenica was also firmly shut and we wanted that open too.

It was Brigadier Roddy's idea to enlist the European Commission Monitoring Mission (ECMM) in the struggle to get an effective ceasefire. He gave me instructions to try to involve them in the monitoring business and suggested that both local sides should have representatives working alongside a 'Commission'. This Commission was quickly established at Brigadier Roddy's suggestion and, amazingly enough, it had high-level representation from both the Croats and Muslims. It was one of the best ideas I witnessed in Bosnia – even if it was sometimes to cause me infuriating problems later. A few days after the Commission had been formally established, Brigadier Roddy suggested that I should chair a meeting of local commanders, UNHCR, ICRC and ECMM at Vitez in yet another attempt to stop the violence in the valley.

We set up the Intelligence Section for such a conference on Saturday 30 January. Nakic Franjo, Timomir's Second in

Command, represented the Croats whilst Djemo Merdan came for the Muslims. Internationally, José de la Mota and Anders Levinson came for the UNHCR and Iris Wittwer for the ICRC. The ECMM Commission Representatives were led by a charming Englishman called Jeremy Fleming who was responsible for getting the now so-called Busovaca Commission off the ground.

I began the meeting by welcoming everyone and then asking Jeremy Fleming to make a report about the Commission's findings into what was causing the problems in the Kiseljak valley. Jeremy made a masterly speech in which he cleverly avoided blaming anyone whilst suggesting that everyone was at fault. I took the same theme when I summed up the meeting just before we broke for a coffee.

Afterwards I decided we ought to get down to what I considered to be the real business. Yet another ceasefire was agreed – this time to start at 8 a.m. the following day. Everyone agreed that all roads had to be opened and I stressed this also meant the valley route to Zenica. The Busovaca Commission's powers were extended and additional local-force representatives were appointed so that teams of roving inspectors could be established with representatives from all sides. This Commission was also required to supervise the withdrawal of those forces brought into the area from outside. All detainees were to be registered with the ICRC. We drafted a document that encapsulated all these tasks and objectives and had it rapidly translated into Serbo-Croat so that it was quite clear to the local forces. Finally we all signed both the English and Serbo-Croat versions at a press conference in the middle of the afternoon.

I believed that we had achieved something substantial with the setting up of this Commission, but felt it would still take some time for the fighting to stop – even if everyone on the ground cooperated. The fighting had indeed forced me to concentrate all my attention into the Kiseljak valley to the exclusion of every other area. Luckily, Tuzla was quiet at the time and the Serbs seemed to have halted their advance into Central Bosnia, maybe as a *quid pro quo* with the Croats for attacking the Muslims, who knows?

In Gornji Vakuf the ceasefire was holding but tension was still very high in the town. As I had not been down there for some time, I decide to visit Alun Jones so that he could brief me in person. The visit was opportune too as it would give me an opportunity to meet Lieutenant-Colonel Alistair Duncan, the Commanding Officer of 1st Battalion The Prince of Wales's Regiment of Yorkshire, that would eventually replace my Battalion. He was arriving at Gornji Vakuf on his initial reconnaissance.

Alun met me as I arrived in Gornji Vakuf on Sunday 31 January and stated in detail what he had been doing to keep his area from exploding again. He felt that the ceasefire there was working but it needed a great deal of effort on our part. B Company was manning four checkpoints around Gornji Vakuf on a permanent basis. With those checkpoints in place Alun had felt able to almost guarantee the safety of soft-skinned-vehicle convoys, which had been running through Gornji Vakuf for several days now. The Company had also been helping to recover bodies from the ruined areas of the town and surrounding villages.

Once Alun and I had talked I drove further south in Juliet on a perilous journey in the ice and snow. I wanted to be at the Makljan Croat checkpoint to greet Alistair Duncan and the new Commander British Forces, Brigadier Robin Searby, when they came into my area with Brigadier Andrew Cumming. I was there in good time and stood looking at a fantastic view across the mountains whilst I waited for them. The country looked fabulous in its snow coating and even the weather did not seem so cold that day. About forty minutes after we arrived I saw Brigadier Andrew Cumming's Discovery edging its way up the very steep hill and eventually the whole Reconnaissance Party arrived at Juliet's position.

I followed the Reconnaissance Party back to Gornji Vakuf and thence onwards to Vitez where a full briefing took place. The two brigadiers then went on to Kiseljak whilst Alistair was to remain with me for a few days. That evening, of 31 January, though we had a shooting incident at the Bulk Fuel Installation near our Echelon's position at the Garage.

The incident was very much like those I had experienced

On a highly successful mission we made it west of Turbe for the first time in December. Here I am talking to Captain Milutin Gruicic of the Bosnian Serb Army, my first contact with the Serbs since I began my official tour.

At Café Boric, accompanied by Beba Salko, wearing the beret. We had an excellent meeting with various Bosnian Serb officers discussing an exchange of prisoners and a possible Christmas truce.

Ice takes its toll on the roads. This warrior slid off the track en route to meet HRH The Prince of Wales.

Above: We had to maintain our patrols of our operational area throughout January and we needed to be well protected against the cold in Warrior.

Left: Recovering a body of a dead Bosnian Serb soldier in no man's land west of Turbe.

A local-force soldier demonstrates his sniper rifle. Such silencers were made locally.

Above: A Croat vehicle stopped by Muslim forces in Travnik. At the time the Croats and Muslims were fighting the Serbs together.

Right: Captain Martin Forgrave and Corporal McConachie, Royal Irish, lift an old lady on to the bonnet of my Land Rover at Turbe where about 2000 displaced persons crossed the lines.

Below: A mid-winter company patrol.

Gornji Vakuf in January 1993: we dug our vehicles in to protect them from fire.

Working in Gornji Vakuf during the battle between Croats and Muslims in January 1993.

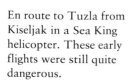

En route to Tuzla from Kiseljak in a Sea King helicopter. These early flights were still quite dangerous.

General Morillon briefs the press at Gornji Vakuf, January 1993, after fierce fighting and the tragic death of Lance-Corporal Wayne Edwards.

Farewell to Lance-Corporal Edwards: Lieutenant Alex Watts leads his Platoon in mourning at Gornji Vakuf at the spot where he was murdered.

Major Philip Jennings negotiating with Bosnian Croat Army engineers prior to removing the mined roadblock at Merdani on the Vitez–Zenica road. Sergeant Thornton translates, Sunday 7 February 1993.

The ICRC were crucial in helping to release prisoners throughout our area. Here Claire Podbielski and Denis Cretenet join me for a drink – to celebrate their luck in avoiding being killed in an accident with my Warrior during early February 1993.

Colour Sergeant Oram commanded our detachment in Sarajevo for several months and was later awarded the QGM. He operated with four armoured vehicles.

Refugees block our way at Cajdras on 19 April 1993. I talk to the people whilst Dobrila Kolaba interprets. Margaret Green sitting down.

With Padre Tyrone Hilary, Esad Denanovic and Captain Matthew Dundas-Whatley at the graves of Derek McBride and Ted Skinner, two mercenaries probably killed by their own side, 3 April 1993.

Company Sergeant Major Beck dealing with Bosnian Muslim displaced persons outside the Garage, April 1993.

Rescuing wounded civilians in Vitez, April 1993.

The withdrawal from Bosnia in May 1993. We took our Warriors with us.

Returning to Hanover with Captain Matthew Dundas-Whatley and Lieutenant Richard Rochester. Mr Archie Hamilton, Minister for the Armed Forces, and Lieutenant-General Sir Jeremy MacKenzie were there to meet us.

in the early days in Northern Ireland. At 11.45 p.m. a white car was driven down the road towards Vitez from the direction of Travnik. As the car passed the Bulk Fuel Installation, a man in it opened fire on some local Muslim forces who were beside the road. The Muslims shot back but the car did not stop. In the Garage, CSM Beck heard the shooting and tried to check that all was well at the Bulk Fuel Installation on the field telephone. He could not get through and so, taking soldiers stood by at immediate notice, he started running up the road towards the place. In fact Lance-Corporal Byrne, the Guard Commander there, had acted on his own initiative. With two soldiers, Privates Hayes and Rooney, he too was following-up the incident by checking on the local forces. Suddenly the car came rushing down the road again. It passed by CSM Beck's patrol and started firing at Lance-Corporal Byrne and his group further up the road. Shots went all over the place. But this time Lance-Corporal Byrne ordered fire to be returned. Twenty-two shots were fired at the car as it sped by and Lance-Corporal Byrne was sure many had struck the vehicle.

In the exchange of fire, he felt a blow to the head but thought it was his helmet striking as he took cover. Later this small wound was treated in the medical centre, not apparently needing further treatment. But three weeks later the wound was not healing properly. Captain Mark Weir, the Regimental Medical Officer, examined it and discovered that a bullet had penetrated Lance-Corporal Byrne's forehead, travelling around between his scalp and skull to a resting place further at the top of his head. Lance-Corporal Byrne had been amazingly lucky. The men in the car were less so. Later we learnt that the man who fired had been admitted to Travnik hospital with severe wounds to his chest and arm. The Croat Military Police even had the cheek to complain to me that one of their soldiers, admittedly a little drunk, they said, had only been firing in the air near the Bulk Fuel Installation when we had opened fire. My initial reaction to such a charge is unprintable but thereafter I was vigorous in my reply citing the time and details of the incident. I told them that the man was very lucky to be alive. I asked if they would

like me personally to visit him in Travnik Hospital to tell him
that. I understand he died later. At the time, of course, I had
not realized that Lance-Corporal Byrne had been wounded.
The Croat Military Police accepted our side of the story completely, only declining my offer of a hospital visit to cheer the
unfortunate man up. At the end of the tour, Lance-Corporal
Byrne was Mentioned in Dispatches for his brave behaviour
that night.

In all, we were very lucky over head wounds. During the
tour, four soldiers were wounded in the head by bullets; only
one of them, Lance-Corporal Edwards, proved fatal. Normally, a shot to the head is almost certainly deadly.

At Kacuni the imposition of our roadblock seemed to be
having a beneficial effect. Progressively, the area seemed to
get quieter and quieter. But there was still the problem of
detainees and both sides seemed to hold a large number of
prisoners. This was where the ICRC came in and they started
to take effective action to get people released as soon as the
area started to stabilize. Many people were saved from misery
by their work. We felt a responsibility for the ICRC in our
area and did what we could to reduce the dangers their personnel were constantly exposed to. Such was the case with
regard to detainees around Kacuni.

Once the situation was quiet enough for ICRC Toyota Land
Cruisers to move into the area, the organization deployed
into Kacuni in search of detainees. On one occasion I was
visiting the Kacuni checkpoint when I learnt that two ICRC
vehicles had just passed through on their way to a makeshift
Muslim prison in the village itself. The area was only just safe
for soft-skinned vehicles and I was still concerned about their
safety. It seemed likely that the two ICRC vehicles had travelled north from the main road past the Kacuni mosque and
so I followed in Juliet. Corporal Gill was driving and Lance-
Corporal Higginson was acting as gunner.

As we left the main road, however, we encountered a
Muslim checkpoint across a minor route leading south-west
into the hills. I commanded Juliet up to a barrier which
blocked our passage. Getting out of the turret, I asked the
bearded Muslim soldier manning the barrier to raise it so that

we could pass. He pointedly refused. In gestures, since I had no interpreter, I suggested that he should reconsider. He refused several times. It seemed to me that this might be the first checkpoint at which I would be turned back but I did not want to give up too easily. I tried to look determined and returned to the turret. I told Corporal Gill that we were to go through. I shouted at the Muslim soldier that I wanted the barrier open. He and the others with him pointed their weapons at us. I told the crew to keep low. Over the intercom I heard one of the others mutter, 'Bloody hell.' Then I ordered Corporal Gill to drive slowly forward to the barricade and push it with the vehicle. He did so. But I stopped the vehicle before the barrier was bent too far. From the hatch again I indicated that the barrier was to be raised. Without waiting for an answer, I indicated I would reverse to give the soldier room to open the barricade. We backed the Warrior a couple of feet. 'Put the barrier up,' I shouted and made encouraging lifting motions with my hands. The bearded Muslim soldier finally conceded and raised the barrier. As we drove through I summoned all the courtesy I could muster and politely saluted and then waved nicely at the guard force behind the officer.

The road thereafter was a narrow, typically suburban street. Vehicles of all types seemed to obstruct our way but we managed to drive around them carefully. Driving on we passed a Muslim Headquarters with a flag flying outside. Then the road seemed to get narrower. I saw the ICRC cars parked near a large building after about two kilometres. We stopped and I dismounted. There were quite a lot of people around – none of them appearing particularly unfriendly or friendly, simply curious, I thought. Again in gestures I asked where I could find the ICRC staff. Someone indicated a doorway into a large warehouse and I walked up to it.

Inside there was a long dark corridor. There were doors on both sides of the corridor and a man was fiddling with the lock of one them about twenty feet in front of me. But there was no sign of the ICRC delegates. I walked up to the man and made a sign of a cross on my arm to indicate ICRC. He pointed to a door further into the building. He took me there and opened one of the doors which led into a makeshift cell, which I think had originally been grain stores. Inside the freezing room was Claire Podbielski registering prisoners with the aid of an interpreter. She looked terribly cold but was working on grimly. All the prisoners, especially the very old ones, were huddled together under blankets. It was the first time I had been to a place like this and it shocked me. I realized that the ICRC had to face these conditions as a matter of routine and I was very glad it was not my job. Claire looked a little surprised to see me, but said things were fine. I asked her if there was anyone else registering prisoners and she told me Denis Cretenet was there too in one of the other cells. I told Claire I would say hello to him and then get out of the way. I found Denis two cells away. He had heard the commotion of my arrival and seemed pleased to see me. Like Claire, he told me that all was well and so I excused myself and left them to their onerous task.

Going back along the narrow road we had no difficulties getting out through the checkpoint again. Once more I saluted smartly and waved as we passed.

A few days later I was to meet the ICRC in the same area once again, but this time under somewhat different circumstances. I was returning from a visit to the Kacuni checkpoint in mid morning. As Juliet rounded a bend some way south of Busovaca she started to slide on black ice. Unfortunately coming from the other direction were two Toyota Land Cruisers, both in ICRC markings. To my mortification we were sliding towards the first of them out of control. My Warrior struck the first and narrowly missed the second ICRC vehicle. The whole of the side of the vehicle we hit, which Denis Cretenet had been driving, had been badly damaged and Denis himself had sustained slight injuries to the head from broken-glass fragments. Claire Podbielski was in the second vehicle. Denis was rather shaken by the experience, for which I don't blame him. My Warrior lost a side mirror. I was really embarrassed by the incident – hitting an ICRC vehicle was hardly good news. But the ICRC delegates were very decent about it, especially Denis who could have been killed. With typical diligence and determination, the ICRC continued on their task of visiting the local detention centre whilst the damaged vehicle was taken back to Zenica. Later I bought drinks for Denis and Claire to go some way towards an apology for nearly killing them.

I was back at the school just in time to catch General Morillon who had decided he wanted to hold his own meeting with Timomir Blaskic and Enver Hadzihasanovic. I introduced Alistair Duncan to the General and they chatted briefly as we waited for the escorts to arrive with both local commanders. Alistair was due to leave the next day having completed his initial reconnaissance.

General Morillon opened the meeting with a short statement in which he declared the hope that this latest ceasefire in Central Bosnia would be a binding one. Then he listened as each side explained its position and complaints about the other's ceasefire violations. General Morillon had to go without staying for lunch but both Enver Hadzihasanovic and Timomir Blaskic were able to join us. After we had eaten, Jeremy Fleming, Chairman of the Busovaca Commission, spent some time making detailed arrangements with the two sides, tying up the arrangements for the ceasefire and the withdrawal of their external forces from the area. Once more, all sides agreed that the valley road to Zenica needed to be opened and that work should start on dismantling the blockages on it within twenty-four hours. I had now lost count of the times I had heard that very same promise being made by these people.

CHAPTER 14

THE REGIMENT SAVED

Skilled soldiers had a knack of knowing when there was water in Vitez Camp and indeed when it was hot enough for a decent wash. For my part I never seemed to get it right. Such was the case on Wednesday 3 February 1993. Someone had told me that hot flowing water was to be had in plenty if I was to get into one of our showers immediately. I rushed to comply with the suggestion but alas the rumour was fallacious. There was a trickle of water, which was not unremarkable in itself, but that trickle was cold. I couldn't bear taking a cold shower. Apart from the severe cold, my head ached badly when I tried to wash my hair in freezing water. Yet I was fairly dirty and needed to do something. I compromised and stripped to the waist in the kitchen and filled one of the basins with some hot water 'borrowed' from a boiler. Using an Army mug, I was in the process of washing my hair when a soldier ran in and told me that I was wanted urgently on the telephone and so, still stripped to the waist, I ran to the Operations Room.

As I went in everyone looked terribly excited and I thought we must have opened fire or something. Tim Park, my Second in Command, just pointed at the Mapper terminal. On its screen was a message. The Secretary of State for Defence had announced that two regimental amalgamations previously planned in the Government's cutbacks would now not take place. Our amalgamation with The Staffordshire Regiment was one of them. My first thought was that someone at the other end of Mapper might have been having a sick joke but then remembered that Brigadier Andrew had wanted to speak. I was unable to speak to him, however, because all the telephone lines to Split were engaged, but after double-checking on Mapper I was convinced that the screen message was no hoax and the celebrations really started then.

A regiment is like a close family. Ours, the Cheshire Regiment, was fully expecting to be amalgamated, and it is impossible to overstate how heartbreaking this was for us. To loyal regimental soldiers the end of over three hundred years of the Regiment's existence could barely be contemplated. It was the equivalent of death. Now that such a death sentence had been removed it was hardly surprising that we were over the moon.

Our 5 p.m. conference included champagne quickly deployed into the school from the Officers' Mess. After the shortest conference on record, we adjourned to the Officers' Mess itself. We had always thought we had ample bottles of champagne for our tour but we were wrong. Within an hour it had all gone. At a later date, when briefing our successor Battalion, Captain Martin Forgrave was asked, if the Cheshires had their time again, what item would they have brought more of for the tour in Bosnia? Martin replied flippantly, 'Champagne.' Certainly he was right on 3 February 1993. We needed much more of the stuff.

Later though we were to receive much sadder news. We heard that the two British mercenaries, Ted Skinner and Derek Arlow McBride, had been found dead in a stream near Novi Travnik. Despite our best efforts, we were really never to find out exactly what had happened to them. Martin Forgrave was despatched by me to assist in the recovery of the bodies and to try and find out what had happened. It seems that they might have been taken from their flat in Novi Travnik in the night. Our best guess was that Mujahaddin had killed them.

As Ted and Derek had worked for the Bosnian Muslims their bodies were taken to the city morgue in Zenica. I spoke to Djemo Merdan about the matter. He knew both men well and was very unhappy about what had happened. He also assured me that they had not been killed because they were

British, or because people thought they were connected to us. Maybe his enquiries ascertained the circumstances surrounding their deaths but he never told me. There was little we could do anyway. Both men were mercenaries and so they did not have British 'protection' as such. We reported the matter to the British Embassy in Zagreb, but I was determined that their remains should have a Christian burial. They were interred quickly in a Muslim graveyard, but I agreed with Tyrone Hilary, the Padre, that some time in the future we should have a proper burial service for both men.

Two months later, on a wet Saturday morning, Tyrone, Matthew Dundas-Whatley and myself found ourselves in that Muslim cemetery on a plateau east of Zenica. An officer from Headquarters 3rd Muslim Corps by the name of Esad Denanovic accompanied us. The cemetery was large – with a great deal of space as yet unused. Ted and Derek's graves were several hundred metres walk from the entrance. Having previously been told that they had Muslim headstones, we came equipped with two crosses provided by the UNHCR. Tyrone quickly dug out the Muslim headstones and replaced them with crosses. Each man had his name and years of birth and death marked on the wood of the crosses with plastic letters.

Standing before the graves I felt terribly sad for them both. They had seemed good men to me, even though they had been mercenaries. They had been the only men that I had any time for in that sordid profession in Bosnia. Neither Ted nor Derek seemed to be in the business for money or thrills. They simply sympathized with the Muslims – yet they may have been killed by the very people with whom they were fighting. I thought too of their families who could not be there, which was the reason why I wanted them to have a proper, decent burial.

Tyrone conducted a very short but moving burial service adapting it a little to account for the fact that both men had been interred some time before. At the end we took photographs and Tyrone undertook to send some to the families of the men. Walking back to the vehicles through the cemetery, Esad Denanovic turned to me and said, 'C'est la vie.' I still

wonder whether he meant anything more than just a plati-
tude when he said it. Maybe he knew what had really
happened . . .

It had taken us two months to give Ted Skinner and Derek
McBride Christian burials because life had become so hectic
by this time. Trouble in the Kiseljak valley simply refused to
die down. Although we maintained the Kacuni checkpoint
and the surrounding area seemed a little less volatile, severe
problems were building up in several villages in the River
Lasva valley, particularly Katici and Merdani. Even the local
leaders seemed to be in despair about it. On one occasion
Santic, the President of Vitez, asked to see me urgently. He
told me he thought all local military commanders deserved
to be 'sacked' as they simply had no answers to anything.
This was a very brave thing for a civilian to say in what was
after all an anarchic state run by warlords and, as I rather
liked him, I warned him to take care with whom he shared
this opinion.

I tried my best to keep in contact with all sides no matter
how bad the situation appeared. From the Croats' viewpoint,
the town of Busovaca seemed under greatest threat from
Muslim forces. Dario Kordich, Deputy President of the Croats,
was also the Commander in the town. He was neurotic about
the impending danger and during one conversation pleaded
with me to go immediately to Katici and Merdani:

'Go there and stop the fighting. Please, go there now.'

On Kordich's mobile telephone I rang Headquarters 3rd
Muslim Corps and spoke to Merdan. I told him that Kordich
wanted me to go to Croat-controlled Katici and then Muslim-
controlled Merdani, but that I was only prepared to do this
if Merdan warned his soldiers that I would be coming. He
agreed and Kordich assured me that the Croats would respect
our neutrality too. It was a little bit of a gamble but I thought
we might just be able to stop the fighting by our presence. I
gave orders for a move into the area from Busovaca and
quickly some Warriors from A Company, commanded by Sergeant Kujawinski, joined me outside Kordich's Headquarters.

I was aware that a very serious battle was taking place but,
with promises from both sides that our presence would be

respected, I hoped we would not become targets. I was far from convinced about this, but felt we had to try.

Moving up the road from Busovaca, I had no alternative but to turn right just before the main River Lasva. As we did so, Kate Adie and her BBC team were passing and they simply followed us in an armoured Land Rover. However, the bridge I had hoped to cross looked far too dangerous for Warriors. Having quickly checked the banks and approximate depth of a tributary of the Lasva, I took Juliet straight across through the water. Sergeant Kujawinski and his second Warrior followed. From there we had to climb a steep embankment to get back on the narrow road, which was not as easy as it looked in the icy conditions. We managed it, however, and slowly progressed down a track towards Katici. We did so cautiously as the ice was treacherous. To minimize the risk of sliding or somersaulting, I ordered Sergeant Kujawinski to leave his second Warrior at the tributary ford and we proceeded with just two vehicles in line astern.

Passing what I knew to be Croat positions on my left about two hundred metres away, a single shot went over my head, not very close, but it immediately confirmed some of my deep misgivings. A few minutes later, a fusillade of small-arms fire was directed at Juliet but now we were all well under cover and so there was no real problem. In our relative safety, we were able to continue without this greatly worrying us. Upon reaching Katici, we drove directly to its eastern edge where the ground opened up and I was able to see Merdani properly. Both Katici and Merdani looked in a real mess. Not only was quite a lot of shooting taking place between both villages but a large number of houses were on fire. Sergeant Kujawinski drew alongside me and we stayed in that highly visible position for several minutes hoping that as many of the fighting soldiers as possible would see us. But our presence made not one jot of difference and the fighting continued unabated.

Next I considered driving across to Merdani, but the road, which had been bad so far, looked even worse between the two villages. In addition I began to worry that we might just become a target for effective anti-tank fire soon. Obviously neither side had any intentions of stopping shooting. I had kept my word and had tried to calm things down with my presence, but to no avail. It was time to withdraw and I gave orders over the radio for both Warriors to turn in a school yard.

We reversed our direction of travel, with Juliet leading Sergeant Kujawinski's Warrior, and Kate Adie in her armoured Land Rover behind that. On the way through to Katici I had avoided some more dangerous-looking bridges that might not have withstood Warrior's weight. Instead we drove down steep banks into the streams and then up out the other side of them. Climbing one bank, however, disaster struck. Sergeant Kujawinski's vehicle started to slide sideways and then toppled over on to its turret.

I was leading and the first I knew of it was when Corporal Gill, my driver, suddenly stopped Juliet and told me what had happened. It looked really bad from our position some one hundred metres in front. Lance-Corporal Higginson and I jumped out of our vehicle and ran down the track towards the overturned Warrior. We were just in front of the Croat positions and in full view of both sides.

As we arrived Sergeant Kujawinski was shouting for responses from his crew to check that everyone was all right. Kate Adie was helping too. From the various positions in which they had ended up, Sergeant Kujawinski's crew hauled themselves out through the upside-down rear door. The driver, however, failed to appear. Sergeant Kujawinski called his name, 'Harrison, Harrison,' but there was no answer. After a couple of minutes though Private Harrison dragged himself out, unhurt apart from a few battery acid burns. I was amazed and delight that no one had been killed. I didn't care about the Warrior.

I suggested we all needed a cup of tea, but the boiling vessel in Sergeant Kujawinski's vehicle was upside down. Juliet came to the rescue there. But as we were trying to work out the best way of righting the Warrior, a severe firefight started. It looked like 12·7mm fire going past about one hundred metres to our north and high. We were certainly not the target for the Croat gunner who was firing from a position

high on a modern factory complex towards the Lasva junction. It was certainly an impressive sight as the tracer sped
past us towards its intended target, some houses in Merdani.

Clearly it was going to be a long night for Sergeant Kujawinski's crew as considerable care would have to taken to
recover his Warrior. The vehicle had overturned in a fairly
exposed place. From Juliet, Lance-Corporal Higginson radioed for a recovery vehicle and I gave instructions that the
second Warrior – originally left at the ford – was to come
forward to join us. Once the firefight had died down and the
second Warrior was with us, I decided there was very little
more I could do. I left Sergeant Kujawinski with the invitation
to 'Have a good night!' and returned to Vitez.

Personally I slept well that night, which was good because
I would need all the strength I had in the traumatic day ahead
of me. In the morning Jeremy Fleming chaired a meeting to
consider the state of the ceasefire. Timomir Blaskic and Djemo
Merdan were there but so too were José de la Mota for
UNHCR and Iris Wittwer for ICRC. The meeting took rather
a long time to get down to the essentials but at the end of it
we agreed, once again, that all firing must stop immediately.
I was losing patience with these discussions of meaningless
ceasefires, but two measures directly affected the Battalion
Group. Firstly, Djemo Merdan asked me to take him to Merdani so that he could explain in person that all firing must
stop. I was reluctant at first in view of what had happened
the night before but was persuaded in the end. Once that had
happened I agreed that the Battalion Group should try to
patrol into and out of the area as much as possible. Secondly,
the Croats were to dismantle the barricade blocking the valley
route to Zenica, and we would monitor the situation starting
at midday the following day.

In the afternoon a small convoy of vehicles set out for Katici
and Merdani. The ceasefire seemed to be working and so I
had less of a problem deciding to use some Land Rovers in
the convoy. Having overturned one the night before, I was
reluctant to consider using Warriors again and in any case it
was dubious as to whether they could physically fit the small
roads in Merdani. We used two Scimitars as a vanguard force

and then I followed with two Land Rovers – mine and Martin Forgrave's. We reached the edge of Katici, where I had turned the night before, and then crossed over the open area between the two villages. I was right, the lanes in Merdani would not have allowed Warriors to pass. We even had difficulty with Scimitars and Land Rovers, especially when trying to turn them around. But nobody fired at us on the way into the village. Once there Merdan alighted from my Land Rover and talked at length to his soldiers. These Muslim defenders of Merdani told me that they had taken some Croat prisoners, who were in a fit condition, and that they had had four soldiers killed in the fighting so far. After about forty-five minutes in Merdani I decided it was time to leave and told Djemo Merdan that we had to return. Going back the two lead Scimitars took the wrong track between Merdani and Katici. Whilst the convoy was manoeuvring to get back on track, someone, probably in devilment, fired some shots at us. I was not too amused with the map reading of the young cavalry officer in the lead and told him so over the radio.

Two days later Philip Jennings managed to open the road-block on the valley road to Zenica. I was delighted by the news and willingly paid my dues. I had bet Philip that he would not get it open that day and the wager was a bottle of champagne. As there was no champagne left in Vitez as a result of the Regiment being saved, I gave him thirty Deutschmarks.

The next day I handed over command of the Battalion to the Second in Command, Major Tim Park, because it was my turn for R & R. It was difficult in these very uncertain circumstances to leave the theatre, but I had little option. Everyone was under orders to take R & R and nobody was indispensable. I had often said that myself and now it was time for me to accept my own philosophy.

As I saw it, the situations in Tuzla, Gornji Vakuf, Turbe and Travnik were relatively quiet and under control by this stage. Kiseljak valley was still more unstable than I would have wished, but at least things seemed to be getting better. Opening the main route into Zenica was a very healthy development, I thought. Matters could have been worse and I felt it to be an opportune time to take a break.

Together with CSM Lawson, Corporal Gill and Lance-Corporal Higginson, I drove down Route Triangle to Tomaslavgrad on 8 February. It had changed tremendously since I had first seen it. The Royal Engineers had done a superb job in improving it by widening the road and hardening its surface over the last three months. At Tomaslavgrad I called in to see my good friend Malcolm Wood at Headquarters of the National Support Element. Malcolm seemed to be living in some kind of splendid isolation there. HQ BRITFOR had redeployed all his support units back to the coast of Croatia and so Malcolm's small Headquarters was all that remained in the town. As ever, it was good to see him. He congratulated me on leaving Bosnia for the first time and we had a good chuckle over events before I reassumed my journey down to Split.

Once there I heard some really good news. Three Sergeant Majors in the Battalion had been selected for promotion to Warrant Officer Class 1: RQMS Gresty, TQMS Salisbury and CSM Lawson. The first two were still in Vitez and so I sent my congratulations to both by signal. But I brought a bottle of champagne from Dijoulje Barracks and waited to 'ambush' CSM Lawson beside my Discovery in the car park.

Innocently he walked up a few minutes later. I gave him the bottle and asked if he would open it for me.

'This looks good stuff, sir.'

'Yes, it's the real McCoy, you know,' I said.

'Looks OK to me too.'

'Not cold enough, though.'

'If you don't mind, sir, what's the celebration?'

'Oh, I'm sorry Sergeant Major. You've been promoted to RSM next year! Congratulations. I'm thrilled to bits for you.'

CHAPTER 15

TURBE AND VISITS

On my return from R & R in Germany on Friday 19 February, it appeared that the situation had become more stable in the Kiseljak valley since I had left. But in Gornji Vakuf B Company had been forced to open fire on three occasions, killing possibly three people. Up in Tuzla, a Royal Marines team from HQ BRITFOR on a fact-finding mission had stupidly driven through Kalesa towards the Serb lines. Their vehicle had been destroyed by an anti-tank round, but by extreme luck the team had been unhurt. They evacuated quickly and jumped into a ditch before more rounds destroyed their vehicle. Unsurprisingly Brigadier Andrew Cumming was furious at this incident and the team had been immediately expelled from the theatre of operations on their return to Split. For my part, I reassured myself that they had been briefed properly before they left Tuzla airfield. It seemed that they had had a full ground briefing but had chosen to ignore it. They were very stupid and very, very lucky too.

Tim Park's leadership of the Battalion whilst I had been away was in fact his swansong as Second in Command. He was being posted to Warminster in Wiltshire and Bryan Watters had already arrived to take over Tim's job. Bryan had just finished commanding the Jungle Warfare School in Brunei and I had known him since 1974. It was good to have him back.

The next day I was immediately thrown back into the old routine, chairing a meeting between Timomir Blaskic and Enver Hadzihasanovic at the French Engineers' Camp in

Kakanj. The aim of the meeting was to hear the latest update report from the Busovaca Commission. Tim Park had been heavily involved in meetings with Jeremy Fleming and the Commission in my absence and some solid working relationships had been developed.

The Commission itself was now being fully supported by us. Three United Kingdom Liaison Officer (UKLO) teams had been attached to it and Brigadier Andrew Cumming had provided these officer-led groups with a new type of vehicle called an RB–44 each with its own INMARSAT telephone. These state-of-the-art communication systems seemed magic to start with, but they never really worked properly in the field. The Commission also had several of Support Company's APCs allocated to it for armoured protection. In theory, two of the UKLO teams were to work in the field, offering armour for when the field teams were entering a volatile area. Transported in these APCs, an ECMM officer and officers from each of the two local sides would investigate a situation together and be returned to their base in safety by the UKLO team. Finally the Commission had decided to move its Headquarters from Busovaca to a house right alongside the school at Vitez, which allowed us to liaise constantly, as well as provide a considerable amount of administrative support to the Commission. The Commission was doing a very useful job and was highly valuable in further maintaining our relations with all sides in the area.

One inevitable adversary whose challenge to routine I had been dreading for weeks was the Yugoslav winter. The weather was getting worse every day. The roads were now so bad that I banned non-essential traffic from moving. Vehicles, both tracked and wheeled, were moving on sheer ice and no amount of good driving could prevent accidents. I cringed as I saw the number of minor accidents on 'orders' steadily increase but decided that, unless a company commander really felt a driver had been at fault, no one should come in front of me for disciplinary proceedings. I was in a couple of accidents myself, both of which involved sliding, totally out of control, into ditches. We were very grateful that nobody was seriously hurt at this time. The roads to Tuzla were impassable too and the Company up there was cut off by the weather for several days.

The Tuzla base was coming under some scrutiny anyway. Brigadier Roddy Cordy-Simpson visited and told me that there was very great British pressure for us to withdraw from the town. I knew this already having had frequent chats about the place with Brigadier Andrew Cumming. My own view was that we should stay, it being the 'jewel in our crown', so to speak. After all, when I had been sent to Bosnia, my main instruction had been to get to Tuzla and ensure it received enough aid. We were just fully establishing ourselves there when this discussion of a withdrawal started. Apparently the main supply route from Vitez to Tuzla, at one hundred and eighty kilometres, was considered too far. The route from Split to Vitez alone was two hundred and forty kilometres. But now that we were managing to make the operation work it was galling to talk about pulling out again. Brigadier Roddy might also have been considering it as a new post for the Canadian Battalion under Tom Gebirt's Command, which had finally been withdrawn from Banja Luka after nearly four months of aggravation by the Serbs. They were in the process of redeploying to Central Bosnia but as yet had no location for a base. Brigadier Roddy suggested that, if the decision were taken, I should expect to start my withdrawal from Tuzla towards the end of March, in four weeks' time. I was not too happy about that, but of course accepted that I may have no choice. Brigadier Roddy told me that General Morillon would make the final decision and I was delighted to learn that when this option was later put to General Morillon, he ruled it out immediately on the grounds that the British presence there was a success. I gather that the staff's advice was that we should withdraw but the General thought such a move was unwise.

Besides the weather, local conditions were becoming unfriendly in other ways that we *could* control. Matters came to head when a Dutch Captain, driving along the Vitez by-pass in the middle of the morning in a Mercedes jeep, was overtaken by a Golf car at great speed which then forced his Mercedes to a standstill by the side of the road. Out jumped two men wearing Croat combat jackets, but with civilian trousers and carrying Kalashnikov assault rifles. Moving sharply to the car they pointed their weapons at the Captain, who had already realized what was happening and had locked his door. When the men found they could not open the door, they smashed through the car window, giving the Captain a severe blow on the side of his head with the rifle butt in the process. He was hauled out and the vehicle was driven off by the men. Not only did he lose his vehicle but also his pistol. The last the Dutch Captain saw of the Mercedes was as it disappeared down the road towards Busovaca following the Golf.

I was at the Garage having snow chains fitted to my Discovery when someone told me about the hijack of the Dutch vehicle. Returning to the school, I walked into the Operations Room to find the Captain being debriefed by Captain Mike Ruddock. The Captain was receiving medical treatment to the side of his face as he was telling his story. We were all very angry at what had happened and I was determined to do something. As soon as the Captain's face had received medical treatment I asked him if he would mind coming with me to the Hotel Vitez where I wanted to have a serious talk with the local Croat Military Police. The Captain was clearly shaken by the experience but was basically all right. He agreed to come with me and we went down there straightaway. Nobody of sufficiently senior rank was at Hotel Vitez but I was very rude about what had happened to what seemed to be a junior officer and demanded that the police do something immediately. Returning with the Captain to Busovaca, we met with Jan de Boer who shared my extreme irritation at what had happened. We decided that we must react very positively, not simply to get the vehicle back, but also to make sure that it did not happen again.

There had been an increasing number of hijackings of vehicles in the Vitez area recently and things were getting out of hand. But this latest outrage was most certainly a turn for the worse, and had to be stopped in its tracks.

When we failed to find Mario Cerkoz, the Croat Commander, in Novi Travnik we again spoke to the Croat Military

Police there who had heard about the incident. An officer explained that the Mafia had probably carried out the hijacking. I had heard about this Mafia in the area before but I had never felt that it would have the nerve to do this sort of thing. Within Vitez the so-called Mafia Headquarters was a place called the 'Al Capone Café'. I stressed that we wanted the vehicle and weapon back and let the Croat Military Police know that we expected them to do something.

When Colonel Filipovitch, the Croat Commander in Travnik, called in to see me the next morning, I laid great stress on the requirement to get the Mercedes jeep back from whoever had taken it. Filipovitch claimed again and again that the vehicle had been taken by 'gangsters'; the Croats had nothing to do with it. In return I argued that the area was Croat controlled and therefore they must assume responsibility for getting it back. I asked him firmly to make sure that every effort was made to get the Mercedes back to the Dutch/Belgian Transport Battalion. Of course such an event, I said, must never happen again.

After a few days the vehicle was returned to its rightful owners. I understand that the Croats had put considerable pressure on to the Mafia. After some very bad feeling, which involved quite a lot of shooting I understand, the vehicle was recovered by the Military Police. The Dutch Captain's pistol, though, was never located.

We never had a subsequent problem with any attempt to take a UN military vehicle but hijackings of international organization vehicles did continue. Finally I decided that I would try to put an end to this altogether and went to see Santic, President of Vitez, about the problem. I complained strongly that the latest hijacking, of an International Rescue Committee vehicle, had occurred outside the very house in which the international staff lived in Vitez. As a result, several international organizations were threatening to quit Vitez for the relatively greater safety of Zenica. Santic seemed only too aware of the possibility that international organizations were likely to leave Vitez and asked for our help to stop the hijackings. I agreed to put the Standby Platoon into Vitez at periodic intervals as a kind of security patrol.

In discussion with the hierarchy in Vitez I also learnt that the Mafia boss was a man called Andric Zarko. His base was Café Boba, about three kilometres west from the school, so I drove directly to the café from Vitez Town Hall, though it was not until my third visit, at about 6.30 p.m. on Monday 15 March, that the café staff agreed to go and find him to talk to me. Shortly afterwards a new Mercedes 500 series vehicle drove up to the front of the café. A blond-haired, thick-set man of about thirty got out of the front seat. He carried two weapons with him.

The man introduced himself as Andric Zarko and he did not introduce the bully-boys who came with him. We sat down at a table in the café and, after coffee had been served, began to talk. He asked me how I had got his name. I replied that everyone in the area knew about him. I told him that I was getting irritated by the number of international vehicles being stolen. He had the nerve to reply that I had come to exactly the right person – as he was Chief of Police for Travnik and Novi Travnik! In that case, I said, I hoped he would retrieve all the vehicles that had been stolen as well as a UNHCR Land Cruiser that had gone a few days before. I did not want any more vehicles to disappear – perhaps he could make that plain to 'whoever it was who was taking them'. He asked if we could meet again the next day but I could not – Bryan Watters was available and went along to see him instead of me and that meeting was inconclusive too. We never did recover any of the vehicles, but the hijackings stopped.

The day on which the list of compulsory redundancies was made public was one which I would not care to repeat. The Army had called for volunteers for redundancy. There were enough soldier volunteers to fill the quota, but not enough officers. Three out of the four of my officers made redundant were not volunteers. I felt terrible about having to tell them. I tried to do it in the best way I could – by going around to where I found them at work and telling them quickly. I was amazed at how well people who had expected much longer careers took the news, but I felt wretched as I told really good people their fates and even worse afterwards.

Towards the end of February rumours abounded, particularly from the Muslims, that there were several thousand displaced persons about to come across the lines at Turbe. I was at Kiseljak, at General Morillon's lunch to say farewell to General Nambiar, when suddenly this was confirmed in a message from Beba Salko, the Muslim Exchange Commission Officer at Travnik. Beba had informed Martin Forgrave that the numbers were enormous and had requested our immediate help in the supervision of a ceasefire. I waited until General Nambiar had gone and then returned to Vitez as soon as possible.

Luckily I had already pre-warned Philip Jennings that, in the eventuality of a mass crossing, he would have to organize everything. Therefore Philip's contingency plan had been put in motion by him even as I was travelling back from HQ BHC. Calling briefly at the school, I then travelled directly on to Travnik where I was to collect my Warrior.

From C Company reports from Turbe, it was clear that an effective ceasefire was in place, so I took both my Warrior and Discovery with me when I drove up to join Philip Jennings. Once in Turbe I followed the Karaula road towards the front lines. A thick layer of fresh snow lay on the ground which greatly hindered our attempts to identify any surface-laid anti-tank mines before we attempted a line crossing. Beba Salko had the solution: producing a plank from the Bosnian Muslim positions, he used it rather like a plough to push the snow aside. It took him and his assistant about twenty-five minutes to locate and remove the mines using this method. Eventually though we were satisfied that all the anti-tank mines that lay in our path had been removed; using Land Rovers, we then drove through the Muslim front lines and proceeded slowly towards the first Serb outposts. Philip Jennings remained on the Turbe side of the lines because no Warriors could cross.

After driving for about a mile or so, we came upon the first Serb soldiers. Mark Laity of BBC Radio News and a few other journalists were with us. Five coaches were parked on the left side of the road facing towards us as we arrived. They were filled with people. Together, Beba Salko and I went up to the house where we had been on a previous line crossing and there found the Serb Exchange Commission officers. They explained that there were going to be large numbers of people crossing over today and the first batch of mainly Muslims from Banja Luka were here now. They were in the coaches and should cross the lines immediately. Beba laughed in rather a hollow way when I suggested to him that we should request that the coaches drive straight across the lines and I would guarantee that they were returned. He did not even bother to pass my question on, saying the idea was simply impossible. Everyone would have to get out of the coaches and walk through the lines. Once they were over the lines many more would follow.

Meanwhile Martin Forgrave was helping the Serbs to recover a Serb soldier's body. It was a very unpleasant task as the man had been killed two months before and his remains were cemented to the ground by ice. From the prints in the snow around the body, it was obvious that animals had been picking at his flesh too. Separating the soldier's remains from the ground where he had fallen was filthy work but the Serbs were most appreciative of the help we gave them in this task.

Together with Dobrila Kolaba, perhaps the most proficient civilian interpreter we had recruited, I climbed aboard the first coach. I explained through her that we were British UN soldiers and that they were now within our protection. They were not to worry and we would do everything we could to help them. Unfortunately, I explained, they would have to walk across the lines. I insisted that this message was repeated on all five coaches before the Serbs started to order people off the transport.

The wretchedness of the situation only really hit us once we saw people start walking across the lines. Old women and men, women with children, an absence of able-bodied men, they started to stumble down the road carrying their treasured possessions in bulging bags and suitcases. Some of the women, particularly the older ones, were weeping. Other people just could not carry their possessions and some of the older ones simply could not walk. Soldiers slung their weapons and started to carry children and bags. The journalists with us did likewise. Nobody was unaffected by what they were seeing. A crocodile file of misery began to move slowly down the road towards Turbe which was over a mile away. We made sure that everyone walked in the tracks made by our vehicles as we crossed the lines. Nobody knew what mines were hidden in the snow. I ordered that our vehicles were to turn around and those people who experienced difficulties walking were to be placed in them. Very quickly they were full and there were even people sitting on the bonnets. We lifted a very heavy old lady and sat her on the spare tyre of my Land Rover. Heavy bags were packed around her so that my driver had the greatest difficulty seeing through the windscreen. The sun was shining brightly and yet it was very cold.

I walked back across the lines with Mark Laity. We each carried a child. At the furthermost outpost of the Bosnian Serb Army some soldiers shouted at us. 'So long, so long. Next time you die', they taunted in broken English. My temper snapped and I shouted back: 'Animals!' Mark, beside me, counselled caution: 'Cool it, Bob.' We walked on and eventually reached the other side.

Once back near Philip Jennings's Warriors, I climbed on one to use the radio. Standing behind the turret, I spoke to the Battalion Operations Room in Vitez.

'Get me as much transport as you can. Use all our trucks and see if the Dutch can give us any.'

I was just finishing with the radio when someone fired a shot at me on the Warrior that came fearfully close. Crouching down, I gave the crew an order to traverse and locate from where the shot had come. But whoever fired did not fire again and so locating the firing point was very difficult. I climbed down from the vehicle and walked back across the lines as my Land Rover was still being used to ferry people down to the refugee centre in Travnik.

About two hundred and fifty people were in that first party of displaced persons. Taking them over was fairly traumatic and upsetting because, again just like after the fall of Jajce, they looked remarkably like people back home in Britain. But when we went back across the lines again it was worse. Many more coaches had arrived and an enormous number of people were waiting to come across. It looked like an exodus. As I walked up the line of coaches, I saw CSM Cusack, the teara-way from Belfast, with his arm around an old woman who was in despair. He started to half carry both her and her bags back down the road. Other people just could not take their possessions and started to abandon them, which we tried to stop them from doing. The first five trucks arrived having been sent across the lines by Philip Jennings. I shouted that nobody was to leave their bags behind. Many of the women were crying. The soldiers looked grimly upset and did every-thing they could to help. So too, in fairness, did some of the Serb soldiers who obviously did not like what they were see-ing either.

I did not go back across the lines but stayed on the Serb side until the very last displaced people were about to leave. Then I ordered that we check every vehicle to make sure that nobody had been left behind. I noticed that some bags had still been abandoned by their owners. With Martin Forgrave and Beba Salko, I checked that nobody else needed to go across and then we started to walk back with the stragglers, carrying bags and children as necessary. Most people still had to walk as we did not have enough transport.

But now it was getting dark. The ceasefire had held – apart from the odd non-effective shot – yet we were all worried as nightfall came. And with just cause, as it turned out. As we left the Serb forward outposts the shooting started. It started first to our south and went straight across the road and it was accurate fire too. We took cover. Nobody must go off the road, Beba shouted. We all knew why; mines were everywhere. I was carrying a child with a sopping wet nappy. When there was a pause in the firing, we half ran on. Then it started again. I ordered those soldiers with us to be prepared to return fire to the points from where the tracer originated.

'Don't do it, Colonel,' Beba said. 'It won't help.'

'All right,' I agreed and we waited lying flat on the road in the half light until the firing died down again. Once more we moved forward as fast as we could. Again the firing started and came right amongst us. The first Warriors were only one hundred metres away. How nobody was hit I just do not know, but we made it back to them.

Angrily I ran to Juliet. She had her lights on and I shouted for them to be switched off. Climbing into position beside CSM Lawson, I spoke to Philip Jennings over the radio. He was to move his Warriors forward into fire positions. If anyone shot at them, they were to retaliate immediately. C Company responded very quickly to that order and within seconds the Warriors were jockeying into fire positions. Typically those that were firing at children, women and old men a few minutes before thought better of taking on Warrior. There was no more shooting.

At the cross-roads just on the eastern outskirts of Turbe there was chaos. So many people had swamped what limited transport we had and a shuttle service was in operation. It went backwards and forwards to the Refugee Centre in Travnik for a couple of hours before everyone was safely away from the front lines.

I returned to the school tired but happy. Just before I went to bed I wrote in my diary:

'This was probably the most satisfying day of my tour so far. True, we have been instrumental in ethnic cleansing but it would have happened anyway. Probably we made it less painful than it might have been and, possibly, by being quick about it, we saved lives.'

Both the UNHCR and ICRC had more difficulty with helping such an operation. By charter, they are duty bound to assist people to remain in their own homes and are most sensitive to charges that they might be helping ethnic cleansing. For our part, we were bound by no such instructions. UNPROFOR was free to do what it felt was best in the circumstances. Clearly we had nothing to do with forcing people to go to the front lines at Turbe from places like Banja Luka. All we did was to try to alleviate the misery of their exodus. It is also possible that without our help the crossing would have extended well into the night. In such circumstances I wondered how many people may have been killed by the crossfire of which we had only had a taste. We had heard reports of

previous instances of crossing lines at Turbe at which displaced persons had been mistreated, many of them forced to
leave their belongings behind before walking across, and of
people dying on the way. At least our presence was discourag-
ing such abuse. I do not imply criticism in any way of the
UNHCR or ICRC by what I have just said about their organizations. Their officials working alongside us in Bosnia were one
hundred per cent behind what we were doing. Indeed they
encouraged and helped us. They also organized excellent
reception arrangements in Travnik. But they certainly had
their hands tied in a way that we did not in such operations.

The Refugee Centre in Travnik dealt with just over two
thousand displaced persons who had crossed over from
Bosnian Serb-controlled territory that day. On debriefing it
was discovered that most of them had had to 'pay' for the
privilege of being transported to Turbe. The going rate seemed
to be about eighty Deutschmarks – ostensibly to offset
expenses of the coach trip. Most didn't even have the choice
as their houses had been sacked to 'encourage' them. It was
appalling that after all that, they still had to give up some of
their precious foreign money. It's like the condemned man
paying his own executioner.

The event was an absolute disgrace. It was one of the most
publicly witnessed instances of ethnic cleansing seen yet in
Bosnia. Most people seemed to be Muslims rounded up from
the Banja Luka area. The international media had a field day
and the Serbs were roundly condemned for their clear guilt.
Watched on television screens across the world, the images
of tired, emotional people dragging their children and belongings through the snow had a dramatic impact. I believe that
it was because of this very negative publicity that the Serbs
never repeated such a blatantly callous act on this scale. True,
they did thereafter use the Turbe crossing point as a means
of pushing small groups of displaced persons over the lines,
but they never risked more than a couple of hundred people.
At first glance this may have seemed an improvement, but I
wondered what horrors the people that had to remain in
Serbia were now having to endure.

Western Bosnia was not the only area where Muslims were

enduring such treatment. For some days now General Morillon had been considering a move across the lines from Tuzla
in order to try to save lives in Muslim 'pockets' in Eastern
Bosnia by organizing the evacuation of displaced persons.
Having flown to Tuzla in two French Puma helicopters, General Morillon's party was met by Alan Abraham. Alan then
took General Morillon from the airfield to Kalesa and across
the front lines in a convoy of two Warriors, two Scimitars,
two Spartans, a Sultan and a Samson. However, the Serbs
would only allow a Spartan and Sultan vehicle to cross into
the area controlled by them. Eventually Alan and General
Morillon reached Novi Kasaba where they spent the night
before negotiating entry into Cerska. The situation in the Cerska Pocket had been much exaggerated by the press and only
some seventy-five wounded civilians were found there.

General Morillon was flown out leaving Alan behind with
a small party in the area of Banja Koviljaca and Zvornik for
a couple of days trying to get local agreement for some Belgian
UN trucks to be brought in to evacuate seventy-five wounded
civilians who were at Konjevic Polje. A Land Rover and a
Foden recovery vehicle joined him having crossed from Tuzla.
But as the procrastination continued, so the resentment grew
amongst local Muslims who demanded that not just the serious wounded be taken out of danger. The next day the Serbs
started to shell the place. On 12 March this shelling proved
to be devastating and at least sixteen people were killed as
they clustered around the B Squadron group. Many more
people were badly injured. Captain Nick Costello, Warrant
Officer 2 McNair, Warrant Officer 2 Sterenberg and Doctor
Simon Mardell, of the World Health Organization, were outstandingly brave in their attempts to save lives.

As shells had landed, hysteria had swept through the crowd
estimated at several thousand at Konjevic Polje. Alan Abraham and his soldiers took shelter in their armoured vehicles
whilst outside the crowd had nothing to protect them. This
was too much for Nick Costello and Warrant Officer 2 Sterenberg who left their vehicles in an attempt to calm the people
down and to direct them to safer refuge. Thereafter they
remained outside protective cover as the barrage continued.

They spent their time running backwards and forwards around the vehicles and buildings carrying wounded victims to shelter.

Suddenly a shell landed in the middle of the crowd. Right in front of Nick Costello a mother became completely hysterical. With horror, Nick suddenly saw why and it was a devastating sight. The baby she was holding in her arms had no head. Its tiny skull had been sliced clean off by shrapnel and blood was all over the woman and Nick. The mother pushed the baby towards Nick who just had no idea what he could do. A man stepped forward and took the baby's body away from the mother and then Nick tried to comfort her. As well as the baby, that shell also killed about five other people who dropped to the ground at the feet of the frantic crowd. Within moments another shell landed and took the legs off several children as well as killing several more of the adults.

In the midst of this panic, a hysterical Muslim soldier, whose nerve had cracked, cocked his weapon and deliberately aimed it at Nick and a Russian UNMO who was with him. Both officers calmly stood still and persuaded the man to put away his weapon. Nick carried many victims to Dr Simon Mardell and Mr McNair who carried out emergency operations in a makeshift hospital or sometimes on the spot, even under shellfire. Some operations were carried out with domestic scissors. The actions of all four men were tremendously gallant and undoubtedly saved many lives that day.

To make matters worse, the Foden recovery vehicle was hit in the radiator, thereby disabling it. As the Foden was towing a Spartan, both vehicles had to be abandoned and were later deliberatedly incinerated by the Serbs. Eventually Alan and his group escaped to Zvornik before finally making it back across the lines to Tuzla after eight days. The whole episode had again commanded high media coverage and was seen across the world.

Whilst Alan was having his Foden recovery vehicle destroyed by artillery fire in Konjevic Polje, our second (and only other) recovery vehicle was destroyed by slipping off a viaduct bridge into the River Bosna at the main checkpoint before Zenica. The vehicle had been towing a Dutch truck which had broken down on its approach to the checkpoint from the direction of Kakanj. As both vehicles came down the gentle slope of the viaduct slipway road they began to slide on ice. Nothing would have stopped them and together they crashed through the barricade falling into the river some thirty feet below. Two soldiers in the front of the recovery vehicle were hurt, though not too badly, and luckily there was nobody in the Dutch truck that was being dragged. It took almost four hours to get the vehicles out of the water. Both were wrecked beyond repair. But again we were thankful we had not lost anyone.

We were lucky too in Gornji Vakuf. Whilst on patrol in the town, Ranger King, a member of B Company, was wounded by a small explosive device. It may have been a bomblet from a rocket which had failed to explode when it first landed some time before. It seems that a child was holding the device and threw it away. As it exploded, the bomb threw shrapnel that struck Ranger King all over his body. What particularly worried the doctors in the surgical team was the fact that an X-ray detected a ball bearing which had gone straight through his head. I saw the films for myself and clearly he was a very fortunate man. Once the potential seriousness of his injuries was ascertained, he was prepared for casualty evacuation by helicopter from Vitez to Split and thence to London by aircraft. At 5.15 p.m. two Sea King helicopters landed. Ranger King was in an intensive care unit in London by ten o'clock that night. It was a marvellous comfort for me to have a surgical team with us and the back-up of effective casualty evacuation by helicopter.

Helicopters were now being increasingly used. They regularly flew from Split to Kiseljak and back along strict air corridors. So far, no helicopters had been attacked in flight and so it gave encouragement for them also to be used to ferry VIPs around. His Royal Highness The Prince of Wales, Colonel-in-Chief The Cheshire Regiment, was the first VIP I saw using a helicopter to visit Bosnia. He did so in mid March when he flew to Redoubt Camp, which was the furthermost point he was allowed to come into Bosnia for security reasons.

I had arranged that an all ranks group travelling in Warriors and Scimitars should journey south to Redoubt in order to meet him. For my part, I took my Discovery and some Land Rovers. Martyn Thomas, Richard Forde-Johnston, Chris Leyshon and RSM Stevens came with me. In addition, I asked Dobrila Kolaba, the Serb interpreter with whom I worked most closely, if she would like to come with us. She was thrilled by the idea and readily agreed. We needed to leave in good time because the road conditions were still extremely bad, especially in the mountains, and so we allowed ourselves nearly five hours to get from Vitez through Gornji Vakuf and down Route Triangle to Redoubt.

The worst stretch of all was in the mountains south of Prozor where the impacted ice on the track was as treacherous as we had yet experienced. The Discovery seemed to cope, provided great care was taken, but Warriors and Scimitars had real problems. One of A Company's Warriors simply slid sideways off the track. Thank God, some trees at the side of the road stopped the vehicle falling more than six or seven feet. Nobody would have survived the fall of at least a thousand feet if the Warrior had not been stopped. Again we were terribly lucky. When my party came upon the Warrior, we joined the awkward recovery operation. I suggested that some of the men started walking up the track, since it was only about five miles before Redoubt, but we later picked them up on our way past.

The Colonel-in-Chief's party arrived in two Sea King helicopters on time. He started his visit by chatting to the Royal Engineers before he walked up to where my party were standing in a line by the guardroom. I introduced HRH to Dobrila Kolaba and he talked to her for a couple of minutes about the problems of the country. I was delighted that HRH paid Dobrila so much attention as she had been with us from the start and had been invaluable in helping not just me but also Mike Winstanley and the liaison officers in our work. Her English was outstandingly good and she was also a very brave woman. Six weeks after our tour ended, on 5 July 1993, Dobrila Kolaba was murdered by a sniper in Vitez, near the 'Captains' house where she had a room. When we were in Bosnia we had moved Dobrila into the officers' accommodation because of the daily threat she faced going backwards and forwards to her parents' house in Novi Travnik. Unfortunately our measures were not good enough and she was possibly deliberately targeted by a sniper who murdered her by a shot to the head. It is beyond belief that any man could so callously line up – presumably with a telescopic sight – on to the head of a woman and then pull the trigger, but someone did. In Germany my Battalion were terribly upset when they heard the news. We flew our flags at half mast and immediately took a collection to help her parents. But anything we could do was really inadequate. Dobrila was a warm, kind but essentially lonely person who was very pessimistic about the chances for her own personal happiness. Very sadly, she was right. But at least nobody can hurt her now. I feel therefore that it is absolutely fitting that I dedicate this book to her, together, of course, with Lance-Corporal Wayne Edwards.

With my small team of officers, we quickly briefed HRH in a room by the front gate of Redoubt. I knew he was well up-to-date already because he had personally telephoned me once and his Equerry had done so on several more occasions. HRH was particularly concerned about the human misery of the people in Bosnia.

Even though everyone was working flat out, it was vital that HRH met soldiers and so, as quickly as was decent, we finished our brief and walked about one hundred metres down the track to where a stand of Warriors, Scimitars and other vehicles had been established. Members of the Battalion Group stood in front and the Colonel-in-Chief went amongst them and talked individually to people for about thirty minutes. He was clearly pleased that the Regiment had been saved from amalgamation and seemed very much at ease with the boys. They thoroughly enjoyed talking to him and so it was a great pleasure for all of us that HRH then had lunch with us in a Mexi Shelter within Redoubt. All too quickly lunch was over and so too was the visit. The Colonel-in-Chief flew off to Meklovic to visit the UNHCR whilst we returned north to Vitez. It had been a long journey down to see HRH but nobody minded that, especially since he had very much wanted to visit Vitez but was not allowed to due to security considerations. Of course, we understood that.

Sometimes though we had unexpected official VIP visitors. Such was the case with a small French convoy of vehicles that got lost trying to find the route to Sarajevo. I quote the following extract from our daily situation report written by Roddy McCauley:

> B Company is presently hosting some of our French UN colleagues. It was reported this afternoon that a convoy of nine Renault APCs was heading towards Bugojno. B Company became suspicious as this was obviously towards the front lines. After heading off the convoy it was escorted to B Company's location where it is now over-nighting. The convoy contained two lieutenants, four colonels and a general. The General now intends to travel on to Sarajevo tomorrow. It is not known whether he will be using the same map reader, although he is more than likely to discard his Michelin road map and use Ordnance Survey maps as issued by B Company.

I always found the French officers I met to be the most fun in conversation. Once chatting to the Commanding Officer of the French Foreign Legion Parachute Battalion whilst having lunch with General Morillon, I offered him a few Warriors to help out his soldiers guarding the airport at Sarajevo. He replied with a twinkle in his eye that he would prefer not to accept British assistance – look what happened to his country last time that happened in 1940!

The stream of official visitors was growing rapidly but I had no objections at all to this. After all, it is vital that those who make decisions on what is happening in Bosnia have some idea of what it's like on the ground. The new Commander-in-Chief United Kingdom Land Forces, General Sir John Wilsey, arrived shortly after HRH The Prince of Wales's visit. By now we had a routine for such visits and we simply decided how we could fit VIPs into what we were doing without too much distraction from our operations. On the occasion of General Sir John Wilsey's visit, though, we were monitoring a cease-fire in Turbe. We were trying to help the first UNHCR convoy come through from Banja Luka and, as we were not certain exactly when it would arrive, we wanted the place to be quiet all day.

I had planned a face-to-face meeting with the Serbs to press for a longer-term ceasefire with the appropriate level commanders on their side of the line. I had picked up General Wilsey from Kiseljak and driven him back to Vitez past the massive destruction quite evident in the Kiseljak valley. The General was keen to follow whatever I advised during his visit and so I suggested he might like to accompany us as we went over and spoke to the Serbs. To this he readily agreed.

Exchanging my Discovery for Juliet at the school, we travelled onwards through Travnik to Turbe. Matthew Dundas-Whatley was already across the lines at the same point where the vast numbers of displaced persons had crossed a few days before. Turbe was quiet and the ceasefire effective and so we transferred back into the Discovery. The front lines were now beginning to look very ragged. I noticed that every time we went over there seemed to be more and more wrecked civilian vehicles and houses. I couldn't think how so much traffic was getting here but they certainly seemed to increase each time I went across. On this occasion the way had been cleared of mines by Matthew and all we needed to do was thread our way past the wrecked vehicles. I was never to get used to the horrid feeling that went down my spine as we crossed the lines. I suppose it stems from the certain knowledge that everyone with a weapon will be watching and fire discipline in Bosnia was hardly good. Any one of them could shoot and then deny he had done so, in the unlikely event of someone challenging him.

I took the General up to the house where we normally met the Serb Exchange Commission. Matthew and Beba Salko were there and I introduced General Wilsey and his party and then got down to business. I wanted a real ceasefire on that Wednesday, Thursday and Friday – all of which were Muslim feast days. In addition, I requested, as I had done on every occasion we had met, that I be allowed to meet the Serb Commanders or go to Banja Luka so that I could talk to the Serb Corps Commander. As normal, the reply was that my request would be passed on to the appropriate authorities.

It was always worth making the point even though, to be honest, I didn't expect any other reply. After a while I took the General and his party back to Vitez, from where, after lunch, he departed.

For my part I went back across the lines again that day, this time at a crossing point further south. I wanted to witness the first UNHCR convoy coming through from Banja Luka. We drove to the wrecked café where I attempted to keep driving on towards Donji Vakuf, but the Serbs had other ideas and said that we would have to wait there for the UNHCR convoy. For the first time the Serbs were fairly hostile in the way they talked to me. They were plainly unhappy about the UN's recent decision to implement a 'No Fly' zone over Bosnia. During the ninety minutes we were waiting around they gave me a pretty rough time about the matter.

In essence the Security Council had resolved that, from a certain date, any aircraft flying over Bosnia could be shot down. Combat Air Patrols of UN aircraft would fly in the skies of Bosnia to ensure compliance with this decision. Any Serb aircraft or helicopter which flew without UN approval was liable to be shot down. The Serb officers were furious. How would I like it if such an order was given to the British about the skies over the United Kingdom, they demanded. How could the United Nations claim it was neutral when it was obviously an order against the Serb Army alone? Why should I consider that I had a right to come across the lines and expect protection when the UN was issuing such threats? It was difficult for a while but in the end the officers softened enough to join me in slivovitz. They produced their own variety which was terribly potent. It was the first time I had seen the Serbs reaction to the 'No Fly' zone decision. I suppose their feelings were predictable but, at least, I was now beginning to see life on the ground from the Serbs' perspective.

While we were arguing with the Serbs we kept receiving reports that the UNHCR convoy was getting closer and eventually it rounded the last bend and came into view. I stopped the first vehicle as it approached and talked to the convoy leader, whom I had never met before. I explained that an effective ceasefire was in place and that we would take the convoy across the lines and then lead them back towards Turbe.

Going through the minefields was not a problem, as the mines had been moved well aside off the road, but a large mound of earth blocked the way right at the Muslim front line. Leko had been unusually intractable about this and had said he would not agree to its removal until the convoy was actually waiting to go through the lines. Now, with his agreement, I ordered one of our combat engineer tractors to remove it. It took less than five minutes to do the job and then the twenty or so trucks could fit through. The Muslims then insisted they should be allowed to search each vehicle. There was a little firing in the area but nothing that seemed to be too close to us and so we ignored it. I grew angry at the attempt to search vehicles and made it clear that this was hardly the sort of behaviour I expected. Although I didn't see Leko around, I made sure he would hear of my displeasure. In particular I was irritated that the soldiers manning a 12·7mm gun seemed to be covering down the convoy. That was simply not acceptable and I ordered them to point the gun in another direction. Surprisingly they did so, after a couple of angry gestures from myself. Then the convoy followed us back through Travnik and we waved it on after Vitez. The next day it returned the way it had come with no problems.

Turbe was once again used as a crossing point to extricate about two hundred and fifty displaced persons a few weeks later. By that time we had developed a system whereby information about a possible crossing would be conveyed or confirmed to us by the ICRC – on this occasion Jean-Luc Noverraz, new head delegate in Zenica, telephoned to warn me of the possibility. He had heard from ICRC in Banja Luka that another bout of ethnic expulsions was about to occur over the lines there.

Matthew Dundas-Whatley talked to Beba Salko in the Exchange Commission Office in Travnik. Beba confirmed that it was to happen on his radio link to the Serbs and Matthew then telephoned me about it. I had already pre-briefed Alan Abraham to command the detailed crossing operation and so it was relatively easy for us to swing into action immediately. Using Scimitars in over-watch positions and Warriors at the front line itself, Alan positioned his forces quickly. We were to use the northern crossing point.

There was a little firing in the area as Matthew Dundas-Whatley, RSM Stevens and I arrived at the front lines but nothing was being targeted at us directly. Although the Muslims said they were not prepared to move the mines themselves, they agreed we could do so. Matthew, RSM Stevens and I half ran up the road and pushed the mines to the side of the track. This time they were clearly visible and were not under a carpet of snow. We went back to our vehicles and then drove slowly over to the other side. We stopped once, to clear a pole obstacle in the middle of the track just before the Serb positions. As we met the first Serbs, we saw that there were five coaches waiting there. Immediately I radioed back to Alan Abraham to send forward Dutch transport that we had pre-arranged. They joined us quite promptly, having been kept in a waiting area within Turbe itself. As the Dutch trucks arrived, we off-loaded each coach successively so that the people from these buses could fit conveniently into them. Once filled with displaced persons, the trucks were led away back across the lines.

I was just thinking how well the operation was going when I heard on the radio that a soldier had been shot at the front edge of the Muslim lines. I leapt into my Discovery and drove back across to the Muslim side. Staff Sergeant Bristo, the Public Information cameraman, had received a head wound from what appeared to be a sniper. He had already been ambulanced out and so there was very little I could do beyond reassuring myself that all we could do had been done. Apparently Staff Sergeant Bristo had been with an ITN news team which had been refused permission to cross the lines. He had been standing at the back of a Warrior when the bullet struck. I calculated that the round had been fired from slightly behind our positions. It could have been a Muslim soldier that fired it; we will never know.

Later in the hospital at Vitez I checked on Staff Sergeant Bristo, another man who was very fortunate to have escaped with such a light wound. The round had been stopped by the new British Army helmet and he was alive thanks to its efficiency. Although the helmet had taken almost all the force of the bullet as it struck, apparently a little of it had penetrated into Staff Sergeant Bristo's skull, detaching a fragment of bone into the brain. The surgical team decided that he must be evacuated to the UK and he went by Sea King helicopter as soon as he was stable enough to travel. Thankfully he was well on the way to full recovery by the end of our time in Bosnia. On 10 June 1993 Staff Sergeant Bristo was awarded an MBE for his work in Bosnia.

Turbe was a very important place for me personally, since in many ways it represented what all our efforts were about. It was a major point of confrontation and as such was as dangerous a place as anywhere – it had become the front line just as we arrived in Vitez when Jajce fell. It had taken us some time to work our way into the place and to get the confidence of all sides. Patrolling and working in Turbe was obviously right at the edge of my mandate and yet I considered it vital to be there. It was also the only place in my operational area where we were regularly to meet all three warring factions. Finally I considered the opening of a crossing point for UNHCR convoys in the west of Bosnia a major achievement, even if it was a relatively low-key event. As with most matters in the country, precedent was a powerful inducement and the UNHCR had long wanted such a route opened to show what could be done elsewhere. This had prompted me to push hard at Turbe from the start. Sadly, though, later events were to stop the UNHCR crossing here again, at least during our tour. An explosion of violence in the area of Vitez itself was to dominate our attention for the remainder of our tour and to make any further progress in opening routes through Turbe impossible.

CHAPTER 16

AHMICI

Tension in Central Bosnia started to explode again from the beginning of April. Over the Easter period Travnik itself started to bristle. Maybe it was the Croats that began it all by hoisting Croatian flags over their buildings, some of which were in front of the Muslim Headquarters. We shall never know the cause for sure, but most certainly a few people were killed by either side. For our part, I decided that the Standby Platoon should patrol through the town and both sides seemed very grateful for this and the situation was calmed by our presence.

But the antagonism remained under the surface. It erupted in further small incidents all the time. For example, one day the ECMM Commission insisted that it needed to go down a certain road towards Bugojno, the very same route on which people had been kidnapped the night before. We advised that they would need armoured protection to do so but they said they were not prepared to wait and intended to carry on immediately. Bryan Watters, my Second in Command, told the Commission over the radio that we would not allow their current escort, a UKLO team in soft-skinned vehicles, to continue with them under those circumstances. Despite this, the Commission insisted on going ahead. Bryan told its members that it was stupid to do so, but it made no difference. On they went. Going down the road they were kidnapped by the Croats as we had feared. Djemo Merdan, Deputy 3rd Muslim Corps Commander, was with them, and had his life threatened. We only learnt about the ECMM kidnapping the next day when they were eventually released. It was one of the very few times I lost my temper with the ECMM Commission and I vented my anger and concern on Jean-Pierre Thebault, its new ambassador based in Zenica. The Commission never again failed to take our advice on security matters. But in the larger sphere, the kidnapping was symptomatic of a marked deterioration of relations between the Croats and Muslims once more.

I decided I would go into Travnik to assess the situation myself and went initially to Muslim Headquarters, but nobody in authority was there. Going outside, I decided I would talk to some of the soldiers there simply to hear their thoughts. Obviously they were terribly concerned about developments. I asked them if they felt we could do anything at all to help. They requested that we keep our patrols on the streets, especially at night. I received this answer from both Muslim and Croat soldiers. They felt that our presence helped calm the situation. Later I made sure that we continued to patrol Travnik at night, at least to around one o'clock. Being where the action is taking place is probably one of the best lessons I learnt in Bosnia on how to conduct peacekeeping. It became a Battalion Group maxim: if there's trouble, get into the middle of it and calm things down by being there.

I was still walking around the streets of Travnik when I received a radio message about a serious disturbance just starting in Zenica of all places. Zenica had always been a place I had considered to be isolated from the troubles. What would happen next?

The catalyst to the trouble in Zenica was the kidnap of a Croat Commander as he drove through the streets on Thursday 15 April. His name was Totic and I knew him. Customarily he travelled with several bodyguards, three of whom had been shot dead as the kidnapping had taken place. Totic's car had been ambushed in broad daylight. A brief firefight had finished off the three bodyguards and a passer-by before the Commander himself had been whisked away from the scene in another vehicle. Clearly the people that had done it were deadly serious in their intent and had demonstrated that

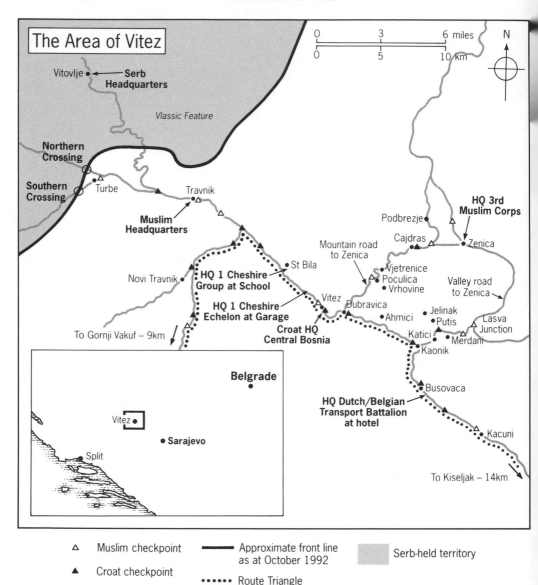

The Area of Vitez

Vitovlje • ←— Serb Headquarters

Vlassic Feature

Northern Crossing

Southern Crossing   Turbe   Travnik

Muslim Headquarters

Novi Travnik   HQ 1 Cheshire Group at School   St Bila

HQ 1 Cheshire Echelon at Garage   Vitez

Croat HQ Central Bosnia

To Gornji Vakuf – 9km

Mountain road to Zenica

Podbrezje•   HQ 3rd Muslim Corps

Cajdras   Zenica

Vjetrenice
Poculica
Vrhovine   Valley road to Zenica

Dubravica
Ahmici   Jelinak
Putis   Lasva Junction
Katici   Merdani
Kaonik

Belgrade

Vitez   • Sarajevo

• Split

HQ Dutch/Belgian Transport Battalion at hotel   Busovaca

Kacuni

To Kiseljak – 14km

△ Muslim checkpoint   —— Approximate front line as at October 1992   Serb-held territory

▲ Croat checkpoint   •••••• Route Triangle

by their actions. They would have no hesitation in killing Totic too – if indeed he was still alive.

Nobody knew who was responsible but, unsurprisingly, the Croats accused the Muslims of the act. Could it have been a Muslim group which was out of control? If it was not the Muslims, then who was it? Colm Doyle, Lord Carrington's

Special Assistant, had once told me that all sides in Bosnia were perfectly capable of killing their own for advantage. Could the Croats do this to themselves? Whoever they were knew what they were doing. It was mischief-making on a grand scale and the implications of it would be enormous.

Jean-Pierre Thebault, the ECMM ambassador, had already arranged an emergency meeting in the International Hotel between both sides and it was due to take place at 3 p.m. Upon receiving my invitation to this meeting, I immediately left Travnik and travelled directly to Zenica in my Discovery, and arrived rather late. Djemo Merdan was present for the Muslims but he denied that the Muslim 3rd Corps had had anything to do with the kidnapping. He undertook to do all in his power to find out who was responsible. For my part I was very undecided about the matter. It seemed to me absolutely stupid for the Muslims to do something like this. I could not understand what they might gain by such actions. Also, despite what had happened, I trusted Djemo Merdan. I suppose it was possible that a Muslim fundamentalist group, out of 3rd Corps' control, could have carried out the kidnapping. Either way, Merdan and the Muslims had to recover Totic — or at least prove it was not they who had carried out the deed. I said as much to Djemo Merdan but the Ambassador suggested that it was also up to the civil authorities to locate and rescue Totic. In the end the meeting put the onus for action on the Mayor of Zenica and the civilian police. I felt that this was wrong but could do little about it. However, I did agree, albeit reluctantly, that we would patrol Zenica that evening, as requested by both sides. Yet I was running out of people and vehicles with which to patrol. I had already given my word that we would patrol Travnik and now I was being obliged to patrol Zenica as well.

Central Bosnia had descended even from the anarchy I had witnessed on my arrival there. This kidnap of a senior Croat officer in a Muslim stronghold created a terribly volatile atmosphere and it was very bad news for all of us who hoped for peace in the region. Unless the perpetrators were found, and quickly, we could all expect a tremendous backlash from the Croats. Both Jean-Pierre Thebault and I fully realized this. The point was stressed continually that afternoon at the meeting in the International Hotel. We agreed to meet mid morning the next day to receive reports on the progress in locating and recovering Totic. But there was precious little time to produce results. Totic had to be returned alive and those responsible found within hours.

And time soon ran out. All hell broke loose in Vitez in the early hours of the next morning. Gun and artillery battles broke out right the way through the area. We started patrolling from the school immediately. By the time I went into Vitez I was able to count nine bodies lying by the roadside on the way to Hotel Vitez. I tried to see Timomir Blaskic but he wasn't there. Neither could I find any Muslim Commanders in their Headquarters. But in truth I knew that the cause of the violence was probably Totic's kidnapping and so I felt that the best thing that I could do in the circumstances was to return to Zenica for the scheduled mid-morning meeting chaired by Ambassador Thebault. This seemed to be our only chance to stop the overnight outburst of violence. Foolishly I was travelling in my Discovery with Colour Sergeant Oram, even though we were escorted by two Warriors. As our little convoy of vehicles travelled through Vitez, we were shot at twice and my heart was in my mouth when someone fired an RPG–7 close by us. Luckily we were not hit and we drove over the mountain road into Zenica.

The meeting was most inconclusive. The civilian authorities in Zenica had made no progress whatsoever. No representatives from 3rd Muslim Corps even turned up. The other Croat Brigade Commander in Zenica was there and demanded effective action. I made a statement outlining the situation in Vitez, emphasizing how many had been killed already. I told the meeting of the nine bodies I had seen in the streets that morning. It was soon obvious, however, that nothing was going to be achieved and people simply drifted away from the meeting with an agreement that we were to meet again later in the day. I went back over the mountain route to Vitez.

Getting back to the school was quite tricky. Colour Sergeant Oram was still with me and clearly enjoying every minute of our journey – especially when we cleared mines together at a deserted checkpoint on the top of the mountain. Although we could see nobody as we did this, I was sure that we were being observed from defensive positions on the high ground about two hundred metres further to the east. As we drove down from the top of the mountain, the whole area looked ablaze with battle. It was a horrific although amazing sight and I was glad to get back to the school.

Once back in the Operations Room I was able to get a feel for what was happening throughout Central Bosnia. Our patrols had been extensive and active since the very first moments of the battle that morning. I had already given orders that we were to recover casualties to hospitals when we found them and that we were to help save lives wherever possible. The Mobile Surgical Team had been dealing with a few people but most locals had been taken directly to Travnik hospital. The Vitez clinic was not in operation – later Bryan Watters discovered two dead bodies, possibly doctors, in its hallway. For the first time, we seemed to be unable to influence events and yet that did not stop our efforts to do so. Wherever we could we went into the fighting in an attempt to stop it by our presence. Inevitably we were attacked, probably by both sides. Warrior was fantastic and took all punishment in its stride. Thanks to Warrior's protective armour we suffered no casualties in that first intense day.

The deterioration of relationships between local forces had been an increasing phenomenon, particularly since January. I felt sure it was related to the Vance–Owen Plan, which divided Bosnian cantons on ethnic lines, and attempts by all sides, particularly the Croats, to get control of as much land as possible. I felt very upset at our apparent impotence but was determined not to give up.

Later I returned to Zenica, this time in Juliet with an escort Warrior. Rather than go over the mountain route I chose the valley one. CSM Lawson beside me in the gunner's seat counted over thirty-five houses destroyed and near the village of Nadioci we saw what looked to be a family of five persons lying in a line where they had presumably been shot dead. Travelling on for a further one hundred and fifty metres or so we saw another man lying dead at his front door. I guess someone had shot him as he came to answer their summons.

In Zenica the third meeting to resolve the recovery of Commander Totic was as inconclusive as the previous ones. It was probably too late by then anyway. The fires had started and they would take much more than Totic's return to quench them. That night I arranged for Warriors to continue patrolling Vitez and for some to be positioned on the mountain road. Additionally I ordered that two Scimitars be stationed at the Lasva checkpoint, with the intention of at least keeping the routes open.

As the worst of the violence seemed to be centred on Vitez, it seemed appropriate to have any further meetings at the school itself. Thus the next morning, Sunday 17 April, I personally picked up the ECMM officers from the International Hotel and Jean-Luc Noverraz from the ICRC offices in order to bring them to Vitez. We used two Warriors, Juliet and Romeo One One, the latter being Corporal Cutting's vehicle. The ECMM officers travelled in their armoured Mercedes and so we positioned this between the two Warriors for the return journey.

Unfortunately about four miles south of Zenica, Romeo One One lost one of its tracks. It ploughed off the road and turned over in a ditch. The Warrior did a somersault much like the one a few weeks before: once again, it was almost miraculous that nobody was hurt, since being thrown upside down in that confined space is exceedingly dangerous. Unable to summon recovery vehicles from Vitez on our radios, even though we were only seventeen kilometres away, I eventually walked to a nearby house and asked to use a telephone. I managed to get through to the ICRC offices where I asked Claire Podbielski to contact our Operations Room at Vitez to inform Bryan Watters of what had happened. As she passed on my message, I continued on to Vitez with Jean-Luc Noverraz in the back of Juliet and the ECMM officers in their armoured Mercedes.

Unsurprisingly we were late for the meeting which had started without us. Bryan Watters was chairing it when we arrived. He had already tried to get a ceasefire in Zenica the day before, had begun negotiations for an exchange of prisoners and the removal of outside troops back out of the area, and had convened the current meeting. The only agreed arrangement which had been fulfilled was that both parties had turned up for the current meeting. Nothing else had changed and the battle was still raging. Our soldiers continued their active patrols, helping to save lives where they could.

I took over chairing the meeting and tried again. Once more we agreed that a ceasefire should come into effect almost immediately. Once again we agreed that prisoners should be exchanged and the ICRC should be involved. Once more we agreed that external troops should be withdrawn from the area. I also suggested that Warriors must continue to patrol the area and that both sides must respect our neutrality. The meeting ended with very little hope that these resolutions would be fulfilled, but we had to keep trying.

In fact the battle seemed, if anything, to be gaining in intensity. Now not only was Nora, the Croat 152mm howitzer, firing from close to our base – we thought into the hills between Vitez and Zenica – but there were also multi-barrelled rocket launchers and mortars pummelling the valley to the east rather than the Serb positions on the Vlassic Feature as they used to. If anything things got even worse overnight. Now we had reports that there was serious fighting in Zenica, where we had no troops.

We were now fully stretched and had no more armoured vehicles available. Only the Standby Platoon was left in reserve and so I had to use it. Together with Alex Watts, once again on Standby Platoon duty, I took the mountain road back into Zenica. At the top, the minefield needed to be cleared once more, which we did without permission from anyone again, although presumably we were watched. Going down the mountain, we passed a vast number of people in the village of Cajdras around the church on our way into Zenica.

The place was very tense and few people were out on the streets of Zenica itself. Roadblocks had been erected everywhere, especially near the HOS Headquarters. HOS were the Croat hardliners and they tended to wear black uniforms. I asked Alex Watts to patrol around the streets whilst I checked that both the UNHCR and ICRC office staffs were safe. Once I was assured of their welfare, I agreed to give Margaret Green of the UNHCR a lift back to Vitez so that she could report properly on the situation there. I summoned Alex to rejoin me for the return journey over the mountain route, and we had no problems whatsoever until we were approaching Cajdras.

Just before entering this small town, however, we came across the Croat Brigade Commander and his staff walking along the road. The Commander was now the senior Croat officer in the Zenica area due to the continued absence of his colleague, Totic, who indeed was never located in our time in Bosnia. Stopping Juliet, I jumped down to speak to him. I never knew his name but I had last seen him at the first meeting I had attended two days before in the International Hotel. He looked worn out and told me that his Brigade was being forcibly ejected from Zenica by the Muslims. All he had left were the troops around Cajdras. He seemed despondent and about to give up the struggle. He told me that 'thousands' of Croats had been ethnically cleansed from Zenica and were taking shelter around the church at Cajdras. Later I discovered he surrendered to Muslim forces a couple of hours later.

As we drove on, we soon came across evidence of what the Commander had said. There was a great crowd of people blocking our way by the church. They shouted and cried out to us. I asked to be let through, but they refused. The local priest stood in front of Juliet with his people. I had Dobrila Kolaba with me as interpreter and through her I learnt what had happened. The priest explained to us that there were nearly one thousand Croats here, all of whom had been driven out of their homes by Muslim forces. Margaret Green and I asked them what they wanted from us. They all wanted to go home. I said we would try to help but I must get through to Vitez to do so. The crowd refused to move from in front of Juliet. It was difficult to hear what the priest had to say at times above noise of the crowd, with women crying and men shouting. We learnt that the majority of people had come from the villages around Podbrezje to the west of Zenica. After about thirty minutes, I agreed to go and see what the situation in Podbrezje was like. I also agreed that I would take a couple of their people with me when I did so. One of these was to be the priest himself. The crowd was still reluctant to let us go through but after a while accepted that we needed to go back to Vitez first. I had to get back to the school to fetch more armoured vehicles before I went into the uncertain area around Podbrezje. Eventually the crowd parted and we proceeded on our way to the school.

There was tremendous activity in the Operations Room when I returned to Vitez. The place was buzzing with activity and reports were flooding in from patrols on the ground. I really needed to stay there but had given my word that I would go back to Podbrezje. I decided that Martyn Thomas should come with me so that if necessary he could tend to the situation in Cajdras and I would be able to return to Vitez. I wanted to delegate responsibility but was unable to do so until I had fulfilled my promise given to the people at Cajdras church.

Martyn Thomas and I took about six armoured vehicles back with us – including Padre Tyrone Hilary commanding an ambulance APC. Margaret Green of the UNHCR was with us too. We picked up the priest at Cajdras and continued on into the outskirts of Zenica before we turned north-west towards Podbrezje. The roads became narrower and narrower as we went. At one point the whole column had to turn around in a tiny space because it just could not proceed any further down one very tight opening.

At last we approached Podbrezje, where we could see some houses were burning. The Croat Headquarters which was close by had obviously been stormed. There was considerable evidence of fighting around it and severe bullet marks all over the walls. Muslim soldiers were standing around the place and it looked like they were holding some prisoners in a truck by the back gate, but I could not stop to check because I wanted to get through the area up to Podbrezje itself.

I identified the place which I thought was the core of the area – Podbrezje seemed to be a sprawl of villages really – and the priest verified that it was where we should head. We climbed the side of a hill towards a church, but now the roads were becoming atrocious. I decided we would split up. I took Tyrone Hilary's APC and Juliet right flanking and contoured around the church halfway up the hill: I wanted to check out what I thought to be a burning house in the dead ground behind the slope. I asked Martyn Thomas to go up to the church and investigate that area.

In fact the smoke was coming not from a burning house but the local rubbish tip that had been set on fire and so we returned swiftly. As we did so, someone fired a shot at us but it was wild. Meanwhile Martyn had gone up to the church and found some Muslim soldiers looting a house. He leapt down from his Warrior but received a very unfriendly reception when he asked what they were doing. Over the radio he advised me that things could turn very nasty. I ordered Martyn to withdraw as quickly as he could. Martyn managed to extricate himself and rejoined me halfway down the hill. We then withdrew past the ransacked Croat Headquarters where, by now, the Muslim soldiers did not look too friendly either. However, Warrior is big, noisy and impressive. It is not the sort of vehicle people tend to argue with, particularly if driven towards them with determination. We drove past the place without stopping.

The priest seemed satisfied that there had not been as much destruction here as the people who had blocked the road at Cajdras had suggested. But now I felt that we should visit the Mayor of Zenica to find out what he proposed to do about the people who had been frightened out of their homes. Both the priest and Margaret Green agreed. We drove directly to the Town Hall but the Mayor was gone. I spoke to a clerk and asked him if we could contact the Mayor on the telephone and about thirty seconds later I was talking to the Muslim Mayor.

I told him what we had found at Cajdras and at Podbrezje. It was obvious that almost a thousand Croats had been driven from their houses by the fighting. What did he intend to do about it? The Mayor, who I knew well, was most sympathetic. I think he loathed what was happening. He told me that he would send a representative that evening to talk to the people at Cajdras. He also said he would organize buses to take the people back to their houses once he had reassured them. I was sceptical about that and asked him to speak to the priest. The priest picked up the telephone and they talked for a couple of minutes. After that I asked the priest if he had been satisfied by what the Mayor has told him. Clearly he was happier and so I suggested to the Mayor that a meeting attended by the priest, Margaret Green and Martyn Thomas should be held in the morning to wrap up the matter. The Mayor agreed.

Martyn Thomas took the priest home to Cajdras and then continued back to Vitez and I dropped Margaret Green off at the UNHCR offices before taking the valley route back to the school. Just after we got there Timomir Blaskic telephoned to say he was terribly concerned about the people in Cajdras. His Brigade Commander, whom I had met earlier, had surrendered to the Muslims and he was convinced that the people at Cajdras would be shelled. He asked me to take some armoured vehicles to Cajdras, but we had none to spare now; everyone was tired out and we were at full stretch. He requested again that I do something, as a friend. But there was nothing I could do, since we were out of front-line armoured vehicles. Then Captain Richard Waltier, the Adjutant, suggested that he could take the Battalion Headquarters APCs, which were normally command-post vehicles, and some of the people who had been in the camp for the last few days. I agreed and told Timomir that two armoured vehicles would be with him within thirty minutes. Later that same evening the Mayor, true to his word, went himself to Cajdras and he organized the return of the majority of the Croats around the church to their homes. Richard Waltier and his two APCs, manned mainly by watchkeeper officers, had a pleasant evening and were very well received by the priest.

That night a truck loaded with explosives was blown up near a mosque in the north-west suburbs of Vitez. We heard the explosion clearly and, once the gravity of the situation was realized, a very tired company commander, Martyn Thomas, went to investigate. There was absolute chaos when Martyn arrived at the scene, he later told me. All the nearby houses had been destroyed. There was no light, people were screaming, many were trapped in the rubble of the collapsed houses, there were dead bodies lying in the street and, just to make matters worse, snipers were still firing at people trying to help.

A Company evacuated nearly two hundred people to the hospital in Travnik where they received overnight shelter. Eight very seriously injured people were also lifted to safety as well as six others with lesser wounds. Martyn did not bother to do anything with the bodies he found that night. They could be left until it was light. He thought there would be quite a few people still buried under the rubble and so some Sappers were also deployed to see if they could find anyone trapped. Rescuing people from the mosque explosion was an arduous, lengthy process, and was made particularly dangerous by the snipers.

I remained in the school and telephoned Enver Hadzihasanovic and Timomir Blaskic. Apparently Mate Boban and President Izetbegovic had agreed a ceasefire, which both Enver and Timomir knew about. The three of us agreed that all fighting should therefore stop at midnight. We knew that this would give time for appropriate orders to filter down to the lowest levels.

Midnight came and went and still the fighting continued with no change in tempo. The next day, together with Brigadier Andrew Cumming, I took Juliet into Vitez. We passed the site of the mosque explosion. It must have been horrific. The area was in a dreadful mess. The exact seat of the explosion was marked by a crater in the road with the skeleton of a truck nearby. All the houses for about one hundred metres were destroyed. I saw a leg and another piece of unidentified body in the road. A woman's body lay sprawled across the remains of an upstairs room in a house. We could see three bodies immediately in one house but there were more partly obscured under the rubble. But, because snipers were still active in the area, I had to order that we stop recovering bodies until a later date.

Together with Brigadier Andrew, I continued into Vitez and asked to see Santic, President of Vitez, and Pero Skopje, the President of the HVO in the town. We had a very heated conversation. Pero accused us of siding with the Muslims, particularly over the way we had taken people to Travnik hospital after the mosque explosion. Brigadier Andrew was more angry than me and was fairly forthright in his answers to Pero's points. We asked both Santic and Pero where the emergency services of Vitez had been when the mosque exploded. They controlled them and yet we were the only people who went there; and as we tried to help the injured, still snipers attempted to exact even more casualties. I began to think that the Croats were working some form of agenda to discredit UN forces.

By now it was clear that both the Croats and Muslims were taking large numbers of prisoners, many of whom being old men, women and children as well as men of conscription age. From Zenica, Jean-Luc Noverraz, head delegate of ICRC, asked me if I would allow him to position a delegate at Vitez so that on-the-spot attention could be given to the registration of prisoners and their eventual release. Jean-Luc felt that travelling backwards and forwards between Zenica and Vitez was too dangerous for his delegates in their soft-skinned Toyota Land Cruisers. Already Margaret Green of UNHCR had spent a couple of nights with us to avoid that journey at dangerous times. Jean-Luc had two of his delegates in mind for the job: François Wuarin or Claire Podbielski. Both of them were very experienced field delegates but were right at the end of their contracts. François felt that he had had enough and did not want to extend his time any further in Bosnia. Claire, however, was prepared to stay a little bit longer and so the choice fell on her. Both she and a lady Bosnian field officer, whose name I will not reveal for security reasons, were therefore sent to Vitez. They were to join several other people who were already living in my house.

Their stay with us could easily have been very short-lived though. Leaving the field officer with some job or other in the school, I was walking to show Claire the house when a large explosion occurred on our right. A mortar round had landed about fifty metres away and it came as a tremendous shock. Richard Waltier and I started running and as we did so I grabbed hold of Claire, almost lifting her off her feet and propelling her towards the cover of the house. In fact only one mortar round fell and nobody was hurt. We all laughed rather hysterically about the matter over a cup of tea. Claire was calmer than anyone else and I had to admire her courage.

The battles were now becoming very serious. Everyone was tired out and the Warriors and Scimitars were working flat out too, with very few mechanical problems. We were on the ground all the time, trying to stop aggression by being there. But violence was everywhere around us and it seemed impossible to halt the flood of it. Locally we would achieve success at one point but then it would break out somewhere else. I assessed priorities carefully and decided that we should concentrate only on the essentials. At my daily conference on 19 April I told the Company Commanders that we were to have three priorities: to save lives, to keep routes open and finally to get what convoys we could through the area.

Many of the routes through our area had descended into free-fire zones. When we were coming back from a meeting with General Morillon in Zenica a sniper nearly killed Lance-Corporal Higginson who was beside me in the turret. It seemed like a small explosion but was in fact a bullet which struck the Warrior six inches behind his head. Behind us the bullet had cut the turret radio aerial in half. From there onwards we closed down.

From our patrols we now estimated that up to possibly three hundred people on all sides had died in the latest batch of fighting. Heavy artillery was pounding away all the time. Most of the dead were Muslims and yet the Muslim Army seemed to have advanced about three kilometres across a broad front between the mountain and valley roads to Zenica.

Meanwhile Ambassador Jean-Pierre Thebault was also doing his very best to get a high-level commitment for a ceasefire. The next day he managed to get the Croat Chief-of-Staff, Brigadier Milivoj Petkovic, and the Muslim Commander-in-Chief, Sefer Halilovic, to the ECMM house beside the school for a meeting. This was the first time I had met either of them. Petkovic was relatively small and thick-set, whilst Halilovic was tall and thin. Physically they were complete opposites, but mentally they were alike – both being fast-thinking and alert. As the top Croat and Muslim Commanders, they were the two people who could control the fighting if anyone could. I asked Bryan Watters to attend the major part of the meeting because I did not want to be tied down too long in a conference. It did take a long time but eventually when Jean-Pierre Thebault had finished both commanders agreed on a number of points.

Firstly, there was to be an immediate ceasefire (of course). Second, both sets of forces were to separate. Within the worst affected area, the territory bounded by the mountain and valley roads to Zenica, there was to be a withdrawal of forces back to the old inter Zenica/Vitez town boundaries. The British Battalion was to supervise this and that particular area was to become demilitarized. Only UN troops should be within it. Thirdly, a Joint Command Headquarters was to be established by the school in Vitez in the ECMM house. Finally, all detainees were to be released under the auspices of the ICRC – Claire Podbielski, also present at the meeting, provided an input on how this should be achieved. In fact she had been registering detainees for the last two days already.

This agreement looked more hopeful but again we were very far from seeing progress on the ground. During the night, the sounds of explosions did seem to lessen a little, but may just have been my imagination. For once, the ball was now back in my court, to some extent. Jean-Pierre had asked me to work as hard as possible to separate the two sides where they had clashed most of all – in the area along the Opstina boundary between Vitez and Zenica. This was where we had to start but nobody had really been deep into those hills since the fighting had started six days before. I decided to lead a patrol there first thing the next morning.

I gave orders for this operation at 9 a.m. on Thursday 22 April 1993. With me went Mark Jones and two Scimitars from B Squadron as well as four Warriors from Alex Watts's Standby Platoon. Mark was to lead followed by Juliet and then Alex's Platoon. We drove down past Vitez on the by-pass and turned up the mountain road towards Poculica where I was surprised to see Claire Podbielski's ICRC vehicle parked on the side of the road right in the middle of a very dangerous area. She was inside a house talking to local commanders. There was no doubt that she was tremendously brave and my admiration for the way she did her job was growing all the time. Later I was to admonish her mildly, insisting that she keep the Operations Room informed of her location at all times. We continued to the top of the mountain pass and there turned east between Vjetrenice and Poculica.

The lane we travelled along was very tight for Warriors and I lost on the branch of a tree one of the pennants that always flew on my radio aerials. Our route took us between the first and second lines of the Muslim positions but as we passed I stopped and talked to the soldiers. Had they heard about a ceasefire? Some had and some had not, they replied. The way eventually became too difficult and so I stopped on a magnificent plateau with tremendous views of the Kiseljak valley. While Mark Jones went off to try to find a route that would take us further to the east, Alex Watts formed a defensive square position around Juliet on the plateau.

After a while Mark came back to me on the radio. We needed to return a little way and then turn down another track if I wanted to go further. We quickly reorganized and went back. Just where we were about to turn left on to the track Mark had found, I jumped down to speak to some local soldiers. They were Muslims. Had they too heard about the ceasefire? Yes, they had but they were not going to stop fighting. Why not? Because too many people had been killed – particularly babies. Where? In Ahmici, in Ahmici, a soldier replied. I didn't believe him but agreed I would go there to see for myself. They showed me Ahmici on the map. It was only a short distance off the route I had wanted to take anyway. We would get there quite quickly.

Mark Jones had found a good track which took us quickly off the high ground. Soon we were going through the first Croat positions. They too had heard about the ceasefire and wanted to stop fighting – I suspect because they realized they were losing. At the main road in the valley we turned right and drove a few kilometres towards the small road that led up to Ahmici.

I had never been there before but the place was now

thoroughly wrecked. What most struck me was what a normal neighbourhood it must have been before and how awful
it was now. The mosque had been relatively new and must
have been rather a pleasant building. Houses had been large
and in good order. Cars had stood in drives before garages.
Gardens had been tended. Windows had been carefully decorated with boxes of flowers and draped curtains. Dogs had
lived in kennels. Horses, cows and sheep had browsed in the
fields. Now the village had been systematically destroyed. The
mosque had been burnt and its minaret toppled by explosives
so that it stood at a crazy angle like a rocket ready to be fired
into the sky. Almost all the houses had been pock-marked
by small arms or shellfire. They had also been burnt out so
that their roofs had fallen through. Later I was to discover
that the houses which had survived had one common charac-
teristic: they were owned by Croats. Cars had been burnt out
too where they had been parked. The gardens were fine,
except for the debris of war like the bodies of pets, downed
power cables running through them and shell cases. Windows
looked like scars on the buildings with scorch marks running
around their perimeters. Pets, horses, cattle and sheep lay
everywhere, bloated by the disgusting chemical reactions that
accompany death. And, of course, that putrid smell was
everywhere. Ahmici had been as badly destroyed as anywhere I had seen. It reminded me of photographs of Second
World War villages that had been razed to the ground.

We drove all the way through the village up the main track.
After about a mile we had passed almost all the houses. At
the far end I stopped the convoy and ordered Alex to dismount the soldiers in the backs of his Warriors so that a quick
check of every building could be made. I was conscious of
the possible danger of anti-personnel mines and booby traps
but felt that risk was probably negligible. Starting from the
top end of the village, the boys slowly worked their way down
through houses checking for bodies as they went, though
this was impossible in some cases where there were
collapsed roofs.

I walked down the main track in the village following the
soldiers as they worked both sides of me. After we had

checked about a third of the way I heard a shout. There were some bodies in a house on the left. I walked there.

On the stairs just inside the front entrance were two blackened corpses. One was obviously the remains of a man but the other looked like a teenage boy. Both were naked, their clothes having been completely burnt off. The boy's arm was pointing into the air but his hand looked like a balled claw. The soldiers told me that they had found more in the cellar behind the house. I walked around there. Through a doorway and a small passage there was a room that had obviously been used for storage. Vegetables hung on the walls and tools of various kinds were still in it. But the floor looked like a charnel house. I'm glad I'm a little colour blind. The human remains on the floor probably did not look as disgusting to me as to others. To me they seemed a blackened, sometimes reddish mess. Here and there the outline of a body was recognizable. Two small bodies appeared to be lying on their stomachs, but their heads were bent backwards over their arched backs at an impossible angle. In one the eyes were not completely burnt. At first I was too shocked to notice the smell but then it hit me. God, I felt sick.

I went outside and leant against a wall. The soldiers and I exchanged glances, saying nothing. There was nothing we could say to each other. Some horses that had somehow escaped the butchers were munching grass within ten metres of us. The sun was shining too and the early spring vegetation across the fields looked fantastic. Yet just behind me was probably the most disgusting sight I had ever seen. The Ballykelly bomb in 1982 had been bad but nothing like this. Who could have done such a thing? It looked to me as though the father and son had tried to protect the remainder of the family at the front door, obviously unsuccessfully. Presumably they had been killed where we had found them. The mother, another adult and maybe four remaining children, all very young, had probably sought shelter in the cellar. But they had been found. There was some blood on the walls of the cellar. Possibly therefore some of them had been shot. I hope so, as their agony would have been shorter. But two young children had almost certainly been burnt alive from the positions their bodies were in when we found them. Poor little devils.

The soldiers continued on with their grim task. Their search was necessarily skimpy but we had already found evidence of the worst. The Muslim fighters in the hills had told the truth. Later we found clear evidence of other killings: the skull of another child in the last house on the left before the main road and several instances where blood and gore had dried. Many of the bodies had been moved from where they had been killed, possibly placed into their homes where they might have been incinerated as the houses were torched. Most of the roofs had collapsed through to the ground floor after burning and this was certainly a good way of hiding bodies.

Martin Bell of the BBC and Paul Davies of ITN were with us and filmed much of what we saw. I had no reason whatsoever to hide anything from them; indeed I felt quite the reverse. After I reported what we had found to the Operations Room over the radio, I received a message back saying that Ambassador Jean-Pierre Thebault would like to see for himself. I agreed and said I would wait for him. As I was doing so, a car containing Croat soldiers stopped. The man in the passenger seat asked if we had had the permission of the Croats to be there. 'I don't need the permission of the bloody HVO. I'm from the United Nations,' I stormed back at him.

When Ambassador Thebault arrived I took him up to the house where we had found the massacred family. He was terribly shocked by what he saw. Afterwards he gave an interview to Martin and Paul. He found it difficult to speak and so I pulled him away. By now he and I were firm friends and I guessed exactly how he was feeling. Both of us knew that all our efforts still had not prevented what we had just seen and that realization was paramount in our minds.

As I took Juliet back to the school someone fired a couple of shots over us, nothing too close though. In the evening Martin Bell showed me a videotape of the footage the BBC had taken that day. It was very powerful. I watched it in silence. Then he asked me if I would like any of it edited out. The scenes were appalling and I knew I was out of line to use the words 'bloody HVO' but that was what I felt like at the time. I said I didn't want to ask him to remove anything but did he think I would be in trouble for anything I had done. No, quite the reverse, was the reply. I thanked him for giving me the chance to self-censor myself. It was typically decent of someone I had come to respect and like over the months. Later that evening I was asked to take part in a live interview on CNN's news-hour programme, which was apparently very influential in Washington. I did so, outlining some of what I had seen that day to American audiences.

Over the next two weeks or so the facts about what had happened at Ahmici started to come out. My main sources were Thomas Osorio and Payam Akhavan, both members of the UN Centre for Human Rights. They had been sent to Vitez to investigate what had taken place at Ahmici. Claire also told me some of the facts that she knew, although she was careful not to breach ICRC confidentiality. For my part, I also spoke to several people who had escaped from the village.

It seems that just after 5 o'clock one morning the village had suddenly been assaulted from two sides. Mortar fire cut off escape routes and men with sniper rifles had positioned themselves so that they could pick off people as they fled from houses. Each house was systematically taken out by squads of soldiers who killed anyone they found. The orders were quite clear. One man, whose name I know but for legal reasons cannot be disclosed, had shouted instructions:

'First kill the men, then the male children and then the rest. Destroy anything that is Muslim.'

After that bodies were thrown into the houses as they were destroyed by fires started with petrol, which the soldiers had brought with them. We reckoned that about seventy soldiers in all assaulted Ahmici. Those soldiers were Croats.

Thomas Osorio offered evidence that a British patrol had probably prevented about one hundred and fifty further deaths too. Some time after the assault had occurred some Warriors had apparently been passing near Ahmici. A large group of inhabitants had been assembled by the attacking troops and were in the process of being marched, they thought, to their deaths. The commander of the Warrior

patrol saw them and stopped. Dismounting he demanded –
in English, he had no interpreter – to know 'What the hell
is happening'. Those people in that one-hundred-and-fifty-
strong group told Thomas that this severely disconcerted the
soldiers guarding them. Their destination was thereafter
changed and they were marched in the opposite direction to
a school where they were subsequently imprisoned – and
later released by Claire Podbielski. All who were present
believed that they would have died but for the chance appearance of that British patrol.

In fact the UN Centre for Human Rights team estimated
that there were about eight hundred people living in Ahmici
when the attack took place. The normal size of the village
was about five hundred but its population had been severely
swollen by an influx of Muslims after the fall of Jajce. The
team had accounted for one hundred and four deaths by
the time I left Vitez and thirty-five people were still missing,
possibly killed too. The survivors of Ahmici either escaped up
into the hills towards the Muslim positions there or were
taken into custody by the Croats to be shot or imprisoned as
detainees. It seems to me that the massacre at Ahmici ranks
as a huge crime against humanity and those responsible for
it should not think they will escape justice. One day, in this
life or the next, they will get their just deserts.

CHAPTER 17

AFTERMATH

The level of activity by the warring factions around Vitez was on the wane. Of course there were still serious breaches of the ceasefire but most definitely there was less shooting and artillery being fired. Cheshire Group Patrols were actively working in the most dangerous areas trying to calm the situation by their presence. We even began to move the odd convoy through Central Bosnia again. I reduced the Alert State so that we did not have to wear helmets and flak jackets all the time. But there were still flare-ups all across the region and we tried to move in to monitor or stop these wherever possible.

The day after we had discovered the Ahmici massacre, I went out on to the ground again in response to a request from Dario Kordich that I see for myself what was happening in the area north of the Vitez–Zenica road, particularly east from Kaonik. A Company was already there. I planned to go to the village of Jelinak where I had heard, from Kordich, that a great deal of fighting was taking place. Together with a few armoured vehicles, I drove down the road past the Lasva junction and then north into the hamlet of Putis. I could hear no firing as I did so but as we went along a minor road I saw a body lying in the fields.

Rather than risk dismounting to walk about one hundred and fifty metres to the body, I swung Juliet cross-country to its location. Once there we dismounted and examined the body of what had been an old man, late sixties maybe, who had obviously been running away when somebody had shot him. He was wearing socks but no shoes. We could not leave him there and so I decided that we would take him with us. Luckily we had some hessian to use as a body bag. Quite quickly we checked that the old man had not been booby-trapped, wrapped up his remains and placed them in Zero Bravo, an APC commanded by the Adjutant, Richard Waltier. But Richard immediately complained that the smell was unbearable and so I agreed to the body being placed on top of the APC rather than in it. Then we continued along the road to Jelinak.

Again all was quiet and nobody was around. Some houses had obviously been sacked though. I entered one, a Croat house with a statue of the Virgin Mary on top of the television set. The house had been looted and television screen smashed, but it had not been burnt. As I was coming out of the Croat house some firing started. Three shots came towards us, but nobody was hit. Then an anti-tank round exploded on the wall of the Croat house. Another one went over our heads. From within my Warrior I heard Lance-Corporal Higginson, who was acting as gunner, shout that he could see the firing point. I called that he was not to engage until I was back and ran across to Juliet. Scrambling over the top – I was too fat to fit quickly through the cage entrance to the turret from the rear compartment – I jumped into position beside Lance-Corporal Higginson. He already had the Raven sights lined up on the target. There were two men right on top of the Gradina Feature to our south. They were holding an anti-tank weapon, an RPG–7. I gave out a quick fire order which, typical for my crew, became a subject of debate rather than a proper command.

'Coax. On. Three hundred. Two men with RPG–7.'

'No, sir, I reckon one thousand, but On,' came the reply.

'Look, I'm sure it's much closer. Let's compromise, go for five hundred,' I said.

'Five hundred. On.'

I suddenly realized that I was about to execute two men. The men looked huge through the sights which magnified their image eight times. They were totally oblivious of the fact that they were about to die and, as they were not actually firing at us, I gave them a chance.

'*Left ten metres – fire.*'

'*Left ten metres – firing now,*' came the reply.

The Hughes Chain Gun burst into life and the rocks ten metres away from the men were sprayed with bullets. But they were landing slightly high. After two bursts I shouted again.

'*Right ten metres. Drop two hundred. Go on.*'

'*Right ten metres. Drop two hundred. Firing now … TARGET.*'

All other rounds hit exactly in the area where the two men had taken cover. My initial range estimation of three hundred metres was absolutely spot on and I have never let Lance-Corporal Higginson forget since! A total of eighty rounds were fired. I then ordered a withdrawal which we carried out without any further fire being directed at us. On the main road again, some three kilometres away, we were shot at once more. But nobody identified the firing point and we just moved away.

Meanwhile in Vitez Bryan Watters was sending an Incident Report up the chain of command on Mapper, our strategic communications system. The report recorded the details of my contact and the fact that I had fired warning shots.

The massacre at Ahmici increasingly became an important issue on the world stage as the days passed. Within Vitez I pressed Timomir Blaskic for action against those responsible. Payam Akhavan, from the UN Centre for Human Rights, felt that those Croats in authority could probably be accused of 'complicity in genocide' as a result of Ahmici. I warned Timomir that this meant him and repeated that something must be done to bring those people responsible for the massacre to justice. Timomir readily agreed that Ahmici was within his zone of responsibility. I also cautioned him that the Security Council was to send some of its ambassadors to Vitez. They were coming specifically to look at what had happened at Ahmici.

Members of the Security Council arrived that very day. We briefed them at the school and then took them to Ahmici under armour. They all wanted to see the site of the massacred family but as a precaution I had ordered that the house be checked by the engineers for booby traps first. All of the Security Council representatives were shocked by what they saw. After that Brigadier Vere Hayes, who had taken over from Brigadier Roddy Cordy-Simpson as Chief of Staff to General Morillon, took the group on to Kiseljak.

On the way back to Vitez I noticed some smoke rising from the hills north of Krecvine and thought we should check it out. In fact it was a ground fire but, as we went there, we approached the Muslim front lines. Four or five shots hit Juliet but we did not return fire. That evening, Saturday 24 April, was Andrew Cumming's last spent with us at Vitez. He was leaving to go back to Wilton where he was to run Operation Grapple from that end. The original team was beginning to break up, which was a sad occasion for me.

During all the events of the last few weeks the Serbs had been amazingly quiet but suddenly I received a message from Beba Salko. He had heard that Lieutenant-Colonel Janko Trivic, Commander 22 Brigade Serb Army, had agreed to meet with me on the next crossing operation, which was to occur the next day, Sunday 25 April. So I accompanied Matthew Dundas-Whatley to Turbe. We went over the lines on the northern route but everything was routine by now. Warriors were in position, mines were moved and then we crossed over in Land Rovers. Martin Bell had come with us and I chatted to him for almost an hour before Trivic came out of the house. 'Well, here I am,' he declared as he entered the room. He was silver haired, well dressed and looked fit.

At first the conversation was fairly adversarial in nature. He was very angry about the 'No Fly' zone decision of the United Nations, saying it was an infringement of his country's sovereignty if Serb aircraft could not fly over their own territory. He was most upset, though, about the statements by Mrs Thatcher that had caused controversy around the world suggesting very strong measures be taken against the Serbs. 'Any bomb that fell on Serb territory could start World War Three,' he declared. In addition if that happened, 'the British Base at Vitez would also be targeted back,' he threatened. It was certainly not the happiest of meetings. I asked if my successor could come and meet him in due course but he responded, 'Why? What's the point?' The whole meeting was conducted outside on the road with Martin Bell present. No cameras were allowed though. Towards the end of the discussion I offered Trivic a drink of whisky from my hip flask. By way of return he gave me a bottle of local slivovitz. The meeting achieved little but simply talking to the man was a start. Of course my hope was that such a basic contact would develop into increased communication with Serb commanders.

Back across from the Serb side of the lines, though, the tensions between Croats and Muslims were a little calmer in the area between Vitez and Zenica but there was most certainly plenty of conflict in both the Busovaca and Kiseljak areas. A Company was actively patrolling Busovaca when I decided to visit the area for myself. With Martyn Thomas's Warriors in the vicinity I could have plenty of support if necessary. Mark Laity, BBC Radio Defence Correspondent and an old friend from my days in Brussels as a Military Assistant, joined us in the BBC armoured Land Rover. I took Juliet and another Warrior down to the town and there linked up with two Scimitars.

From the centre of Busovaca we then drove north-east towards where the fighting had reportedly been fiercest. We had trouble at a narrow but, more significantly, weak bridge over a small river just as we started to leave the town and go up into the hills. The Scimitars went over the bridge with no problems and then took up over-watch positions on the far side. With considerable care, we guided the two Warriors over as well. Mercifully, they made it after a great deal of complaining from the creaking bridge. We then slowly wound our way up into the hills along a dusty track towards Kula. With the Scimitars leading, we reached the forward Croat lines. The whole place looked like a First World War trench system which extended over the hills.

Considering that the fighting had only started a relatively short time ago, I was amazed at how far advanced the fortifications were. Claire Podbielski had already warned me that many prisoners were being used to construct front-line trenches. She believed that one prisoner a day, on average, was killed in the construction of such trenches. Seeing the amount of work completed I fully accepted what she said. The ICRC was doing all in its power to stop detainees being used for such a purpose as it was most definitely against the Geneva Conventions.

The Croats did not stop us as we went through their lines and we carried on towards Kula. Half a mile later we came upon the Muslim outposts. They relied on a bunker rather than trench system. I dismounted from Juliet and noticed a dead soldier alongside the track. The soldiers there told Nick Costello, who was interpreting, that it was a Croat who had been killed in an attack that morning. Having asked to speak to the Commander, I was directed up a hill through the trees to a couple of large bunkers. Nick Costello, Mark Laity and I walked up there.

From the local soldiers we learnt that the Muslims had only very recently taken these positions. They confirmed that Muslim detainees were being used to dig Croat positions further down the valley. Everyone we spoke to had heard about the ceasefire but they were not yet prepared to stop fighting.

Suddenly, as we were talking, a massive firefight started. The Croats were directing heavy fire at our position. We took immediate cover behind a bunker and stayed there for the next twenty minutes or so whilst bullets ricocheted off the trees and fortifications all around us. It was quite a frightening exchange of fire as some of the incoming bullets were passing very close. As many of the Muslims as possible crammed into their bunkers. The UN had to take its chances outside, which I suppose was fair enough as we had not been invited to be there. After a while Mark Laity decided to interview me whilst the firefight continued. Mark asked me to explain what was happening and other questions about what was going on at the time. To finish he asked me if the present outbreak of troubles made it a very sad end to our tour. I was just about to answer when two bullets pinged off the cover we were hiding behind. 'I think it would be a very sad end to the tour if we were killed,' I responded. We stayed in position behind the bunker until the firing died away of its own accord. Then I walked across to the Commander's bunker.

'I know it's difficult but can you keep the ceasefire?' I said.

'OK, then. You've been here. Have we fired?' he asked in reply.

'No, I accept you have not on this occasion, but can you please try to keep restraining yourselves.'

I think Mark's recording was a bit of a 'scoop' for him. It was certainly well played on all radio programmes for the next twenty-four hours or so. Probably over four thousand small-arms rounds were fired during that twenty minutes. Mortars were employed too, although not too close, I'm pleased to say. Whilst all this was happening Juliet, without my knowledge, was away being used to pull the second Warrior out of a trench system into which it had fallen. In the process the Warrior in the ditch threw its track. When I went down the slope, finding Juliet missing was just about the last straw. Together with Nick Costello, I hitched a ride with Mark's BBC Land Rover. He drove down the track towards Juliet's position and we mounted up there.

I had very little hope that either side would stop fighting in the Kula area. Both the Muslims and the Croats were very jumpy and the slightest noise was enough to scare them. One man would fire, the other side would respond and very quickly a full-blown firefight would be manufactured. Leaving the Warrior which had thrown its track to be recovered later, I went back to Vitez along the route we had just come.

Later I was sitting in my house when Claire, her field officer and a little girl walked into the room. Claire had told me a couple of days before about a girl of six who had been orphaned at Ahmici. They had found her in a prison. Although she was being looked after as well as possible by the other Muslim prisoners, she had no relatives with her. Claire and her field officer had managed to get Croat agreement to take the girl out of prison. Her name was Melissa. Could she stay here until the ICRC located some relatives? asked Claire. Naturally I agreed she could and I gave some money to Private Jones, a member of the Officers' Mess staff, to buy her as much chocolate as possible at our NAAFI. Meanwhile we arranged for some clean clothes for Melissa from 'Feed the Children' whose house was next door to mine.

Melissa was taken off by the field officer and given a good bath. She had not been washed for over thirteen days – since the massacre – and all that time had been imprisoned. We brought Melissa some clean clothes before she was out of the bath and shortly thereafter she returned looking clean and beautiful. She was a lovely little girl with fair hair, big eyes and long lashes. The field officer told us what Melissa had said about Ahmici.

'Some soldiers took us out of the house. We were made to lie down on the grass with Mummy and Daddy. There was a lot of noise. Then I was taken away by the soldiers. My Mummy and Daddy stayed lying down on the grass.'

We made up a camp bed for Melissa in the ICRC bedroom and she spent the night there. The next day the women managed to locate her uncle who lived in Travnik. She was reunited with what was left of her family and I never saw her again.

By now though it was obvious that both Claire and her field officer had a full-time job on their hands. Because of the risks of travelling around the Vitez area, the ICRC had taken the very unusual step of withdrawing its armoured Range Rover from Sarajevo and issuing it to Claire in Vitez. Not only that but when the ICRC delegates wished to visit some parts of our area I insisted that they travel under armour to do so. This was undoubtedly the first time that Warrior has ever been used in the service of the International Red Cross. Extraordinarily ICRC Headquarters in Geneva had given its permission for Claire to make use of Warrior too. Once, when Claire was travelling in the back of my Warrior, I turned around in the turret and saw she was covered in dust because she insisted on standing up to see what was going on around the vehicle.

'Are you OK, Claire?' I said through the intercom.

'I am peeesed off,' came the immediate reply from the small, dark and obviously uncomfortable figure.

All in all, Claire estimated that there were perhaps up to

one thousand people detained in makeshift prisons in the Vitez area. She and her field officer had to visit, register and then, if possible, release them. The problem was that many who had come from places like Ahmici had no homes to go back to. We estimated that about five hundred houses had been destroyed in the Vitez area alone during the current fighting. Both ICRC girls never finished writing their reports before late at night and they departed for the field first thing in the morning. Even trying to get them to stop for dinner was well-nigh impossible. Whilst we did all we could to stop the fighting, this very small sub-delegation of the ICRC did all in its power to assist the living victims of that violence who were held in captivity by one side or other.

Often I would meet the ICRC in the field. They were frequently taken to places where we would never be allowed, such as secret prisons on the front lines. During this time in Vitez, both Claire and her field officer were often under fire. They relied almost exclusively upon the ICRC symbol to protect themselves. But in Bosnia everyone knew how the Red Cross symbol was sometimes misused by all sides to move troops around. In my view the ICRC symbol was not a good guarantee of security. The work being carried out by the ICRC was gruelling, time consuming and very personal as the delegates were dealing directly with each prisoner in turn. I was amazed at the results achieved sometimes. Yet the cost to both girls was increasingly evident. As the days went by they lost weight, they looked more and more drawn and very tired.

They lost their spark and they became flat. They were driven by the requirement to release 'their' detainees. But the impact on them both physically and emotionally was obvious to all of us who saw them.

Technically the ICRC can sometimes be responsible for the recovery of bodies and so Thomas Osorio, of the UN Centre for Human Rights, requested that Claire supervise the recovery of some further victims of the Ahmici massacre. From interviews with survivors, Thomas had taken me to a house identified to me as Number 5 at Ahmici and there we had discovered the burnt remains of the Ahmic Nasser family: the father was aged thirty, the mother twenty-eight, son eight and baby three months. From Zenica came agreement for Claire to coordinate the recovery but clearly no local undertaker was available and so naturally we agreed to assist. We had already recovered the eight bodies from the original house and we used the same system again. Older soldiers who were medics picked up the bodies while Claire and her field officer supervised with a local imam, an officiating priest from a mosque. Revoltingly, as we arrived, a puppy dog was eating the remains of the family. Poor thing, it was probably starving, but the incident was disgusting. The remains of the Ahmic Nasser family were quickly placed in plastic bags and then put in an ambulance. Claire made a statement to the press after which the ambulance, Imam and ICRC delegation then departed for a local mosque. Once there Muslims from the area emptied the plastic bags and placed the burnt bodies out on the grass. Both Claire and her Muslim field officer stayed until the bodies were interred.

My admiration and feelings for Claire Podbielski grew remarkably whilst I watched her work in Vitez at this time. Having seen her under fire, I knew she was a very courageous woman. She was utterly devoted to her work and never gave up until she had done all she could. What she and her field officer achieved in the three weeks they spent based in Vitez was amazing. She was terribly good at dealing with difficult commanders, yet they all respected and liked her a great deal. Unsurprisingly so did I.

For my part, dealings with the Croats became increasingly difficult after Ahmici. Personally I felt that Timomir Blaskic and I were still 'friends' but, at an official level, matters were not easy at all. I had warned him point blank that I considered the Croats were responsible for what had happened at Ahmici. That is not to say that the Muslims did not commit atrocities too, they most certainly did and we had evidence of it. For example, five Croats were taken from a village north of Vitez, lined up against a wall and shot purely for being Croats. However, it was clear to me that the attack on Ahmici was a well-organized and systematic Croat operation. It took place only four kilometres away from Blaskic's own Headquarters and only five hundred metres from a local Croat

Headquarters. When talking about it, Dario Kordich, Croat Commander in Busovaca, had suggested that the Serbs had been responsible. I was quick to retort that was absolute rubbish. From the time I discovered the massacre until the very last moment of my time in Bosnia, I continued to press for action against those who were responsible.

We were continually discovering other massacres too. Just a few days before my tour ended, I was in Jelinak to discuss with the Muslim Battalion Commander there whether he had received orders about withdrawing to the agreed ceasefire line. In fact he said he had none. It was clear anyway that he had no intention of withdrawing from the place. He said he would show me why and took me around the back of some buildings.

A foul smell struck me as I went. I knew I had to steel myself for something awful again. And I was right. The Commander pointed out a pair of boots positioned in some ashes. But sticking out of the top of the boots were two leg bones. Beside them was the burnt upper torso of a man. There was no bottom half of the body. The torso was dark brown rather than blackened like the bodies at Ahmici. The man's features might have been recognizable too to someone who had known him in life. The Muslim Commander said some of his men *had* known him. Three victims in all had been shot, he said. He showed me where. It was ten metres away in front of the house. Bullet marks had scarred the walls and there were dark stains on the ground. After the men had been shot their bodies had been dragged over to the place where we found them. There they had been incinerated. It had clearly only been a small fire, but it had consumed two whole bodies and some of a third — assuming the boots had belonged to the man whose upper torso we had seen. The Commander gave me the names of the three men, all of them Muslims from Jelinak.

On Monday 1 May General Morillon passed a message to me via radio that he wanted to meet. I was at the Busovaca junction just on time to see his Renault arrive. As I had just driven down from Jelinak having seen the bodies, I thought he might like to view the kind of bestiality that was taking place in my area. He agreed and we drove back there, with me abandoning Juliet to sit with the General in his car. General Morillon met the Muslim Commander in Jelinak, had a few words with him, saw the remains of the three men which clearly disgusted him and then we left for Vitez. As we went I called in at Dubravica School. The General had expressed an interest in seeing the condition of detainees and I knew Claire Podbielski had been in the place earlier trying to get the last remaining prisoners released. But we were too late. She had already succeeded and left the place: Dubravica School was a prison no more. Back in Vitez, we gave General Morillon update brief on what had happened since his last visit to the area and then had some tea in the Officers' Mess. I made a short speech saying that it was likely that this was the last time we would see him – at least under command – and thanking him for his help. I presented him with some Regimental mementoes and he was very nice by way of reply. After that he returned to Kiseljak.

Alistair Duncan, Commanding Officer 1st Battalion The Prince of Wales's Regiment of Yorkshire, arrived on 5 May to start his take-over of command. We started our handover immediately and one of the first visits we made was to see Anto Valenta. Like Dario Kordich, he was a Vice President of the HVO. He had once been an academic and was considered to be the philosopher of the HVO political party. Valenta had only recently come to live in Vitez and so we had never met before, but I had heard about him. I went to the Hotel Vitez and found him occupying Timomir Blaskic's office. To be honest, I was much disconcerted by this man. He was clearly a fanatic – maybe even more so than Kordich, if that was possible. Valenta gave both Alistair and me a copy of his book. He outlined what he had written in it to us. Everything he had forecast was happening, he suggested. In short, the Serbs, Croats and Muslims should all be confined to their own cantons. His book, he said, had stated this and even planned the outlines of the boundaries of each canton. There was no doubt that the Serbs, Croats and Muslims could not live together. Although I do not think he said it directly, he at least suggested that each canton should be 'ethnically pure'.

On the lighter side, however, I have to own up to the fact that we did make one of God's creatures into a refugee. Between a garage and restaurant on the Vitez by-pass, just west of Dubravica, a brown European bear had its home. The bear had been there throughout our tour and belonged to the restaurant owner who was a member of the Vitez Hunting Club. The bear was about three years old and looked in good condition. The boys often went to see him when they were passing for a little bit of light relief. Few of us liked seeing animals in cages but this bear did seem to have a relatively big cage and was well looked after by its owner. Apparently he had been captured when a small cub and so had known very little else in his life. I say 'he' because the bear was called MacKenzie – presumably after General Lewis MacKenzie, the man whom General Morillon succeeded in Sarajevo. Unfortunately the fighting in Vitez had destroyed the restaurant and its owner had evacuated leaving the bear on his own. Personally I checked up on him once and was vaguely satisfied that some Croat soldiers living in the garage were looking after him. I even took General Morillon to see the bear once. However, I was also worried about the bear's old age. It seemed to me that his life expectancy could not be great in the middle of a battle zone.

Talking to Mark Laity one day he told me that he was a 'bear enthusiast'. Why not get in touch with Libearty in London, he suggested. It sounded a good idea and so I telephoned them and asked for advice. They were most enthusiastic to help and asked if they could come and look at the bear. I agreed and immediately decided on the appropriate officer for the job of liaising with Libearty. Captain David Sherlock, Second in Command of A Company, was just the man for the task. After all, he had a dog at home that looked like a bear and he was a fanatical animal lover. He got the job.

Two Libearty personnel were with us in Vitez within days. David Sherlock went to the Vitez authorities and asked them if the bear could be taken away. Reluctantly they agreed it could and so we built it a travelling cage. The most difficult job of all was getting MacKenzie out of his cage into our much smaller one. Winnie the Pooh was fond of honey, so we all assumed this might appeal to our bear. Not so, MacKenzie would not move for a pot of it. But he moved rapidly into the smaller cage when offered a pot of Army jam. All those children's stories about honey and bears are rubbish. In future, think of Army jam, the bear enticer. I last saw Mac-Kenzie being craned on to the back of an Army truck and taken away down to Split Zoo where he was very happy when I last checked. I hear he is now in the Netherlands.

Throughout the operational area, things were much quieter, all sides seemingly having run out of steam, but the situation remained uneasy. Travnik was a particular worry. Both Alistair and I were fully aware that the tensions there were ready to explode. The Croats had moved their Headquarters out of the town and apparently started to position artillery and mortar ammunition at gun and mortar emplacements in the surrounding area. That was ominous. Beba Salko and others warned us that trouble was brewing and would not be long in coming.

The lines of conflict had not really changed throughout our tour: Bugojno, Turbe, Tescanj, Maglaj and Tuzla had all held through the winter. But the summer was approaching and I did not envy Alistair his task. We had been sent to do our best to ensure that as few people as possible either starved or froze to death in Central and Northern Bosnia over the winter months. To my knowledge, nobody starved or froze to death. When I consider the forecasts about such deaths last autumn – hundreds of thousands were going to die, they had said – it puts our tour into perspective. The Battalion Group had carried out what it had been sent to do and done it well.

As I packed my equipment on the day before my departure, I picked up my gloves in the office. They were made of wool and nylon, and were showing serious signs of old age. Looking at them, I was reminded of everything I had touched in Bosnia. They made me feel dirty and, although I knew I was being a little sensitive and silly, I decided to burn them. Rather like Lady Macbeth, I just didn't feel clean. Watching them burn in my steel wastebin, I felt better for it.

I handed over the British United Nations operational area to Alistair Duncan at 8 a.m. on Tuesday 11 May 1993 and departed for Split. My Battalion Group's tour in Bosnia was over.

CHAPTER 18

REFLECTIONS

Everyone expects so much of the United Nations, especially when it comes to solving the problems of the world. This was particularly so in Bosnia. The truth is that it is only because problems are so intractable that we look to the United Nations for a resolution. If there were straightforward solutions to such breakdowns in human affairs, they would have been cleared up long before. The United Nations is thus a court of last resort and from it the world seems to expect a fair and just settlement acceptable to all sides.

A founding principle of the United Nations is unanimity of purpose. But unanimity is impossible without compromise in any political system and the United Nations is most certainly that. For us in the field that means that any instructions we receive are likely to be a compromise between the political aspirations of all the nations drafting our instructions. Mandates will thus normally be the sum of the 'bottom line' option that each state can accept. This is a fact of life and it is no good ranting and railing about it. We have to get on with the job. In my view people should be realistic and thankful when a mandate can be agreed. It is up to us in the field to implement the mandate in a practical way and interpret events on the ground in a way that perhaps the Security Council cannot. If we are careful those on operations can have much more freedom in the matter than at first it seems. The decisions of those under pressure of real events in the field and against the clock are viewed with much more sympathy than those decisions examined in great detail and with no deadlines in a debating chamber. Fewer questions are asked when actions are taken in direct response and with a gut feeling for what is right.

My mission in Bosnia came directly from Security Council resolutions and basically it amounted to operations in support of the UNHCR to deliver humanitarian aid. Taken literally we could have simply put a Warrior at the front and back of each UNHCR convoy and tried to escort the column to its destination. Some UN contingents might indeed interpret the mission in that way. It would have been taking the Security Council exactly at its word. But that was not the way either I or, for that matter, my superiors in the British chain of command interpreted what was required. I felt that the mandate must be interpreted in a much more wide-ranging way than that.

I took the mandate we were given and examined in detail what it implied. Within NATO this process is often called Mission Analysis. It involves a detailed investigation into the purposes and intentions behind an action. I felt strongly that the main reason we had been sent to Bosnia was to support the operation to save lives – anyone's life, for that matter. Moreover any action taken with that intention was not simply defendable, it was an imperative. For example, sending two Warriors to escort an ambulance through Gornji Vakuf on 13 January with the ultimate result that Lance-Corporal Edwards was killed, was most certainly an implied task from my mandate, no matter what my feelings of guilt were at the time.

It also made great sense for us to create a climate of peace and stability in which to operate. After all, if conditions could be improved then perhaps we would be able to escort convoys through areas with much greater ease. Indeed if circumstances did improve, we might not even need to provide so much aid. This suggested, therefore, that we should do all in our power to help stop the fighting and arrange ceasefires. Many might suggest that this interpretation was pushing our mandate to its very limits: we helped escort military units whose deployment in one area was upsetting the local balance of forces, we transported commanders from one place to another in efforts to get the fighting to stop, and we cleared mines, recovered dead bodies from front-line positions, evacuated casualties – both military and civilian – and crossed lines to help displaced persons move in safety from one part of their country to another. Some of these operations may seem quite a long way from 'operations in support of the UNHCR to deliver humanitarian aid', but I do not think they were. Everything we did was ultimately in support of that aim. I feel I was not 'extending' the mandate but 'interpreting' it.

Again, going back to fundamentals, I would always ask myself whether a course of action was essentially good or bad. If I felt it was morally defensible, then I would consider doing it. When Malcolm Rifkind, the Secretary of State for Defence, was visiting Vitez he asked me if I had any problems with my mandate. I replied that I had not and explained how I looked at problems in simple terms of whether an action was essentially right or wrong. He agreed with my approach. I had a method of working to it and that is what I did. Never again did I concern myself with worries about the mandate. From then onwards I concentrated all my efforts on dealing with the situation as I found it.

However, we had no mandate for forcing a passage through regardless. Negotiation was the way we always intended to achieve our aims. Launching a convoy towards a certain destination in the hope that it would get there eventually was not good enough. We had to create favourable conditions for our work with local contacts, which is why I established a comprehensive system of liaison officers who concentrated on improving relations in a particular area. Their own personalities were vital since they had to be able to operate on their own, in a style which both attracted and suited local commanders. It was vital that they were considered professional and trustworthy. Local commanders often only considered us 'neutral' if we were seen to be favouring their viewpoint and they were very quick to make accusations of bias if we suggested that there may be two sides to an argument. I myself and the liaison officers I selected were frequently questioned closely about how much time we were

spending with the 'opposition'. I felt that our liaison officers
– Jimmie Askew, Mark Cooper, Matthew Dundas-Whatley,
John Ellis, Martin Forgrave, Mike Hughes, Ken Lonergan and
Bob Ryan – were fundamental to our successful tour. They
worked in advance, warning and preparing the ground as
well as being trouble-shooters when things went wrong. In
Tuzla, Mark Cooper and Bob Ryan lived on their own for
several months as they liaised with Headquarters 2nd Muslim
Corps and all other local authorities prior to the deployment
of a company to the airfield there. When the Kiseljak valley
was in flames, Matthew Dundas-Whatley was shuttling
around Novi Travnik and Travnik at a tremendous rate trying
to keep the situation there under control. It was a very tall
order for a captain acting alone at a time of great tension, but
he did it. Mike Hughes worked the Gornji Vakuf area quietly
and effectively right through our six months. For his part
John Ellis was appointed to look after the Kakanj, Breza,
Vares and Olovo area relatively late in the tour but built up
an amazing knowedge of commanders and local conditions
astonishingly quickly. Finally, first Jimmie Askew and then
Ken Lonergan were our crucial link to the UNHCR and they
too established excellent reputations for themselves. The
work of these officers was perhaps the most important contribution to our success in Bosnia and I acknowledge a tremendous debt to them for their work in a highly complex
situation. But here I would also like to acknowledge the out-
standing work of our very young and courageous local
interpreters, whose names, apart from the late Dobrila Kolaba, I have refrained from mentioning. Like the liaison
officers, their work was crucial to the achievement of our
mission.

Bosnia is certainly complex beyond anyone's dreams. There
are far more than three sides – Serb, Croat and Muslim – we
hear about in the media. There are factions within groups
and groups within factions. And without an established order,
these different elements had created a situation as close to
anarchy as I have yet witnessed. Bosnia does not even recognize itself as a country. The main political parties and armies
are all newly created. Even the differentiation between mili-

tary and civilian is impossible. Bosnia is undergoing a classic civil war, fought by civilians against civilians. A civilian one minute is a soldier the next. Bryan Watters, my Second in Command, remarked to me when we were looking at an appalling atrocity that there were few noble acts in a civil war. Clemençeau once stated that war was now too terrible to be left to professionals. In Bosnia the war is mainly being fought by civilians. But maybe what Clemenceau said does not apply completely to a civil war. A civilian soldier probably knows little about the established 'rules of war'. The use of detainees for digging trenches in the front line, where they are liable to be shot by their own side, might make sense to him. But both the ICRC and we were incensed by it. It is strictly against the Geneva Convention, we shout in exasperation. What's the Geneva Convention, comes the reply? How can someone like Commander Leko in Turbe be expected to know all the details of the 'civilized' conduct of war? Less than two years ago he was a teacher. He's had very little military training. What he is actually doing, of course, is defending his home, or what is left of it.

UN officers in such situations have to be highly professional in the way they handle themselves. They must start by establishing their credentials to authority with local commanders. In Bosnia this just does not come with a UN beret. Officers must get out on the ground and meet key personalities. This may not be easy but it is essential. Liaison officers have a duty to ensure that their commander meets the key players in his area. Impressing them with the strength of his personality is then up to the commander himself. Personal relationships are vital in a situation that has no established order and often a problem which seems impossible one moment can be solved almost instantly in a conversation. I would often embarrass people with a sudden visit that would spur them into taking effective action. Officers must obviously lead in this matter. Indeed I believe that UN duties are primarily 'officers' wars'.

All sides in Bosnia are still trying to establish themselves as players in a political, social, economic and military sense. There is no experience for them to fall back upon. Yet we from fully established countries are inclined to expect recognizable reactions and behaviour to problems that confront them. We should not. We have the luxury of being able to be dispassionate about this because our own people are not directly involved. In Bosnia life is for real. Decisions are made without past precedent and against the clock. I wonder how many times I saw a certain look in the eyes of commanders with whom I was dealing that seemed to say, 'You simply don't understand, my friend. It's so easy for you to come and tell us what to do. It's not your family and home that's being crucified, is it?' No one ever said this to me, but I could sense it was what they were thinking and I would have done so too in their circumstances.

But we have to be involved in Bosnia even though it is not our own people who are suffering. It's just that we shouldn't expect instant remedies. Houses, gardens, cars, clothes and the look of the people are not so very different in Bosnia to those back home. Above all, the people look like us. But their attitudes were so alien. On the face of it everything looked normal and civilized but then something seriously disproves this. How can those Croats whose houses still stand in Ahmici look at themselves in the mirror? They must have watched or at least known what was happening to their long-standing neighbours. During the fighting around Vitez my soldiers found a child shot dead with his dog wrapped in his arms. Who could have done that? What kind of man – I presume it was a man – could line up the sights of his telescopic rifle on Dobrila Kolaba's head and then deliberately pull the trigger? Is he so inured to violence by that time that, without emotion, he can watch a young woman's head burst like a melon when struck by a high velocity bullet?

The answer, of course, is that he can probably justify anything he does by the hatred he feels for the 'opposition' and anything within his sights becomes the enemy. Certainly I found very few commanders in Bosnia who exhibited any regret or remorse for what had happened. Massacres can be 'handled' in Bosnia. Those responsible are still free and no meaningful investigation seems to be happening. At the very least those who were allegedly responsible for the Ahmici massacre should be investigated and, if necessary, brought to trial later. In Bosnia anarchy is king and gun law prevails for the moment. I hope that will not be the case for ever.

For our part we had to have very clear rules as to when we could open fire and when we could not. The Rules of Engagement had to be known intimately by everyone, yet in their full form they stretched to several pages of complicated instructions. For a soldier operating on the ground, under fire and under very great time pressure, something much shorter is required. A card was produced which encapsulated the main circumstances when fire could be returned, but even that was a little complicated. The simple fact was that whenever a British UN soldier was operating in the field he could open fire provided two conditions were fulfilled: firstly, he or the people he was protecting had to be engaged with effective incoming fire; and secondly, he could identify the firing point and had a chance of hitting it, thus stopping the threat to his or other lives.

Naturally, as we were in Bosnia in the service of peace as such, we had to avoid opening fire if at all possible. Shooting, whether justified or not, can often be counter-productive. Yet sometimes when complaining to one local-force commander or other about his troops shooting at mine, I would be asked, 'Why didn't you shoot back?' In a gun-law country, they expect that to happen. In fact we only opened fire seven times throughout our tour. We certainly killed four men when we did so. I do not think we killed more than that.

How many times have I asked why Bosnia is happening? How many times have I read definitive accounts of the origins of the war to try and find the answer? And how many times have I finished reading these authoritative accounts and still not known the answer to that fundamental question? In truth, nobody knows why the Balkans have chosen self-destruction as the primary means of forward progress. Surely it is not over questions of race. They are all South Slavs in origin but simply follow different religions. But then it's not religion either. Most certainly I saw both churches and mosques being destroyed, but they were attacked not out of real hatred but rather just to aggravate the other side, since the destruction of religious places is always guaranteed to goad people who worship there. Neither is it satisfactory simply to say that the South Slavs are like that. When we first took over the school at Vitez to start with we used the Teachers' Common Room as an Officers' Mess. There were a lot of teaching books still around and one of them made a distinct impression on us all. It was an illustrated history of the Second World War and on almost every second page there was a photograph of some atrocity or other, presumably used to maintain a sense of injustice in the children. Yet I met many very civilized people in Bosnia despairing about what was happening to their society. Ultimately, if we do not know what is causing the troubles in the Balkans, we cannot really hope to find a solution. More than that, might not the troubles in the Balkans infect the rest of Europe if they are not resolved? Consciously or unconsciously, the rest of Europe is concerned about the area because it is frightened by the implications. If it can happen there, and we do not know why, then maybe it could happen to our countries too. For reasons such as these, it is vital that those UN troops sent to Bosnia do everything in their power to achieve something positive and good.

It is also vital that UN troops are seen to be effective both internationally and at home, which is where the media enter the equation. Surely there are no real secrets when working on a humanitarian or indeed peacekeeping mandate. This is a fundamental difference between general war and peacekeeping. I agree that if the UN were to be involved in peace*making* then things might be different, but in my operation there were no real secrets. Therefore the press can have almost unlimited access with the proviso that they do not get in the way too much. The media can also be used by the UN as a form of weapon and to inform people in the theatre. I'll expand on both these points.

Getting the message across in Bosnia required an approach at two levels. In Central and Northern Bosnia there were many local television and radio stations. I volunteered to appear and speak on these as often as possible. I remember doing so in Tuzla, Maglaj, Tescanj, Zenica, Vitez and Travnik.

My broadcasts were never censored at all. What I said went out. In Bosnia people believed whatever they heard on the media. Thus it was vital that we gave our message frequently, if only to counter the 'big lie' someone else would almost certainly be feeding them elsewhere. Martin Waters, who ran the Public Information Office in Vitez for most of my tour there, arranged a weekly slot on TV Vitez to put our side of the story. It was most effective and thoroughly worthwhile.

At the international level it was also important that people back home saw what we were doing and how we were doing it. People have a tendency to believe what the media states whatever they say to the contrary, and that can include military officers. On one occasion a Sky News report suggested that a soldier had been wounded in an incident. In fact no one had been injured but a demand rapidly came down the chain of command as to why we had not raised such an incident report. Our response that it did not warrant one was almost disbelieved at first.

I feel that in UN operations the press must be considered as part of the action. After Bob Ryan had been attacked, on 7 November 1992 while finding a route to Tuzla, I led the next reconnaissance in four Land Rovers. Nine press vehicles followed me. I could not stop them and so decided then and there to include them in my planning. They were fully briefed by me and they travelled at what we call a tactical bound behind us – not close enough to get in the way and yet able to see what was happening. As a tit-for-tat for a little cooperation, I would try to help the press get their pictures and stories.

The press can also help in tricky negotiations. On a number of occasions a media presence produced a marked improvement in attitudes. 'Commander, I understand that you do not wish to allow us to pass through your checkpoint despite the fact that your Headquarters has authorized it,' said in front of cameras, often had an immediate effect. The mere presence of cameras was also sometimes enough to change the situation. They can thus be a very useful adjunct to our armoury – and there are no Rules of Engagement we have to comply with before using them.

There is no reason for UN forces to be backward about helping the media. They too are at the end of an extended supply route, but without our back-up support. We are normally in a much more favourable situation than theirs when it comes to daily supplies. Thus if they need rations or spare parts for their vehicles and it does not hamper our own operations, why not offer them? The press will always pay for what they take, and a grateful journalist is much better to have around than a spurned one. Their copy is normally much more obliging too.

In the military, we tend to think that even the slightest criticism made by the media is a disaster. Ninety-five per cent of an article can be glowing and yet we torture ourselves over the five per cent of criticism. That is madness of course and yet we still do it. I am afraid we have to get used to accepting a little bit of the rough with the smooth.

The Cheshire Group was always on a humanitarian mandate in Bosnia. We were not there to 'make' peace, we were not enforcers of it, but naturally we had to encourage it as much as possible. Helping to create conditions for peaceful resolution of disputes was one thing but forcing a cessation of hostilities was certainly outside our charter. Peacekeepers have largely to react to events whilst enforcement troops may help create them.

I believe the United Nations has achieved a great deal in Bosnia. We were sent there last autumn at a time when some people were forecasting that hundreds of thousands of people were going to die in Central and Northern Bosnia that winter. Thanks to the collective efforts of UNHCR and UNPROFOR who worked closely together this did not happen. Of course many people died as a result of the appalling war but we were not sent there to stop that. Hunger and cold were the enemies we went into Bosnia to tackle, and I think we succeeded.

It is all too easy to castigate the United Nations for its failures and forget its successes. I, for one, am proud to have served with the United Nations in Bosnia over the winter of 1992–93. So too are my soldiers, because by so doing they were instrumental in saving a great many lives. I have not heard one of them say they would not go back.

So what then is the future for UN operations in Bosnia and maybe elsewhere? I do not think anyone should be surprised to hear from me that I believe that there is most definitely a future for UN military operations in Bosnia. Nobody who has been there can fail to be affected by what he or she has seen. The place is crying out for help and it is in Europe. We are talking about our back door; maybe we should remember what Churchill called it, 'the soft underbelly of Europe.' The rest of us could easily be vulnerable to what happens there and the sooner everyone realizes that the better. And so it must be sorted out. But how best to do that is the question.

Obviously the origins of any effective use of UN troops derive from national perspectives. It is no good blaming the United Nations when its troops are hamstrung by ineffective mandates. As I have said, I believe that mandates can be interpreted rather more widely than some have done in the past. But clearly the starting point must be the operating instructions given to a UN force by the collective voice of the United Nations, the Security Council.

However, committing troops to ground situations necessarily demands an over-arching strategy with clear objectives. I suppose the Vance–Owen Plan might have been considered a strategic objective when I was in Bosnia, but the instructions on how it might be carried out were never clear. In fact I had very little direction from the United Nations at all. I do not complain about this; in many ways it gave me a free hand which suited me. However, it is probably not the way to proceed. There should have been a strategic concept of how Bosnia-Herzegovina Command operated and detailed objectives for each UNPROFOR Battalion. This is something for New York to sort out, and I must stress I imply no criticism of either General Morillon or indeed Brigadier Roddy Cordy-Simpson with whom I had almost daily contact. Brigadier Roddy was under tremendous pressure. He was brave, absolutely honest and often 'gripped' me for mistakes. I have the highest regard for him and now consider him a good friend. The direction I received from Brigadier Roddy was always straightforward and practical. But the point is that it came from his experience and not from some strategic or tactical directive.

I believe in robust intervention by United Nations forces. Bosnians respect strength and have little time for weakness. In their experience any sign of indecision is a precursor to defeat, a principle that I believe normally applies throughout the world. When UNPROFOR arrived in Bosnia the locals mentally paused to assess what impact UN forces would have on their country. They expected that the UN would make a big difference. It had some impact but overall UNPROFOR often appeared to be ineffective. So-called experienced peacekeepers applied their methods too rigidly. Negotiation followed by retreat hardly inspired confidence. Therefore, after UNPROFOR's first arrival, the Bosnian conflict carried on much as before, with the United Nations' forces simply being regarded as an annoyance that was sometimes in the way. That should not happen. When the UN goes into a country, it should become a major player. With the right people in decision-making positions, and the right troops, even a loosely worded mandate can be interpreted to make a successful mission.

If the United Nations really wants success, its members should also be prepared to send their best troops into such operations. To be fair, it is not just military officers who are aware of the fact that certain armies are not suitable to carry out duties where they will be expected to adapt, be flexible and even a little bit aggressive in order to make their point. Some armies in Europe, just as much as the rest of the world, are just not up to dealing with the stresses, strains and intricate politics involved in peacekeeping and they should not be employed. United Nations duty pays well for some nations. I am also aware, of course, that the United Nations sometimes has no option or choice but to include such armies in its forces. I will say no more on the subject.

There is also clearly a need for specific United Nations training. At the moment this is a national responsibility but it should not be in future. A peacekeeping doctrine requires to be provided in a written form and from this training can then be evolved. Officers being sent on UN duties should start by learning about the organization itself and how it functions. They should then receive common teaching on principles and procedures. The UN needs to run its own peacekeeping staff college, in my view. It also needs a much more effective operational staff who would keep a firm control of what is happening in the field. Much as I appreciated being allowed to make almost all my own decisions in Central Bosnia, that is certainly not the way to proceed. It would be nice to think that a standing force of peacekeepers could be established but I know that this is an unrealistic proposition, at least in the foreseeable future. Each UN operation at present requires states to decide on the specific composition of a force and this in fact runs counter to the creation of standing forces, which may not include the right sort of armies and special skills for a specific task. The whole business of training and operational control of UN peacekeepers certainly needs to be addressed, however, because it is, to my mind, the future of international military intervention.

Bosnia is one of the most vicious wars ever. Few can doubt that. An end to it all is not in sight. That is what is so depressing. With this apparent lack of progress, some might suggest that we all give up. But then those who argue for this have not looked into the eyes of the people who live in that stricken country. There, but for the grace of God, go all of us. Bosnia may be an intractable problem and might cost us all many more lives but we cannot abandon the place to its fate. The United Nations may be an imperfect instrument for dealing with Bosnia's problems but it is all we have got. I cannot see any solution without UN involvement and I hope I will not see UN withdrawal either.

MEMBERS OF 1ST BATTALION
THE CHESHIRE REGIMENT GROUP IN BOSNIA

Pte P G Abbott
Pte T E Abbott
Rgr W H Abraham
Maj A M Abraham
Pte M Acton
Cpl B P Adams
LCpl D L Ainley
LCpl F T Allen
WO2 R Amery
Cpl A An-tAthair-
 siorai
Sgt S T Anderson
LCpl J J Antrobus
LCpl N A Armitage
Pte M A Armitt
WO2 S P Arthur
Capt J M Askew
WO2 B E Atherton
Sgt W Atkinson
LCpl G Atkinson
LCpl M W Bailey
LCpl M J Bailey
LCpl R Bain
Tpr L I Baker
Cpl D G Ball
Capt J B Balls
Rgr D J Bamber
WO2 R A Banwell
LCpl D K Barker
LCpl W A G Barley
LCpl D Barlow
Rgr P F Barlow
SSgt G R Barnes
Pte D P Barnett
LCpl I C Barnett
Rgr D S Barrett
Pte P J Barrow
Pte G I Barrow
Cpl L Bartlett
Pte R E Bartley
Cpl J W Barton
Pte L J Barton
Rgr J C Barton
Pte P J Bate
LCpl C C Bate
CSgt E W A Bates
Pte D J Bates
Pte P W Baxter
Sgt S G Beale
Pte M F R Beanland
LCpl C A Beasley
LCpl P A Beatty
WO2 T F Beck
Lt B V Beddard
2Lt G P Bellis
Capt D M Bennett
Rgr G N Bennett
Pte M A Bennett

Pte P A Bennison
SSgt W Bernard
Cpl C Berry
Cpl S T Beswick
Pte C P Bibby
Rgr T Bill
Pte C Bills
Cpl A Bithell
Cpl M A Black
CSgt B D Blackburn
Pte T M Blackshaw
Cpl S N P Blockley
Tpr M Blunt
Pte C Booth
LCpl C Bowcock
Pte P O Bowers
WO2 J A Bowles
Sgt S M Bowmar
Cfn S J Boyd
LCpl A M Boyd
Rgr K N Boyd
Capt R J Boyd
Cpl R Bradley
Cpl N J Bradley
LCpl G M Bradley
Sgt K F Bradshaw
Pte M S Bradshaw
Cpl S G Bragg
Pte K J Bragg
Pte R Bratchell
Pte E G A Bratchell
Cpl G Bremridge
Cfn S Brennan
Rgr P V M Brennan
Pte I J Brennan
Pte P G Brennan
Pte A Brierley
LCpl A Brookes
Cpl K Broomhall
Cpl T J Broughton
Cpl A D CBroughton
Cpl S C Brown
LCpl I M Brown
Pte S Brown
Pte M T Brown
Pte A Bruce
Pte C R Brunt
Pte W H Budworth
LCpl D J Bunting
Pte S Burgess
LCpl M P Burn
Cpl K M Burnett
Pte I R Burns
Pte D Burrows
LCpl I C Butcher
LCpl D Cailceta
Cpl A R Callan
Rgr W D Camblin

Pte C E W Cameron
Pte C A Campbell
Pte L E Canner
Rgr T L Carey
Pte J P Carless
Pte N Carlson
Rgr J T Carragher
Rgr A A Carroll
Cpl S Carter
Cpl G M Chambers
Tpr S R Chambers
LCpl A J Chapman
Pte C P Chapman
Pte J L Chapman
Pte K J Chappelle
Cpl A J Charles
Sgt P S Chase
Pte S W Chase
Pte C D Cheetham
Pte S J Childs
Rgr A D Christian
LCpl D A Clamp
LCpl J Clark
Cfn T M Clark
Sgt J R Clarke
Cpl D A Clarke
LCpl P D Clarke
Pte J A Clarke
LCpl S M Clarke
Pte P W Clarke
Rgr A P Clephan
LCpl P G Clewes
Pte K Clewes
LCpl D Coard
Rgr J N Colfer
Rgr C Coll
Rgr J R Collins
Bdsm A Collis-Smith
CSgt P A Collister
Cpl G Colwell
Sgt J O Connelly
Cpl C M Connor
LCpl R Connor
Rgr E D Conway
LCpl J Coogans
LCpl C M Cooper
Lt M A Cooper
Pte M C Cope
Cpl G C Copeland
Pte M P Coppenhall
Pte A P Corlett
LCpl J L Cornthwaite
Sgt K Costello
CSgt T A Cotgrave
Pte R Coventry
Cpl G Cowan
LCpl R L Cox
WO1 M S Craig

Pte C A Craven
Pte D Crawford
LCpl J M Crimes
Cpl S Cromie
Cpl K J Cross
Pte A J Cross
Rgr W P Crothers
LCpl D J Crump
Sgt J D Cubbins
WO2 S J Cusick
Cpl J Cutting
LCpl J Dabell
Pte D A Daley
Pte S Daley
Sgt P J Dalton
Pte J L Daniels
LCpl G A Davenport
LCpl P G Davidson
LCpl B Davidson
LCpl K J Davies
Pte R Davies
LCpl D K Davies
Pte C T Davies
Rgr S Davies
Pte A S Dawson
Pte I Dean
Pte S A Dean
Pte A P Dean
Pte K D Dennis
Cpl E P Dent
LCpl P Dent
Pte C K Dentith
LCpl M P Dernley
LCpl A F Dicken
Sgt G T Dickinson
Pte S D Dingle
Rgr J Dinnen
Sgt P Disley
Rgr R S Dixon
Cpl P Dodgson
Cpl D Doherty
Tpr C P Doherty
Tpr D Dolbear
Maj J P S Donnelly
Cfn S L Donoghue
Pte S T Doolan
Lt M S Dooley
Cpl S D Downey
Pte R Draper
Cfn S C Dryden
Cpl C H Ducker
Pte S J Duffey
Cpl R L N Duncan
Capt M J Dundas-
  Whatley
Rgr W J Dunlop
Pte S M Dunn
Pte M N Durston
Sgt S J Dutton
Pte D J Dutton
Cpl P A Dyer
LCpl A J Eardley
Pte J R F Eaton
Pte D J P Eccleston
LCpl K J Eccleston

LCpl M A Eddie
LCpl C R Eddison
Sgt D J Edmonds
Sgt P A Edwards
LCpl W J Edwards
Pte S P Edwards
LCpl M R Egan
Pte A J Elliott
Pte R M Ellis
Pte C R Ellis
Pte R L Ellis
Capt J R Ellis
Capt S E H Ellis
2Lt T Ellis
LCpl J B Elms
Rgr W J M Emmott
Pte J J England
Rgr D J Esdale
Rgr W Eskins
LCpl A W Evans
Sgt B D C Fairbrace
Pte P G Fairbrother
LCpl K J Faloon
Rgr P S Farmer
Tpr J D Farquhar
Cpl B M Farrell
LCpl M I Farrer
Sgt D B Feetham
LCpl C P Fenton
Capt M R Fenton
Capt J A Ferguson
LCpl D J Ferns
LCpl N S Fidler
Pte E J Fielder
Sgt A D Finlay
Cpl C W Finnerty
Cpl P Fisher
Rgr R A Fitzgerald
Tpr R A Fleetwood
Sgt K J Fletcher
SSgt A L Flower
Lt W J O Fooks
Capt R Forde-Johnson
Capt M W Forgrave
Pte P B Forster
Pte J E T Fowles
Rgr I R Fowlie
LCpl S G Fox
Pte A K Fox
Cfn S M France
LCpl M J Frankham
Tpr M P Franks
Sgt J Frearson
Lt J P B Freeland
Pte C J Frodsham
Cpl A Furniss
Capt T D Furphy
Pte G M Gallagher
Rgr G D Gardner
Pte C P Garvey
Pte Gaskell
LCpl R F Gaskill
Sgt P Gaylor
Cpl T C Gelsthorpe
Pte T J Geraghty

Pte A W Gibbons
Sgt M J Gibbon
Pte P M Gillard
Sgt M Gilbert
LCpl T J Gill
Cpl C F Gill
Pte J W L Gill
2Lt P M Gill
Rgr A B Gilmore
Rgr S Gilmour
LCpl T Gilpin
Pte K Gleave
LCpl S R Goddard
Tpr T J Godfrey
Pte K A Godkin
LCpl R A Goodridge
Cpl M C Goodson
Sgt R A Goodwin
Cpl V R Gough
Rgr J D Graham
Rgr J P Gratton
LCpl N J Green
Pte H G Green
Pte N M Green
Tpr N D Green
Pte S R Greenfield
Pte D A Gregson
WO2 P J Gresty
Cpl J C Griffiths
Pte A J Griffiths
Pte M K Griffiths
Cfn P A Grimwood
CSgt A L Grundy
Rgr D D Hagans
LCpl D Haighton
Cpl M Hall
LCpl M Hallam
LCpl D Hallewell
Pte M E Halsall
Pte D J Hambleton
LCpl S H Hamilton
Sgt R P E Hand
Rgr P V Hanlon
Rgr B T Hanna
Rgr J W Hardwick
Pte D J Harman
Sgt A N Harper
Cpl S A Harraway
Cpl A D Harris
Cpl C P Harrison
Pte M J T Harrison
Tpr J D Harrison
Rgr C W Harrison
Pte P E Harrison
Pte N M Harrison
Pte P L J Hart
Pte T Hartless
Cpl S C Harward
Cpl D Haslam
Pte P Hather
Pte C Hay
Pte B J Hayes
Pte R A Hayes
Rgr G A Hayter
Cpl A N Heath

Pte P A Heath
Pte M P Heaton
Tpr T J Heely
Sgt S A Hempsey
Cpl D A Henderson
LCpl K R Hendrie
Pte M C Henry
Pte J W Herbert
Capt T R Hercock
Cpl B Heslop
Pte D Heverin
LCpl D C Hewitt
LCpl D P Hehoe
LCpl S M Hibbert
Pte A E Higginbottom
LCpl A J Higginson
Cpl D A Hill
CF4 T Hillary
LCpl C R Hillman
CSgt I Hindley
Pte D A Hitchmough
Cfn I M Hoffman
LCpl C Holden
Pte K J Holland
LCpl G B Holland
Pte D T Holland
Pte S P Holland
Pte T L Holland
Cpl K W H Holley
Sgt D R Holroyd
Pte L M Holt
Rgr R Hooson
Pte A D Hopping
Pte G Horrocks
Pte W J Houghton
Pte C Hourihan
Cpl S Hoxworth
Cpl J W Hudson
Pte J D Hudson
WO1 J A C Huggins
WO2 S N Hughes
Cpl J W Hughes
Cpl D M Hughes
Tpr J P Hughes
Pte J J Hughes
Capt M L Hughes
LCpl S Humphries
LCpl A M Humphries
LCpl A H Hunter
LCpl G C Hunter
Pte A R Hunter
Pte M K Hurley
Sgt M Huxley
Pte C S Huxley
LCpl P A Hyde
LCpl R Ingram
Sgt D Ingram
Pte P W Irving
Capt W G Irving
Pte K A Isherwood
Pte M A Ives
Cpl D A Jackson
Cpl P A Jackson
LCpl M D Jackson
LCpl S D Jackson

Pte M A Jackson
Rgr H M M Jackson
Capt M Jakubowski
Tpr L R James
LCpl L J Jarman
LCpl A K Jarvis
Pte F L Jeffrey
Maj P F A Jennings
Pte C J Jervis
LCpl S M Johnson
Tpr Johnson
Pte G E Johnson
LCpl I J Johnston
Rgr W A Johnston
Rgr R D L Johnston
Maj A D Jones
Cpl I A Jones
LCpl E J Jones
Pte T H Jones
Pte I P Jones
Pte P A Jones
LCpl A E Jones
Pte W B Jones
Rgr J A Jones
LCpl J W Jones
LCpl A Jones
Pte S Jones
Lt M Jones
Sgt E R Judge
LCpl S P Kane
Cpl D J Kearns
Pte S P Kee
Sgt A G Keenan
Cpl N Keery
LCpl P J Kelly
2Lt D Kelly
Pte M Kendrick
Cpl N P Kenton-Barn
Pte S G D Kerse
Pte D King
Rgr A King
Rgr M J Kinnear
Pte A Kirkham
Sgt I Kite
LCpl J A Kivell
LCpl G J T Knowles
Sgt A P Kujawinski
Tpr S N Kusbish
Tpr M E Large
LCpl J W Larmour
LCpl T J Latham
Pte A J Latham
Cpl R J Law
Cpl G Law
Pte G B Lawler
LCpl A Lawrence
LCpl L D Lawrence
WO2 I P Lawson
Sgt S Lawton
Cpl W P Leadbetter
Tpr D G Ledgard
Rgr L A Lee
LCpl A Lee
Cpl P M Leek
Bdsm M Leers

Pte J Legge
Cpl R A Leigh
Pte J J Leigh
Pte G P Leighton
Pte D Levy
Cpl P B C Lewin
Capt C J Leyshon
Pte R P R Light
Sgt S Lindsay
Pte D K Lindsay
Rgr R P Linehan
Pte K J Lister
Pte S J Littler
Pte G J Lloyd
LCpl T Lomas
Pte M Lomas
LCpl I G Lomax
Pte D G Lomax
Pte C P Long
Capt K N Lonergan
Rgr P A Loughead
Sgt Lutton
LCpl M A Lyddon
LCpl M Lynch
Cfn R J Lyon
Pte D J Lyttle
Maj A R MacDonald
Tpr R J Machen
Cfn G G Mackie
Rgr J J Mahood
Cfn A J C Main
Cpl S L Maini
Pte M T Mainwaring
Tpr G J Manger
Tpr S M Mansfield
Cfn A J P Marks
Capt S Marsh
Pte C J Marshall
Tpr P J Marson
LCpl A Martin
Tpr D J Martin
Cpl P S Mason
Sgt A Mason
LCpl N J Matthews
Pte H A Mayers
Rgr B Mayne
Cpl D McBride
LCpl G T McCaffrey
LCpl N E McCall
Capt D C McCamackey
LCpl S J McCandless
Pte A N G McCann
Rgr C A McCann
LCpl J E McCaw
LCpl W S P McCleery
Cpl A S McConachie
Rgr J N W McCrea
Rgr C D McCready
Cpl I W R McDonald
LCpl A J McDonald
Pte T R McGaw
Rgr H R McGeehan
Cpl M McGrath
Pte P R McIlwraith
Pte A I McIntosh

Pte G McKee
LCpl G A McKenna
Cpl B McKinney
Rgr A F McKinney
Cpl W McManus
Cpl J T McNair
Rgr J M McShane
Cpl A Meadows
Tpr S B Meadows
Rgr G A Meehan
LCpl A P Melbourne
Pte A Melia
Pte A M Melling
Cpl D Meredith
LCpl C E Metcalf
Sgt J M Mewett
LCpl R A Middleton
Cfn S A Miles
Rgr K Millar
Tpr P Millband
Cpl J Miller
LCpl P J Millns
Tpr P D L Mills
Cpl A Millward
Pte T Millward
Cpl C M Mitchell
Cpl C A Mitchell
LCpl I Mitchell
Pte A Mitchell
Cpl K Moffitt
Pte S Molyneux
Pte S C Mooney
Pte S A Mooney
LCpl R Moreman
Pte R J Moreland
LCpl P J Morley
Cpl A Morris
Cpl R H Morris
LCpl B C Morrison
LCpl S Morrison
Pte T J Morrison
Cpl R T Mortimore
LCpl S A Morton
Rgr J T Mullally
Cpl S J Mullender
Pte J D Mulligan
2Lt M B Murdoch
Sgt M Murdoch
WO2 P T Murphy
Rgr S B Murray
Pte L G Murray
Cpl G M Murrell
Pte R J Murtagh
Tpr D R Nardone
Pte A R Nash
Rgr G E Naughton
Pte S R Nelhams
Cpl L G Nesbitt
LCpl J D Nicholls
LCpl J D Nimmo
Rgr M H Noble
Pte R A Nolan
Pte Noon
LCpl N J Norkett
LCpl J D Northrop

Pte A Nutter
Pte A T Oakes
Cpl D G O'Callaghan
LCpl F P J O'Connor
LCpl J P O'Donaghue
Sgt D M O'Hara
Cpl M B Oliver
CSgt J C Oram
Tpr S C Orr-Munro
Pte H E Osborne
Sgt S J O'sullivan
Cpl J W Ottaway
Pte P J Owen
Pte L E Owen
Pte I J Owen
Pte D E Owens
Pte E Owens
LCpl N M Pagan
LCpl R J Panter
LCpl D J Park
Maj T A Park
LCpl D J Parker
Pte B Parker
Pte L J Parker
Sgt I S Parrott
CSgt P Parsonage
Pte S A Parsons
Cpl M J Pascall
LCpl H R Pashley
Pte G J Patmore
Pte N Patterson
Pte W J Patterson
Cpl B Patton
Cpl C M Payne
Tpr M C Payne
Pte S Peacock
Rgr W J Peacocke
SSgt J Pearce
Pte D R Pearce
Pte M A Pearce
Cpl N H Peers
Pte M Pennington
WO2 G D Percival
LCpl S Perry
Cpl D A Peters
Cpl R E Phillips
LCpl T N Phillips
Sgt M A Philpott
LCpl P R Phoenix
LCpl G Pickersgill
Sgt L M Pilcher
Capt M J Pimblott
LCpl S M Pinches
Pte M A Platt
LCpl P L Plum
Pte L Pollitt
CSgt A Poole
Pte L Portis
Pte A J Postles
Cpl B W Potter
Pte A D Powell
Bdsm A J Prescott
Cpl R W Price
Cpl A G Price
LCpl C S Priestley

LCpl S Pritchard
Tpr R O Pritchard
Pte S D Pritchard
Pte K M Pritchard
Pte G R Pulford
Pte R A Pumford
LCpl S Purcell
Cpl P J Quinn
Rgr I Quinn
Cpl A G Quinn-
  Williams
Rgr A S Rainnie
Cpl R Ramsden
Rgr I Ramsey
Sgt M J Randles
Tpr N P Ransome
LCpl W R Rawlinson
Pte M A Redgrift
LCpl N R G Redgrift
Pte R A Redpath
WO2 M C Rees
CSgt R A Rhodes
SSgt I S Richardson
Sgt D R Richardson
Cpl J Richmond
LCpl D D Rickford
Pte D Riley
SSgt B Roberts
Tpr M W Roberts
LCpl M O Roberts
LCpl M Roberts
Tpr O R Robinson
Pte P J Robinson
Lt R W Rochester
LCpl J D Rocke
CSgt W Rodaway
Cfn D Rodden
LCpl A P Rogers
Pte E J W Rogers
Pte B Rogerson
Pte A B Rooney
CSgt W Roscoe
Rgr P S Ross
Pte C P Roughley
Sgt D M Rowlinson
Pte D R Rule
Maj A W Rule
Tpr S Russell
Rgr H J Russell
Sgt S R Ryan
Sgt L A Ryan
LCpl G R Ryan
Pte R J Ryan
Capt R P Ryan
WO2 J M Salisbury
LCpl N D H Salt
Sgt N D Sanders
Pte S J Sands
SSgt P D G Saunders
Cpl P Savill
Pte C J Sawley
Pte Scarisbrick
SSgt D C Scott
Rgr W J Scott
Pte M R Scott

Pte K P Scott
Sgt P R Seed
Sgt D T Senior
Pte T J Shaunessy
LCpl D J Sheen
Rgr M J Sheil
Sgt M S Shepley
Sgt M Sheridan
Capt D K Sherlock
Rgr N A Sherman
Rgr R A J Shilladay
Pte S D Shrewsbury-
Gee
LCpl D J Sidebottom
Cfn T R Simmons
LCpl M N Simpson
Tpr M J Skates
Pte J M Skellern
LCpl A Skelly
LCpl D Skelton
Pte J J Skillen
Cpl D Smallwood
Sgt C D Smith
Sgt C L Smith
Sgt M T Smith
Cpl N M Smith
Cpl K P Smith
Cpl G L Smith
Pte S R L Smith
LCpl C A Smith
Rgr F E P Smith
Pte A W Smith
Cpl S Smithurst
LCpl A Sommerville
Rgr R Sommerville
Cfn S R Sorbie
Tpr J South
LCpl D P Southern
Tpr C W Sparkes
Bdsm C Sparks
Pte P B Spencer
Pte P W Spilsbury
Cpl D Spoors
SSgt G A Stace
Capt A N Stansfield
WO2 A F Sterenberg
WO1 C S D Stevens
Rgr N R Stevenson
Rgr J M Stewart
Lt Col R A Stewart
LCpl N A Stewart
Rgr J A Stirling
LCpl S Stone
Pte L J Stone
Cpl N Storer
Cpl H W Strain
Pte D S Strain
WO2 R A Straney
Cfn S A Stroud
LCpl K L Swift

LCpl A P Symmons
Pte J A Taberner
Sgt P Tatters
WO2 W J Taylor
CSgt A P Taylor
Sgt D M Taylor
Sgt T P Taylor
LCpl S J Taylor
Cpl S C Taylor
Cpl G J Taylor
Pte G M Taylor
Pte R T Taylor
Pte A G Taylor
Pte N Theaker
CSgt W Thomas
Cpl R J Thomas
Pte J W Thomas
Maj G M Thomas
Tpr A J Thomas
LCpl K M Thompson
Sgt D M Thorley
Pte C T Thorpe
LCpl A P Tidbury
Cpl A N Till
Cfn E M Tindall
LCpl D W Toole
LCpl R G Topping
LCpl K J Townley
LCpl D W Townsend
Rgr W J Trainor
Pte J M Traynor
Pte A Trowell
Pte I A Tunstall
CSgt C J Turley
Cpl M Turnock
WO2 G R Tweedy
Pte P J Upton
Pte S J Valentine
Pte J Vernon
LCpl J W Visser
Pte G D H Voss
LCpl S Vyse
Pte C D S Wade
Pte L W Waldron
CSgt M J Walker
LCpl S M Walker
LCpl C J Walker
LCpl M H Wall
Pte P L Walmsley
Pte N S Walmsley
LCpl S Walters
Capt R D F Waltier
Cpl S W Ward
LCpl R A Ward
Capt S J I Ward
LCpl J D Waring
Rgr S G Warnock
Sgt R F Warren
Cpl T J Warren
Pte E W Warrington

Cfn A P Watmuff
Rgr I G Watson
Rgr A J Watt
Maj B S C Watters
LCpl C E Watterson
Lt A A Watts
Sgt H J Waugh
Cpl G P Webb
Capt M J S Weir
Cpl A K Welch
CSgt S H R Westcott
LCpl M H Westley
Cpl M K White
LCpl C L White
Pte C Whitehead
LCpl R J Whitlow
Tpr B R Whittaker
LCpl P M Wick
Cpl A Wickham
Pte G A Wiggin
Pte J C Wild
Pte P R Wilde
Cpl C Wilding
Cpl P A Wilding
Cpl R A Wilding
Tpr J P E Wilkinson
Cpl M W Willett
Sgt A D Williams
LCpl R M Williams
Cpl G P Williams
LCpl A N Williams
LCpl D A Williams
LCpl C Williams
Pte M L Williams
LCpl E Wilson
LCpl D Wilson
Tpr T J Wilson
Capt M J Winstanley
Pte Winstanley
Tpr R B Wiseman
CSgt S Wohlleben
Sgt A C Wood
Pte L A Wood
LCpl I M Woods
Pte B Woods
LCpl P R Woolley
Lt M R Woolley
Cfn M R Wootton
Cpl D Wragg
Sgt J T Wright
LCpl S L Wright
Maj Wright
Rgr D C Wright
Tpr A C Wright
2Lt G S Wright
LCpl G M Wyatt
Pte M C Yeardsley
Pte S J Yeo
LCpl S F W Young

INDEX